Nadia von Maltzahn is Research Associate at the Orient-Institut Beirut, and has in the past lived and researched in Damascus. She holds a DPhil in Middle Eastern Studies from St Antony's College, University of Oxford.

The Syria-Iran Axis

Cultural Diplomacy and International
Relations in the Middle East

Nadia von Maltzahn

I.B. TAURIS

LONDON · NEW YORK

New paperback edition published in 2015 by
I.B.Tauris & Co Ltd
London • New York
www.ibtauris.com

First published in hardback in 2013 by I.B.Tauris & Co Ltd

ISBN: 978 1 78453 169 0
eISBN: 978 0 85773 374 0

A full CIP record for this book is available from the British Library
A full CIP record is available from the Library of Congress

Library of Congress Catalog Card Number: available

Typeset by Newgen Publishers, Chennai

To my parents

CONTENTS

ACKNOWLEDGEMENTS

This book would not have seen the light of day without the support of a host of people and institutions in several countries. Since it is based on research conducted for my DPhil thesis at St Antony's College, Oxford, I would first of all like to express my gratitude to my supervisor, Philip Robins, for his guidance throughout the process of researching and writing. His continuous support and enthusiasm for my project has always encouraged and motivated me. I am grateful to Raymond Hinnebusch, Edmund Herzig, Eugene Rogan and Michael Willis for their constructive feedback at different stages of my research. The Middle East Centre at St Antony's College has offered a welcoming and stimulating environment for my research during my time in Oxford. Special thanks go to Julia Cook for tracking me down and sending me feedback while I was in Syria and Iran. The Middle East Centre library would not have been the same without Mastan Ebtehaj, whose sense of humour has lightened many grey mornings.

I have profited from the financial assistance of several institutions throughout the course of my research. I would like to thank the fellows of the Middle East Centre and the late Foulath Hadid for electing me to the Hadid scholarship. My thanks also go to the Abdullah al-Mubarak al-Sabah Foundation at the British Society for Middle Eastern Studies, the British Institute for Persian Studies, the Institut français de recherche en Iran, the Alastair Buchan Grant Committee at the Department of Politics and International Relations at Oxford, and the Oriental

Institute in Oxford. The British Institute for Persian Studies and the Institut français de recherche en Iran have provided me with an institutional home in Tehran. The Institut français du Proche Orient in Damascus generously hosted me as an affiliated researcher throughout my prolonged research in Syria. To all I am grateful, in particular as institutional affiliation greatly facilitates research in Syria as well as Iran. I would like to thank the directors and staff of the Iranian cultural centre in Damascus and the Syrian cultural centre in Tehran for receiving me, answering my many questions and letting me become part of their daily activities. The Orient-Institut Beirut provided an institutional home at a difficult time, when working in Syria became increasingly frustrating during the on-going crisis. I am grateful to the OIB team for welcoming me in their midst to finish working on the book manuscript in the summer of 2012 while organizing a conference for the institute.

I owe particular thanks to Elvire Corboz, Refqa Abu-Remaileh, my godmother Soraya Antonius and my father for reading through all or parts of my thesis at different stages. Their comments and feedback have been invaluable. My thanks go to all my friends who have accompanied my journey over the years, rich in adventures in Iran, Syria and even Oxford. You know who you are. Refqa Abu-Remaileh, Nisrine Jaafar and Nahid Siamdoust have not only been brilliant friends, but also hosted me in Oxford, London and Tehran, have brought me my mail across countries, and have always been there for me. I thank Maria Marsh at I.B.Tauris for guiding me through the publishing process. Last but certainly not least, I would like to thank my family, without whom this book would never have been written. My parents and brothers have always supported and encouraged me in every way, and it is through them that I first became fascinated with Syria and Iran. I am truly grateful to my family, to my husband's family for their warmth and generosity, and to my husband for his love and support.

All of the images and photographs were taken by me. And needless to say, all errors of judgement are entirely my own.

NOTE ON
TRANSLITERATION

Transliteration follows a modified *International Journal of Middle Eastern Studies* system. For the purpose of simplicity, *'ayns* are the only diacritical marks included in the transliteration of Arabic terms, indicated by ('). Names with an established English spelling appear in their anglicised form – i.e. Ali, Hezbollah, Khomeini. Arabic names are given in a standardised form that reflects the Arabic pronunciation, i.e. Hafiz al-Asad, Persian names in a form that reflects the Persian pronunciation, i.e. Sadegh Ghotbzadeh. Vowels are transliterated as *i* and *u* in Arabic and *e* and *o* in Persian, the *ta-marbuta* is given as *a* in Arabic and *eh* in Persian.

INTRODUCTION

THE ROLE OF CULTURE IN FOREIGN POLICY

The Syrian-Iranian relationship has frequently made the headlines in recent years. US-led attempts to separate the leading states of the 'Axis of Resistance' have only brought the two allies closer together. Today, in the on-going crisis in Syria that started in March 2011 and has turned into a regional and international power struggle for control in the Middle East, the Syria-Iran axis is part of the debate over Syria's future. Iran, as the Syrian regime's principal ally, has stood by the latter's side. The same held true during the 2009 presidential election crisis in Iran, when the Syrian president was quick to declare full support to his Iranian counterpart. In an increasingly polarised environment, however, popular support for the alliance came to reflect people's stances towards their own government. The Syrian uprising is unfolding and no end to the crisis is in sight. While Syria's creative resistance has been continuously reinventing itself, Syrian-Iranian cultural diplomacy has largely continued unabated since the start of the uprising.

What role does culture play in foreign policy, and why is it an important aspect to consider when analysing a relationship such as the Syrian-Iranian alliance? It has been suggested that cultural diplomacy, while it 'may seem to be far removed from the high politics of alliances, international law, rising powers and new security challenges, in fact provides the glue that holds alliances together'.[1] To what

extent does this hold true in the Syrian-Iranian case? The close partnership between Syria and Iran had been very visible in some areas
of Syria, with Iranian religious tourists dominating some quarters of
Damascus and its surroundings, and Shi'i mosques taking on a more
and more Iranian Islamic-style architecture, rich in ornamentation and
geometrical patterns. However, while relations between the two states
continue to be strong, relations between the two peoples are limited.
What were the two states doing to improve the (largely negative) view
each side had of the other, in view of their close political relationship?
What image did each country want to project in the other country?
How could such a large number of Iranians visit Syria every year and
still insist that Arabs had no culture? How had things changed since
the Islamic revolution? Did a genuine exchange take place between the
two peoples, or did relations largely play out at the official level? These
are some of the questions I am attempting to address in this book,
trying to understand to what extent Syrian-Iranian cultural diplomacy
has been successful in bridging the cultural divide between the two
peoples. Understanding the dynamics of the Syrian-Iranian relationship
through their cultural interactions provides an insight into the nature
of the alliance, and how the two peoples perceive the latter. It also
provides a case study of the state of cultural diplomacy in the region.

The Syrian-Iranian relationship has proven remarkably durable,
having lasted for over three decades despite being labelled as the 'odd
couple'.[2] Why would Syria, a secular state that considered itself at the
heart of Arab nationalism, and Iran, an Islamic republic, enter into an
alliance? Syria and Iran refer to their relationship as a strategic alliance.[3]
Both sides had clear geopolitical interests in a partnership. Initially, an
alliance with Syria gave the Islamic Republic a crucial Arab ally in its
war against Iraq, and provided it with access to the Shi'i community
in Lebanon, where Iran hoped to increase its influence. For Syria, an
alliance with Iran brought it out of regional isolation. Iran's change of
strategy vis-à-vis Israel and its commitment to the Palestinian cause
turned it into a powerful new partner in Syria's struggle against Israel.
That was how the Syrian leadership justified its partnership with
the Islamic Republic to its own public. While not competing with
each other ideologically, the shared values of anti-imperialism and

anti-Zionism allowed for a close political alignment – Syria and Iran becoming the leading states of the 'Axis of Resistance'.

As the relationship evolved, developed into an alliance and became consolidated, the two states emphasised the need to institutionalise relations on the cultural level, to foster interaction between the two peoples. The drive for this dialogue came from the Iranian side. As the Iranian Islamic Republic had a revolutionary agenda and wanted to promote its ideas and values abroad, it had a particular motivation for cultural diplomacy, at the core of which lies the idea to attract the people of another state through the use of culture and political values. Iran wanted to convince other nations to follow it, by promoting itself as the standard bearer for Islamic values. Syria in contrast had no tradition of propagating its culture abroad, least of all outside the Arab world.

In this book, I examine the motivations, content and reach of cultural diplomacy between Syria and Iran, considering to what extent a state-directed cultural exchange can foster bilateral relations as well as to what extent cultural diplomacy efforts reach down to the popular level. I aim to establish to what degree the two states have been successful in bridging the cultural divide between the two nations. Looking at the Syrian-Iranian relationship through the lens of cultural diplomacy helps our understanding of the perceptions each side have of the other, beyond pragmatic foreign policy considerations. It shows the place and role of culture in the bilateral exchange, and its limits. To set the framework, we will first look at the role of culture in foreign policy by defining the concepts of cultural diplomacy, public diplomacy and soft power before turning to cultural diplomacy in action.

The Role of Culture in Foreign Policy

'Any program of cultural relations is a program of communication. A nation's culture is the sum total of its achievement; its own expression of its own personality; its way of thinking and acting. Its program of cultural relations abroad is its method of making these things known to foreigners.'[4]

'What is cultural foreign policy? It is nothing less than an instrument of foreign policy [. . .]. It is not simply about promoting culture abroad, but about how cultural work can support the goals of foreign policy.'[5]

The role of culture in foreign policy is constantly evolving. Culture constitutes a nation's identity that is being communicated abroad through cultural relations, culture being a pillar and an instrument of foreign policy. This book is concerned with cultural diplomacy, and to what extent government-directed cultural initiatives can succeed in building up ties between peoples. Attracting and co-opting the people of another state through the use of culture and political values lie at the core of cultural diplomacy. A study undertaken by the British think tank DEMOS asserts that culture has a vital role to play in international relations today; 'as culture incorporates wider, connective and human values, it is the means by which we come to understand others'. According to the study, 'cultural exchange provides the forum to appreciate points of commonality and understand motivations and humanity that underlie differences'. We should think of culture as providing the operating context for politics.[6] The term culture is understood in a broad sense, to include not only the arts and heritage, but also value systems, traditions and beliefs.

Anthony Haigh, former Director of Education and Cultural and Scientific Affairs of the Council of Europe, applies the term cultural diplomacy to 'the activities of governments in the sphere – tradition-ally left to private enterprise – of international cultural relations.'[7] Former British Council officer John Mitchell in his work on inter-national cultural relations distinguishes between 'cultural diplomacy' and 'cultural relations', the former being essentially the 'business of governments', in short, to negotiate cultural agreements between states and put them into action, the latter being more comprehen-sive and not limited to government activities. Ideally, the execution of cultural exchange would be carried out through cultural relations rather than through diplomats or cultural officials, as the latter are closely aligned with official policy and national interest. Writing in the mid-1980s, Mitchell maintains that while there was a trend in that direction, it would be too much to expect of all modern states to handle their cultural representations objectively and not link them with national interest – 'after all, cultural diplomacy is probably still the only realisable mode for countries that have not been able to evolve beyond a high degree of government control'.[8] While our understanding of cultural diplomacy today is moving away from the state and towards greater involvement from civil society and non-state actors, this differentiation between cultural relations and cultural diplomacy is still applicable when talking about states with a strong degree of government control.

As diplomacy expert Jan Melissen points out, coordination and control have always been easier in non-democratic regimes, and they are not incompatible with traditional images of public diplomacy – China being a classic example of a state that excels in central coordination of its public diplomacy activity.[9] In states where government control is more diffused, cultural institutes do engage in cultural relations in the broader term, and 'prefer to serve the national interest indirectly by means of trust-building abroad, representing the non-governmental voice in transnational relations'.[10] Syrian-Iranian cultural diplomacy is directed by the two governments, which are in control of the cultural content promoted in the other country. In this study, the term cultural diplomacy will therefore be understood as the efforts of a country's government to build up understanding and relationships with the people of another country by way of official cultural relations.

Public Diplomacy

Culture is a vital component of public diplomacy, the latter being the way in which a state communicates with foreign publics. The American international relations theorist Joseph Nye attributes three dimensions to public policy:

> 'Daily communications, which involves explaining the context of domestic and foreign policy decisions [. . .], strategic communication – in which a set of simple themes is developed, much like what occurs in a political or advertising campaign, [which] plans symbolic events and communications over [a period of time] to brand the central themes, or to advance a particular

government policy – [. . .] and the **development of lasting relationships** with key individuals over many years through scholarships, exchanges, trainings, seminars, conferences and access to media channels.'[11]

Three levels of public diplomacy activity have been suggested, namely promoting a country's national goals and policies, communicating a nation's ideas and ideals, beliefs and values, and building common understanding and relationships.[12] Public diplomacy aims to increase familiarity, increase appreciation, engage people and influence people's behaviour.[13] In sum, public diplomacy is based on communication, engaging people and building lasting relationships. Cultural activity has an important contribution to make to public diplomacy in terms of strategic communication and relationship building. Public diplomacy is about building relationships, by way of understanding the needs of other countries, cultures and peoples, communicating points of views, correcting misperceptions and looking for areas of common cause.[14] Through the use of culture, a nation can promote understanding by transmitting its ideas and value systems, and build up lasting relationships through exchanges and educational initiatives. Cultural diplomacy is one section of public diplomacy where communication, engaging people and building lasting relationships is achieved through culture and values. It can be carried out through different channels such as cultural centres, through educational and artist exchanges and by way of tourism.

Cultural Diplomacy and Soft Power

Cultural diplomacy is an instrument of soft power. The concept of soft power was coined by Joseph Nye, who argues that

> 'a country may obtain the outcomes it wants in world politics because other countries want to follow it, admiring its values, emulating its example [. . .]. In this sense, it is just as important to set the agenda in world politics and attract others as it is to force them to change through the threat or use of military

or economic weapons. This aspect of power – getting others to want what you want – I call soft power. It co-opts people rather than coerces them. [. . .] It is the ability to entice and attract. And attraction often leads to acquiescence or imitation. Soft power arises in large parts from our values. These values are expressed in our culture, in the policies we follow inside our country, and in the way we handle ourselves internationally.'[15]

Soft power is based on attracting others, co-opting people rather than coercing them, and emphasises values and culture. Soft power refers to the outcome of having the ability to attract others; public and cultural diplomacy are means to reach that outcome.[16] So whereas soft power can largely be influenced by government policies as policies play an important part in the formation of a country's image abroad, its success in the end very much depends on perception. At times a country's soft power gains its validity by not being directly identified with the country's government – if government policies are seen as lacking legitimacy, for instance. As Nye explains, 'soft power does not belong to the government in the same degree that hard power does.'[17] In that sense, soft power is more closely connected to the definition of cultural relations as given above, cultural diplomacy being one instrument of it. While cultural diplomacy as it stands is a way of building up relations through government policies, there has been a debate to what extent the responsibility for performing cultural diplomacy should be shared with sub-state actors, in particular considering the evolving access to information.[18] Cultural diplomacy, by speaking out to foreign publics, involves a broader set of interests that go beyond those of the government of the day.[19] The concept of cultural diplomacy has in fact evolved over the last few years, putting larger emphasis on non-state actors.

Cultural Diplomacy and Propaganda

Cultural and public diplomacy are linked to propaganda. Like public diplomacy, both propaganda and nation-branding are about the 'communication of information and ideas to foreign publics with a view to changing their attitudes toward the originating country or reinforcing existing beliefs'.[20] There is a fine line between propaganda and public diplomacy. An early definition of propaganda explains the latter as being 'a process that deliberately attempts through persuasion techniques to secure from the propagandee, *before he can deliberate freely*, the responses desired by the propagandist'.[21] Government departments of propaganda were set up during the First World War, and developed thereafter, 'designed to make a contribution to the war effort by impressing upon public opinion in other countries a sense of the rightness, and of the efficacy, of the political aims and military methods of the propagandising department's governments'.[22] The term propaganda, while initially a neutral term, gained a negative connotation during the interwar period, when it was used by governments to impress their ideas and half-truths on their own and other peoples. Joseph Nye affirms that cultural diplomacy can at times be seen as propaganda, the latter being very much a question of perception – what is cultural diplomacy for one can be propaganda for another. How a country's cultural diplomacy is perceived depends again on legitimacy; government policies that are seen as arrogant for instance will be dismissed as mere propaganda and not produce the soft power of attraction.[23] Cultural diplomacy is more likely to succeed and be understood if it is based on dialogue rather than monologue.

Cultural Diplomacy Practices

Cultural diplomacy is thus an instrument that governments use to mobilise resources – resources that arise from values a country expresses in its culture – to communicate with and attract the publics of other countries.[24] Most programmes of cultural relations abroad have been initiated and controlled or supervised by foreign ministries, who also carry a large proportion of the cost. In some cases, the education ministries are also the instigators. Traditionally, cultural diplomacy is conducted through cultural institutes abroad, like the British Council or Goethe-Institut. Important components of these cultural centres are language teaching and coordinating artists' exchanges and exhibitions, organising lectures, concerts and exchanging books. Another important channel for cultural diplomacy, in particular for building up lasting relationships, are academic exchange programmes, as well as the exchange of technical experts and leaders in various fields of intellectual and artistic expression.[25] Tourism plays a role in cultural diplomacy as it enables people to visit another country and observe its culture. At the same time, tourists themselves project an image of their own country abroad. The huge increase in a new kind of Chinese tourist, for instance, has tended to project a more positive image of a wealthier, more confident Chinese elite.[26]

The institutionalised use of culture as a foreign policy tool emerged in Europe. Europeans were the pioneers of cultural diplomacy, first amongst them the French. In the nineteenth century, the French and Germans started setting up schools abroad. The first French lycées opened in 1846 in Athens, 1868 in Constantinople (Istanbul) and 1875 in Rome; Germany opened schools in Constantinople, Cairo, Belgrade, Athens and other cities in the mid-nineteenth century.[27] France opened schools in order to spread French language and thought, Germany more to provide for its own nationals abroad. Cultural institutes followed suit. In the period between the two world wars, a competition for cultural influence ensued between the European nations. The British started an organised programme of cultural relations with other countries in the 1930s, motivated by the other European examples. A correspondent of *The Times* commented in March 1935:

> 'No country to-day can expect to be understood by others if it remains aloof and passive. Foreign policy alone, however wisely conceived, cannot remove misunderstandings unless it can work on a background of knowledge. Some form of national publicity, if wisely directed, with the Government, education and industry in a working partnership, can do much to provide a fruitful ground of policy.'[28]

European cultural diplomacy largely developed out of a desire to promote or maintain languages and values abroad, and took on a more organised manner in the period between the two world wars. Following the Second World War, each government restructured its cultural relations department and re-launched cultural diplomacy as it stands today. Cultural diplomacy efforts were largely directed through foreign ministries, either directly like in the French case, or indirectly by being responsible for financial support like in the case of the British Council or the Goethe-Institut; the ministries of education have been important partners. Education and language teaching played major roles, as well as training teachers and introducing one's culture in other countries.

A country that has greatly increased its cultural diplomacy efforts during the last decade is China. China cares deeply about its image abroad and has an ancient culture to build upon. At the same time, as an authoritarian state, it wants to control this image. This held true for Mao's China as much as it holds true for present-day China. In recent years the concepts of public diplomacy, soft power and cultural diplomacy have been discussed. From China's point of view, cultural diplomacy should underline its peaceful development to counteract the fear of its rise, and more generally develop the Chinese cultural industry. Soft power is seen in China as an important indicator of a state's influence in the international arena. It is understood in Nye's terms as discussed above, with an emphasis placed on the domestic dimension – using the concept for national cohesion – and on traditional Chinese culture. The latter is seen as the most reliable source of Chinese soft power.[29] China has also invested in developing its media abroad to work on its image and discuss what it considers non-controversial subjects such as its ancient history and culture.[30]

In terms of institutionalised cultural diplomacy, China decided to set up a worldwide network of Confucius Institutes in 2004 in order to provide Chinese language and cultural resources to host countries and present a softer image of China.[31] The main aim of these institutes is Chinese language teaching and teacher training, but also to foster research on contemporary China and to inform about Chinese education, culture, economy and society. In contrast to the European cultural centres, the Confucius Institutes are set up by the Chinese Ministry of Education and coordinated by a Chinese Language Council called Hanban, which works under the patronage of the ministry. The institutes are established in cooperation with local partners, usually by forming partnerships between Chinese and local universities.[32] The impact of Chinese cultural diplomacy is still to be judged, but it seems to have been successful in spreading Chinese language teaching thus far.

Cultural Diplomacy in the Middle East

Middle Eastern states on the whole have not been great proponents of institutionalised cultural diplomacy. Although rhetoric and image control play a large role in politics, the concepts of soft power and cultural diplomacy as foreign policy tools are little developed, as evidenced by the general lack of institutionalised cultural activities abroad. A number of Gulf states have engaged in social power diplomacy, investing some of their oil wealth into development and aid projects abroad. Saudi Arabia, Qatar and Iran are clearly competing for influence in the region, and mobilise their resources to keep and gain friends. Where existent, cultural diplomacy and soft power have been very much state-produced.

Very few Arab countries have cultural centres abroad, and those that do count only a very limited number. Algeria for instance has one cultural centre abroad (in Paris), Tunisia has allegedly been planning to set up a network of cultural centres (Maisons de Tunisie) around the world, and Syria has a handful of centres. Cultural policies on the whole lack vision and clear strategies. In most countries, several actors are responsible for cultural diplomacy, ranging from the Ministry of Culture and the Ministry of Foreign Affairs to the Ministry of Higher Education. Some countries have specialised agencies, such as the 'Cultural Influence Algerian Agency', a body affiliated to the Algerian Ministry of Culture and responsible for Algeria's presence at international cultural events, or Morocco's 'Supreme Council for Culture' set up in 1975 to discuss cultural policies. The concept of culture is often mobilised for political ends, with the state taking on the role of gatekeeper limiting private initiatives. Notable exceptions are Lebanon and Palestine, where governments are weak and private initiatives and civil society drive the cultural sector. However, this takes place largely on a local level, collaborating with other countries for fundraising and exchange activities.[33] While cultural diplomacy has been underdeveloped in most Arab countries, a debate about cultural policies and the need to move away from a state-centric model to a more diverse and independent approach has started amongst a number of civil society actors in the region. The advent of the Arab uprisings in early 2011 has shown that people power counts in the region, and countries like Tunisia have greatly enhanced their regional attractiveness – at least momentarily.

One phenomenon of the last two decades is the rise of Arab satellite television channels. Al Jazeera, launched in 1996 by the Emir of Qatar, serves Qatar's diplomacy as an instrument of prestige and influence.[34] In 2003, Saudi Arabia followed suit and launched Al Arabiya, its satellite channel based in Dubai. Following the success of first Al Jazeera and then Al Arabiya, and wanting to influence Arab public opinion following growing hostility against it after the US led-invasion of Iraq in 2003, the United States launched its own Arabic satellite channel, Al Hurra. However, the latter never succeeded in attracting audiences, and was not taken seriously by the Arab public.[35] As asserted above, cultural diplomacy depends on perception, the latter being connected to legitimacy – since the US presence in Iraq was not considered legitimate, its public diplomacy attempts were dismissed as mere propaganda efforts.

One country in the region systematically employing cultural diplomacy is the Islamic Republic of Iran. Iran has engaged in an active programme to promote its ideas and values abroad since its inception, believing in the power of culture in foreign policy. As Joseph Nye has affirmed: 'I think one can say that Iran believes it has soft power'.[36] In the first decade of the Islamic Republic, Iran was driven by a desire to export its revolution. This transformed into a more subtle effort to project its values abroad during the 1990s, when Iran set up an institution to coordinate its cultural diplomacy work, the Islamic Culture and Relations Organisation (*sazeman-e ertebatat va farhang-e eslami*), ICRO in short. Like the Goethe-Institut or British Council, the ICRO administers Iranian cultural centres abroad that actively implement official Iranian cultural policies.

To sum up, culture has been used as an instrument of foreign policy. Cultural diplomacy is the attempt by governments to build up ties between peoples, and attract and co-opt the people of another state through the use of culture and political values. It is based to a large degree on communication, engaging people and building lasting relationships. Soft power is one outcome of cultural diplomacy: when a country is successful in attracting the people of another country, one can say that it has soft power. This can fall outside of the control of government policies – soft power is in the eye of the beholder. Cultural diplomacy on the other hand is still very much the business of governments, in particular when considering authoritarian states.

This book is an in-depth study of the case of cultural diplomacy between Syria and Iran, against the backdrop of their bilateral relationship and the international relations of the Middle East.

Outline and Sources

First, I establish a historical narrative of Syrian-Iranian relations in order to give a framework for the emergence of cultural diplomacy between the two countries. Syria and Iran have been located in their historical context drawing on the contemporary history of both places, comparing their structures and policies towards each other. In this introduction, the concepts of cultural diplomacy and soft power have been explained before looking at a number of examples of cultural diplomacy in action, setting the frame for analysis. Chapter 1 gives the historical backdrop for the book by presenting an overview of Syrian-Iranian relations from the pre-revolutionary period until the present, essential for putting cultural diplomacy between the two allies into the right context. This is followed up in Chapter 2 with a study of the foreign policy formulation and cultural policies in Syria and Iran, as well as key themes and political values that characterise the shared Syrian and Iranian worldview promoted in their dialogue.

Attention has been given to institutional practice through which cultural diplomacy is fostered. I have aimed to develop a profile of the institutions involved in the process. In Chapter 3 I examine to what extent cultural relations were promoted by the two sides prior to the Islamic revolution in Iran, and introduce the foundations and guidelines for post-revolutionary exchange. The next chapter, Chapter 4, deals with Iran's cultural diplomacy in Syria, looking at the motivations, content and reach of the activities of the Iranian cultural centre in Damascus to evaluate the effectiveness of Iran's cultural diplomacy efforts and its limits in Syria. Chapter 5 looks at the Arab-Syrian cultural centre in Tehran and Syria's cultural diplomacy in Iran, showing that Syria's cultural presence in Iran is primarily an expression of the strengthening of the Syrian-Iranian alliance in the face of external challenges.

Finally, I explore the directions and limitations of cultural diplomacy in practice using a case-based approach. Having examined the main institutions involved in bilateral cultural relations, we will look at two groups of actors. Chapter 6 focuses on language students in both countries, as well as Iranian students in Syria and Syrian students in Iran, whereas Chapter 7 concentrates on the case of Iranian religious tourists to Syria, which draws on the shared cultural heritage between both countries while showing the limits of interaction between the two peoples.

Due to the nature of my subject, sources include not only archival material and publications of official institutions, but also rely on interviews and conversations, as well as participant observation. Websites of institutions have proven a valuable source in particular to provide data on foreign cultural centres and cultural diplomacy practices. In addition, a survey of news articles from the Syrian, Iranian and international press has complemented my research.

In terms of archival material, the most important findings were made at the Iranian Foreign Ministry archives in Niavaran, Tehran. I went there hoping to obtain a copy of the 1975 cultural agreement between Syria and Iran, after I had received copies of the 1984 cultural agreement and subsequent implementation programmes between the two countries from the Syrian Ministry of Culture. I did find the draft text of the 1975 agreement, and much more. The archivists gave me access to the folder of the Iranian embassy in Damascus, covering the period between 1950 and early 1978. Allegedly due to a 30-year confidentiality rule, documents from the revolutionary and post-revolutionary period were not accessible in the summer of 2008, when I spent over a month at the archives. Documents consulted included

Iranian embassy correspondence with various ministries back in Tehran as well as with the Syrian Foreign Ministry, news articles of the time and Syrian and Iranian reactions to them, consular matters, memoranda of understanding between the two countries, reports on political and cultural bilateral relations, and correspondence about university affairs and pilgrimage.

Another source of useful official written material proved to be the library of the ICRO, the main institution for coordinating Iran's cultural foreign policy. There I managed to obtain a number of internal reports and correspondence between the Iranian cultural centre in Damascus and its mother organisation, the ICRO. These provided an invaluable insight into the workings of the Iranian cultural centre in Damascus as reported back to Tehran, documenting not only activities of the centre and reporting on official visits of Iranian delegations, but also introducing the Syrian cultural landscape as viewed from the Iranian centre.

These reports were complemented with a survey of publications of the Iranian cultural centre in Damascus, which included articles in the centre's journal, *Islamic Culture*, quarterly brochures announcing the programme of activities of the centre, various pamphlets, reports on the centre's activities, books and studies. While examining the material available at the Iranian cultural centre, I also engaged in participant observation to understand the dynamics of the centre, becoming part of its regular activities as well as interacting with the visitors frequenting the centre. This allowed me to form my own opinion about the content and reach of the centre's activities.

While it was unproblematic to keep track of the activities of the Iranian cultural centre in Damascus due to the mountain of material proliferated by the Iranian side, it was more difficult to find out information about the Syrian cultural centre in Tehran, which had next to no publications – neither did it offer reports about its activities, nor did it have a written programme available. A glossy brochure about the centre and the draft of a lecture given by the centre's first director at several Iranian universities in the academic year 2005–2006 were about the only two pieces of written material that could be obtained from the centre. Information on the Syrian centre has thus largely been taken from the Syrian press, *Tishrin* newspaper in particular, and interviews and conversations with people involved in the centre, such as its director and staff, and students frequenting the centre. The imbalance in quantity of sources about the Syrian and Iranian centres reflects the level of motivation and productivity of both countries' cultural diplomacy.

Interviews and informal conversations form a core source of information. Interviews were held in Syria and Iran with Syrian, Iranian and European diplomats, former and present directors and staff of the two cultural centres, university professors, officials at the Syrian Ministry of Culture in Damascus and the ICRO in Tehran, students and others. Conversations were held with teachers, students, shopkeepers, travel agents and taxi drivers. Personal observations made during my regular participation in events of the two cultural centres over the course of several years gave me precious insights into the dynamics of both countries' cultural diplomacy efforts, obtaining an idea of who the audience was that each centre managed to reach out to. I also observed Iranian pilgrims in Damascus, in the crowded streets of the old town, in the market thoroughfares, in the shrines they visited, in the areas around their hotels.

Through use of rich empirical data collected in both Syria and Iran, it will be demonstrated that while cultural diplomacy has provided bridges between the two countries, its reach remains limited. Relations continue to be strongest on the official level.

CHAPTER 1

HISTORICAL BACKDROP: OVERVIEW OF SYRIAN-IRANIAN RELATIONS SINCE 1946

This chapter will provide an overview of bilateral relations between Syria and Iran from the mid-twentieth century until the present, which presents essential background information for understanding the context of cultural diplomacy between the two states. I first discuss the period prior to the Islamic revolution in Iran, concentrating in particular on the 1970s after Hafiz al-Asad took over the Syrian presidency. Relations in the pre-revolutionary period played out on two levels, between the two states on one level and between Syria and the Iranian opposition on another level. I then deal with the first decade of the post-revolutionary period, during which the strong Syrian-Iranian partnership emerged and became consolidated through continuous cooperation and consultation, in particular during times of crises. I then analyse bilateral relations during the 1990s up to the US-led invasion of Iraq in 2003, before focussing on relations since 2003. Throughout the 1990s, which were dominated by the Arab-Israeli peace process, Syria and Iran continued to maintain their relationship despite differences and grew closer together by the end of the decade. Syrian-Iranian relations received a boost following the 2003 invasion of Iraq, the two partners presenting a united front against the challenges they faced in the region. Syria stuck to its ally when the latter faced domestic challenges following the 2009 presidential election, and Iran has continued to support the Syrian regime throughout the on-going crisis that started in March 2011. While this overview is far from exhaustive, it will give an insight into how the Syrian-Iranian relationship has developed since the two countries established diplomatic relations in 1946.

Diplomatic and Undiplomatic Relations: Syria and Imperial Iran

Relations between Syria and Iran in the decades preceding the Islamic revolution in Iran were generally poor. Ideologically, the two countries had not much in common. Syria was Arab nationalist, pro-Soviet and did not recognise Israel. Pahlavi Iran was Iranian nationalist, pro-Western and – while never officially recognising it – maintained close relations with Israel.[1] In the 1970s, interaction between the two countries increased: the Syrian government established limited relations with both the Shah and his opposition. Diplomatic relations between the two governments have to be largely seen in terms of the broader regional shifts in alliances throughout the 1970s – neither the Shah nor Asad were set on a close relationship. Whilst the Shah for strategic and personal reasons was more interested in the Persian Gulf and Egypt than Syria – the Shah and Egypt's president Sadat maintained a personal friendship – Asad still opposed the Shah's positive stance towards Israel and his submission to the United States.[2] Therefore Syria established ties with members of the Shah's Islamic opposition parallel to official relations.[3] How Syrian-Iranian relations developed in the decade leading up to the revolution will be examined in the following, by first looking at diplomatic exchanges between Syria and Imperial Iran before turning towards relations of the former with the Islamic opposition to the Shah.

Diplomatic Exchanges between Syria and Imperial Iran

Asad in conversation with Muhammad Reza Shah: 'The two countries Iran and Syria have friendly relations. Of course it is possible that sometimes there are matters of difference between two friendly countries and this is natural.[4]

Tense Beginnings

Syria and Iran established limited relations in the period leading up to the Islamic revolution. Full diplomatic relations between the two countries had been established in 1946 after Syria gained independence.[5] While initially trying to consolidate diplomatic ties – exemplified by the signing of a friendship treaty in 1953 – relations between the two states in the late 1950s and 1960s were tense.[6] Arab nationalism was at its height, with Syria – next to Egypt – as its most outspoken proponent. The Shah was considered an agent of Western imperialism, for whom the Arab nationalists had no sympathy.[7] Iran was signatory to the Baghdad Pact of 1955, whereas Syria's refusal to join the defence agreement put her further in the anti-Western camp and moved her closer to Egypt.[8]

The Bahrain episode exemplifies Syrian-Iranian differences during this period. When in November 1957 the Iranian Council of Ministers approved a bill that designated Bahrain as the fourteenth Iranian province and reasserted Iran's claim to the island, the Syrians strongly denounced this move. A Syrian Foreign Ministry spokesman stated that Syria considered Bahrain part of the 'Arab Nation'.[9] The Syrian press of the time was full of reports of the 'Iranian conspiracy to conquer Bahrain', to the extent that the Iranian embassy in Damascus complained to the Syrian Foreign Ministry about Iran being misrepresented in the Syrian press.[10] More tensions arose in the mid-1960s. Egyptian-Iranian relations had been full of differences, especially with regards to Iran's policies in the Gulf, and Syria did not want to be outdone by Egypt in proving its Arab credentials. In November 1965 Yusuf Zu'ayyin's Ba'thist government in Syria claimed that the Iranian Arab province of Khuzestan was an integral part of the Arab homeland and referred to it as 'Arabistan'. The Syrian government later denied that it had intended to damage relations between the two states, but the harm was done: in reaction, the Iranian regime protested and withdrew its ambassador and most of its diplomatic staff from Damascus, downgrading the level of bilateral ties.[11] Diplomatic relations developed again after the 1967 Arab-Israeli war, when the Iranian Red Lion and Sun Society sent medical personnel and humanitarian aid to Syria to assist with Syrian war casualties.[12]

During the 1970s, bilateral relations improved due to significant regional changes. As Hafiz al-Asad set Syrian foreign policy on a new course whilst Muhammad Reza Shah started to take a greater interest in regional affairs, relations between the two states warmed up. During the 1973 Arab-Israeli War, Iran provided logistical, medical and non-military assistance to the Arab side. It received Syrian and Egyptian wounded soldiers in Tehran and cared for them in its hospitals.[13] It was not until late 1973, however, that diplomatic relations returned to ambassadorial level. On 5 December 1973 Iran's ambassador Muhammad Pursartip presented his credentials to Syrian president Hafiz al-Asad. Syria also appointed an ambassador to Iran, Ali Mohsen Zifa.[14] This followed an improvement in Syrian-Iranian relations after the October War due to several factors. Syria under Asad had started to become a more important regional player – and thus more significant for Iran. With a shift in foreign policy from a state mainly driven by ideology to being a more realist actor, Syria reconsidered its posture towards Iran.[15] This coincided with Iran's decision to play a more active role in the region following British withdrawal from the Gulf in 1971 and its new found economic power after the oil price revolution of 1973, which drastically improved its financial situation.[16] The death of Nasser in 1970 and the relative decline of Pan-Arabism also contributed to Iran taking a more pro-Arab stance. As the oil price boom shifted the regional balance of power in favour of the Gulf States, non-oil states such as Syria were more willing to make political compromises in exchange for economic assistance.[17] Against this background, relations between the two states warmed up and diplomatic relations expanded.

Increased Diplomatic Activity and Asad's State Visit to Iran

Starting in 1974, a series of high-level exchanges took place. This began on the economic level: whilst some Iranian businessmen and industrialists had taken part in the 1972 Damascus Trade Fair, it was not until May 1974 that an economic agreement was reached between

Syria and Iran following the visit of Muhammad Imadi, the Syrian Minister of Economics and Finance, to Tehran. Shortly after, in the summer of 1974, the Iranian Foreign Minister visited his counterpart, Abd al-Halim Khaddam, in Damascus; the latter returned the visit in November.[18] Moreover, a tourism agreement was signed in the same year, as part of the stipulations of the economic agreement.[19] In 1975, a cultural agreement was drafted between the two countries in Tehran, but never put into practice.[20]

This diplomatic exchange culminated in Asad's state visit to Tehran in December 1975 to consolidate the growing interaction with Iran. Asad had a number of motivations for this visit. Syria felt increasingly isolated in the region: Sadat had adopted a pro-US policy after 1973 and concluded an interim agreement with Israel in September 1975; Syrian relations with Iraq remained tense, whilst Iran's bilateral relations with Egypt and Iraq improved – the latter in particular following the Algiers Accord of March 1975 in which Iran and Iraq temporarily settled their dispute over the Shatt al-'Arab waterway.[21] At the same time, Iran was becoming a more important regional and international player, and since it had adopted a more pro-Arab stand, Asad felt a rapprochement between Syria and Iran could be useful.[22] Moreover, he was hoping to use the Shah's close relationship with the United States to assert influence on Washington to approach the Arab-Israeli conflict in a more balanced way.[23] However, although the visit paved the way for further ministerial exchanges to expand political, economic and cultural ties between the two countries, the Shah refused to back Asad stance regarding Israel. On the contrary, he supported Sadat's decision to make peace with Israel and continued to maintain clandestine ties with the latter.[24] Officially, both sides issued a joint statement following the visit, calling for an end to occupation of Arab lands and the right of a Palestinian homeland, a just peace in the Middle East and the withdrawal of the Zionist regime from the occupied territories.[25] Overall, however, relations cooled down after the visit.

Regional Power Balancing

The process of the mid-1970s has been described as at most a limited rapprochement. Neither state was of primary concern in the foreign policy formulation of the other. Bilateral relations between Syria and Iran before the Islamic revolution were largely influenced by regional power balancing. Keeping Israel in check was a major concern for Syria, albeit one not shared with Imperial Iran that continued its clandestine relations with Tel Aviv. Syria's move toward Iran had been out of pragmatic reasons; Asad still saw the Shah as a Western proxy and enemy of the Arabs, and despised his partnership with Israel.[26] The two states drifted further apart again in the late 1970s and Syria became increasingly isolated as a Saudi-Iranian-Egyptian axis developed under US approval, Sadat visited Jerusalem in November 1977 and signed the Camp David Accords in March 1979, and a Saudi-Iraqi-Jordanian entente was formed.[27]

Common interests in neighbouring Iraq played an important role in both countries' foreign policies. Agha and Khalidi suggest that the détente between Syria and Imperial Iran had no lasting effect on either bilateral relations or on the regional balance at large, but may have shaped Syria's perception of Iran as a balancing force against Iraq and vice versa.[28] Syrian and Iraqi relations were tense throughout the 1970s. The two Ba'thist countries were divided by power rivalry and party schism, which was intensified by personal tensions between Asad and Saddam Hussein.[29] After it had signed the Algiers Accord with Iran in 1975 and thus temporarily secured its eastern borders and outlet to the Persian Gulf, Iraq announced in April 1976 that it would stop using the trans-Syrian pipeline to export its oil, which damaged Syria's economy and made it more dependent on loans from the Gulf States and Iran.[30] However, Asad was prepared to put these differences aside in pursuit of larger interests concerning strategic parity with Israel. Thus between October 1978 and July 1979 he attempted to create a coalition with Iraq to counterbalance Egypt's peace agreement with Israel. This attempt failed, however, as mutual distrust and differences were too great. The uncovering of a plot against Saddam Hussein with alleged Syrian involvement brought talks to a standstill.[31] Thus by the end of the decade, a rapprochement between Syria and Iraq seemed remote. Likewise, Iran's relations with Iraq were historically characterised by border disputes and rivalry over access to the Persian Gulf. Tensions eased after the Algiers Accord of 1975, but never transformed into a friendship.

Relations between Syria and the Iranian Opposition

Sadegh Tabataba'i, on a visit to Damascus in October 1979 in his position as Deputy Prime Minister of the new Islamic Republic: 'I came to Damascus several times before the victory of the Iranian revolution...Syria was an arena for the Iranian revolutionaries who were fighting against the Shah's regime and who were supported by the Syrian government.'[32]

Parallel to establishing limited relations with the Shah's regime, Asad also maintained close ties with the Shah's opposition and supported Iranian activists in Syria and Lebanon. Syrian-Iranian relations in the Lebanese context for instance mainly took place between the Syrian leadership and the Iranian Shi'i opposition to the Shah. They were based not so much on power considerations as on personal ties, and formed the basis for the Syrian-Iranian alliance following the Islamic revolution.

Musa al-Sadr and Iranian Opposition Activists

The most prominent of these personal connections is Asad's relationship with Imam Musa al-Sadr, the head of the Lebanese Shi'i Supreme Council and one of the main figures behind the Lebanese Shi'a's awakening of political consciousness.[33] Born in Qom and educated at Najaf and al-Azhar, Sadr had been based in Lebanon since 1959 and soon emerged as the most authoritative spokesman for the Lebanese Shi'i community.[34] Sadr sought an alliance with Syria as he felt that the Lebanese Shi'i community could profit from a powerful external ally, whilst Asad viewed the Shi'a as an important potential partner in his bid to consolidate Syria's position of dominance in Lebanese politics. It has also been suggested that relations with the Lebanese Shi'a could be helpful in increasing the Alawite's religious legitimacy in Syria. In 1973 Sadr issued a fatwa proclaiming that the Alawite community constituted an authentic part of Shi'i Islam, after a prolonged dialogue with Alawi religious shaykhs in Syria.[35] Asad's personal relationship to Sadr that had developed during the latter's frequent visits to Damascus allowed him to establish links with the Lebanese Shi'a and the Iranian opposition.[36] For instance, Sadr acted as a go-between with Khomeini, whom he periodically met with in Najaf.[37]

A network of prominent Iranian, Iraqi and Lebanese Shi'i clerics had been set up in the 1950s and 1960s. These clerics had studied together in Najaf and Qom where they established not only intellectual but also family links.[38] The development of close personal relationships between key figures from the Iranian opposition movement to the Shah and Lebanese Shi'a as well as members of the Palestinian movement enabled Iranian opposition groups to train in Amal and Fatah camps in Lebanon.[39] As Alpher, writing about what he calls 'The Khomeini International', reports:

> 'Together the exiles, the Syrians, and the Palestinians prepared cadres for revolutionary activity inside Iran. They organized arms smuggling operations into the country, using food transport trucks leaving Beirut to conceal weapons and explosives. They recruited supporters from the pro-Khomeini Iranian student movement, which they organized throughout the Middle East, Western Europe and the United States. They prepared and infiltrated propaganda and agitators back into Iran. They were free to move about Lebanon and Syria, visit Libya and Algeria, and organize revolution.'[40]

The list of Iranian revolutionaries coming out of Fatah camps is remarkable and comprises a high number of officials who took power after the fall of the Shah, including Khomeini's two sons.[41] Some of the Iranian opposition activists were even given Syrian passports, most notably Sadegh Ghotbzadeh who was to serve briefly as Iran's Foreign Minister following the revolution.[42] As a student in the United States, he had been active in anti-Shah activities; after the Shah revoked his passport and the USA subsequently expelled him, Musa al-Sadr helped Ghotbzadeh to obtain a Syrian passport as well as training in revolutionary organisation.[43] Ebrahim Yazdi and Mustafa Chamran were given diplomatic coverage by Syria – in 1979 Yazdi became Deputy Prime Minister in charge of revolutionary affairs (and later

Foreign Minister), and Chamran was appointed Defence Minister of the Islamic Republic after having played a leading role in the formation of the Revolutionary Guards.[44] Sadegh Tabataba'i, related to Khomeini and a nephew of Musa al-Sadr, served as a useful connection between the Syrian government and the Iranian opposition around Khomeini. He became government spokesman and Deputy Prime Minister following the revolution.[45] Another activist – and student of Khomeini in Najaf – who went to Lebanon in the 1970s was Ali Akbar Mohtashemipur, who served as the Islamic Republic's ambassador to Syria from 1981 before being appointed Minister of the Interior in 1985.[46] Mohtashemipur spent some time in the seminary Musa al-Sadr had set up in Tyre to learn about the position of the Lebanese Shi'a. However, he was dissatisfied with the teaching and became concerned about the way the southern Lebanese ulama dealt with the Palestine issue, fearing that they might create an atmosphere that would divide Muslims and only serve Israel. He returned to Khomeini in Najaf to inform him of the situation.[47] Mohtashemipur became an important actor in Syrian-Iranian relations following the Islamic revolution.

This support of the Islamic opposition to the Shah proved useful to the Syrians after the fall of the Shah. Syria was one of the few countries that had offered Khomeini asylum when Saddam Hussein expelled him from Iraq in October 1978. A former Iranian cultural attaché to Syria in the 1980s put great weight on the Syrian offer to take in Khomeini in 1978, as it 'left a good impression on Khomeini and laid the ground for the relationship that followed'.[48] Thus when the Islamic revolution took place in Iran and Khomeini created the Islamic Republic, limited relations with the new leadership had already been established. The limited rapprochement between the Syrian republic and the Iranian monarchy in 1975 contributed to enabling an increased interaction between Syria and Iranian oppositionists.

Ali Shariati

Ali Shariati, the Islamic intellectual whose ideas played an important role in shaping the Islamic Republic's ideology, provides another link between Syria and Iran. After his death in London under suspicious

Ali Shariati's shrine next to the shrine of Sayida Zaynab, 1 July 2008.

circumstances in June 1977, Shariati's body was flown to Damascus to be buried next to the shrine of Sayida Zaynab,[49] in conformance with his last wishes. Musa al-Sadr seemed to have encouraged this plan, and officiated at Shariati's funeral.[50]

Zaynab, Imam Husayn's sister, was greatly admired by Shariati for her courage and resistance.[51] According to Shariati's biographer Rahnema, Shariati 'had argued [in his speech "After martyrdom"] that every revolution had two aspects, blood and the message. Imam Husayn was the symbol of martyrdom and blood, while the grave responsibility of communicating and disseminating Husayn's revolutionary message after his martyrdom was left to Zaynab.'[52] Following the revolution, the shrine of Sayida Zaynab became the main destination of the quickly developing Iranian religious tourist industry to Syria.

Syrian-Iranian relations prior to the Islamic revolution in Iran thus developed on two levels, the state-to-state level and the state-to-opposition level. On the state-to-state level, bilateral relations started off tense as post-independence Syria followed a radical Arab nationalist ideology in conflict with the Shah's regional policies. Relations in the 1970s improved with a shift in Iran's regional policies and the Shah's acknowledgement that Syria under Asad had become an important player in the Middle East that could not be ignored. The diplomatic exchange between Syria and Iran in the mid-1970s has to be understood in terms of both leaders' attempts to maintain a regional power balance most profitable for their respective countries. Official relations reached their peak in 1975 with Asad's state visit to Tehran, after which they declined again. On the state-to-opposition level, Syrian involvement with the Iranian opposition to the Shah's regime increased throughout the 1970s, culminating in Syria's offer to host Khomeini in 1978. Asad realised it might prove useful to maintain relations with both the Shah's regime and its Islamic opposition, and thus extended an arm of support to Iranian opposition activists in Syria. Syria was attractive to these activists as they could profit not only from the Palestinian training camps situated in Syria and Lebanon, but also from the pre-existing clerical networks linking neighbouring Lebanon to Najaf in Iraq and Qom in Iran. The fact that a number of Iranians who were to play a prominent role in the Islamic revolution and subsequent republic had been supported by Syria in the run-up to the revolution set the scene for the formation of an alliance between Syria and the Islamic Republic.

The First Revolutionary Decade

Bilateral relations developed quickly after the fall of the Shah. Asad welcomed the revolution in Iran, as the Islamic regime's hostile position towards Israel allowed for a Syrian-Iranian alliance, bringing Syria out of regional isolation. In fact, Syria and the Soviet Union were the first to recognise the new regime in Iran.[53] Syria and revolutionary Iran's common stance vis-à-vis Israel and the United States, both countries' interests in Lebanon, their animosity towards neighbouring Iraq and their mutual need for a regional partner turned their relationship into a close alliance. In the following, the development of Syrian-Iranian relations in the 1980s will be mapped out, by first looking at diplomatic exchanges in general, before examining bilateral relations in various regional contexts: Iraq, the Persian Gulf and the Lebanese arena. It will become clear that the emerging alliance was not without its ups and downs, but had survived several tests by the end of the decade and become consolidated.

An alliance proved useful to both sides. For the Islamic Republic, an alliance with Syria gave it a much needed Arab ally in its eight year war with Iraq, preventing the war from turning into an all-out Arab-versus-Persian affair. It moreover provided Iran with access to the Shi'i community in Lebanon, an area where Iran hoped to increase its influence. For Syria, revolutionary Iran constituted a new and potentially powerful partner to replace Egypt in its struggle against Israel. Iran's change of strategy towards Israel, expressed through its commitment to the Palestinian cause and anti-Zionism, brought Iran ideologically closer to Syria.[54] Both countries shared not only their anti-Zionist attitude, but also an anti-imperialist one primarily directed against US foreign policy in the region. Syria supported Iran in its war against old rival Saddam Hussein, although it was opposed to Iran occupying any Arab land in the process. Syria also had economic incentives: in exchange for its political support and military assistance in Iran's war with Iraq, Syria received a large quantity of free or discounted oil from Iran. It has also been suggested that an association with Khomeini's Iran would be useful for Hafiz al-Asad in bolstering his religious credentials and avoid Iran backing the Islamic opposition in Syria, with whom Asad had been struggling since the late 1970s. Having Iran on his side would prevent Iran becoming an adversary.[55] Thus although some scholars have emphasised the theoretical incompatibility between the two countries – Syria the socialist republic and bearer of pan-Arabism vis-à-vis Iran the radical Islamic theocracy opposing the concept of a nation-state[56] – both sides had clear geopolitical and material interests in an alliance.

Diplomatic Exchanges

Abd al-Halim Khaddam in his position as Syrian Foreign Minister, August 1979: 'Syria has supported the Iranian revolution prior to its outbreak, during it and after its triumph.'[57]

Iranian President Khamene'i, July 1987: 'Fortunately, our Syrian brothers have always proved that they are strongly committed to expansion and deepening of relations with the Islamic Republic of Iran.'[58]

Following Ayatollah Khomeini's arrival in Tehran in February 1979 and the fall of the imperial government in Iran, President Asad sent a telegram to Khomeini congratulating him on his triumph over the Shah. A month later, the first senior Syrian official, Information Minister Ahmad Iskandar Ahmad, visited Iran and presented Khomeini in Qom with a Quran as a gift from Asad.[59] Then, during his visit to Tehran in August 1979, Syria's Foreign Minister Khaddam proclaimed the Iranian revolution to be the 'most important event in contemporary history' and that Syria supported it 'prior to its outbreak, during it and after its triumph'.[60] These steps taken by the Syrian regime clearly indicated to the new leadership in Tehran that Syria looked favourably at the transformation in Iran. Thus when Iran tried to win Arab support for its case against the United States in the aftermath of the US embassy takeover in Tehran in November 1979, the Iranian Foreign Minister Bani-Sadr at first turned towards Syria. In ensuing talks with the Syrian ambassador Younes, the scope for political and economic cooperation between the two countries was discussed.[61]

From this point onwards, high-level diplomatic exchanges took place between Syria and Iran. The intensity of bilateral consultations varied according to regional developments. Whenever a crisis loomed on the horizon, Damascus or Tehran dispatched a high-ranking official or delegation to the other side's capital for briefings and to discuss further cooperation. The drive for these discussions seems to have come primarily from the Iranian side, seeing that Iran sent a larger number of envoys to Syria during the 1980s than vice versa. All in all, visits of Iranian officials to Syria exceeded visits of Syrian officials to Iran by roughly a third.[62]

Whilst the Iranian Foreign Minister and his deputy made the highest number of trips to Syria in the 1980s, closely followed by the Minister for the Revolutionary Guards Corps, the Syrian envoys seemed to have been more economically orientated. The Syrian Ministers for Oil, Economy, Commerce and Industry paid nearly as many visits to Tehran as the Syrian Foreign Minister. This reflects the nature of the alliance in the early period: whilst Iran's interests in the alliance were primarily of a political and military nature (as indicated by the presence of the Revolutionary Guards), Syrian interests were political as well as economic. Iran's need for Syrian support was moreover often immediate, for example in the context of the war with Iraq or in the Lebanese arena, which accounts for a high number of Iranian official delegations to Syria.

The signing of a ten-year trade pact between Syria and Iran in March 1982 marked the formal beginning of extensive bilateral relations, as it to some degree constituted the institutionalisation of their relationship. In this pact, Iran agreed to supply Syria with a substantial amount of crude oil in exchange for phosphates, textiles, glass, barley and other foodstuffs; Syria moreover agreed to provide services to Iranian tourists.[63] It is true that the intensity of diplomatic exchanges increased after 1982, as we shall see by looking at the various areas of Syrian-Iranian cooperation in more detail.

The Iraq Factor

Patrick Seale: 'Asad condemned Saddam's war as the wrong war
against the wrong enemy at the wrong time. To fight Iran was
folly: it would exhaust the Arabs, fragment their ranks and
divert them from "the holy battle in Palestine".'[64]

The consolidation of the Syrian-Iranian alliance has often been attrib-
uted to Syria's support of Iran throughout the eight-year long Iran-Iraq
war. Asad was against the war. However, to avert an Iraqi victory and
to prevent an all-Arab front against Iran that might lead the latter
to turn towards Israel for military assistance, he opted to support
the Islamic Republic. In September 1980, a few days before the Iraqi
invasion of Iranian territory, the Iranian President Bani-Sadr sent a
special envoy to Damascus to seek diplomatic and military assistance.
Whilst Asad at this stage refused to declare publicly support for Iran
or to send troops to Syria's eastern border with Iraq, he did agree to
provide Iran with arms and medical supplies.[65] Asad's siding with
non-Arab Iran against fellow Arab Iraq was not a popular decision in
Arab public opinion, which is why Asad wanted to keep a low profile in this matter. It could only be justified by portraying Iran as a
committed force in the general struggle against Israel – Syria was in
effect protecting Iran against Iraqi aggression with the aim of ending
the hostilities as quickly as possible to concentrate all forces to fight
against 'Imperialism and Zionism'.[66] During the Arab summits in Fez
in November 1981 and September 1982, Syria had to defend its position in front of its fellow Arabs, but could not be persuaded to drop
its support for Iran.[67]

Syria helped Iran in several ways. In April 1981, Syrian airspace
was made accessible to Iran in order for Iranian warplanes to refuel
during their raid against al-Walid, the base for much of the Iraqi strategic bomber force.[68] Under Iranian pressure, Syria closed the border
with Iraq as well as the pipeline carrying Iraqi oil via Syria to the
Mediterranean in April 1982, depriving Iraq of about 40 per cent of
its oil revenue.[69] It moreover supported oppositional forces in Iraq,
especially Kurdish resistance groups.[70] Syria weakened Iraq not only

directly, but also indirectly. For instance, it used its influence in Arab circles to block any Arab moves to help Baghdad militarily following Iraqi demands for Arab military assistance in May 1982.[71] However, when the tides in the Gulf war turned after the summer of 1982 and Iran went on the offensive against Iraq, Syria faced regional and international pressure to reconsider its position in the conflict.[72] Asad remained loyal to his Iranian ally, although he tried to pressure Iran to ease tensions and prevent further escalations in the war. It had become apparent by early 1985 that Iran could have ended hostilities with Iraq between 1982 and 1984, but had misjudged Iraq's strength and the wider support the latter received, and decided to fight on. Iran's obstinate behaviour in the war alienated many of its Arab neighbours and polarised the situation, thus increasing the importance of the Syrian-Iranian alliance from Tehran's point of view.[73]

The years 1984 to 1987 were problematic in the alliance. Not only were both Iran and Syria suffering economic difficulties that hindered the former to deliver oil supplies and the latter to pay its outstanding debts, but also Jordan tried to mediate a Syrian-Iraqi rapprochement that would drive Syria and Iran apart. However, although limited talks between Syria and Iraq ensued, Syria remained close to Iran and the two countries continuously declared their ties firm. Diplomatic activities were at their height during this period – dialogue was perceived as crucial to sort out their differences and increase cooperation.[74] Syria was generally informed about forthcoming Iranian actions in Iraq. A notable exception was Iran's acceptance of UN resolution 598 in July 1988, which ended the eight-year conflict. Syria had apparently neither been consulted nor informed about this decision – which was grudgingly taken by Ayatollah Khomeini following an extraordinary meeting with senior Iranian political and a military officials – but welcomed the decision nevertheless.[75]

Gulf Mediation

Hafiz al-Asad, September 1987: 'After Mecca, some Arabs wanted to change relations with Iran... It is against the interests of the Arabs to break relations with Iran.'[76]

'Both in Amman and Algiers [at the Arab League summits in November 1987 and June 1988 respectively], Syria did not try to swim against the strong anti-Iranian current and paid lip service to the pro-Iraqi bloc by endorsing its position, but it refused to abandon its strategic relationship with Iran.'[77]

Particularly in the second half of the Iran-Iraq war, Syria played an important role in mediating between Iran and its Arab Gulf neighbours. Whilst Saudi Arabia was working towards helping a Syrian-Jordanian reconciliation as well as Syrian-Iraqi rapprochement starting in the mid-1980s, Syria acted as a go-between for Iran and the Arab Gulf states. This proved crucial especially following the Mecca incident in July 1987, when Iranian pilgrims clashed with Saudi security forces during the hajj season in Mecca, resulting in over 400 people killed. This incident revived fears amongst Arab Gulf states of Iranian revolutionary expansionism. Syria managed to ease the damage done to Arab-Iranian relations and to modify an Arab League resolution calling for the severance of diplomatic ties with Iran, which was drafted at the Arab League meeting in August 1987. At the following Arab League meeting a month later, at least seven Arab states – led by Syria and Algeria – advocated dialogue with Iran, which prevented the break-off of Arab-Iranian diplomatic relations.[78] The Amman summit in November that year again condemned Iran for not accepting UN resolution 598 of July 1987, which demanded an immediate end to hostilities between Iran and Iraq.[79] Although it was anything but easy for Syria to stand by Iran against an anti-Iranian Arab front, Syria repeatedly declared its support for its ally and criticised the Arab League's attempt to isolate Iran by misrepresenting the Gulf War as an Arab-Persian conflict.[80] Syria thus proved a useful partner for Iran in the Arab world. For Syria, its relations with Iran increased its leverage in the Gulf. The alliance raised Syria's regional status; the Gulf states granted economic aid to Syria and acknowledged Syria as an Arab counter-balance to Iraq and a channel to Iran.[81]

The Lebanese Arena

Abd al-Halim Khaddam: 'We greatly value our alliance with Iran, but our regional allies must respect our position . . . our role

[in Lebanon] is above all other considerations. In their operations, our allies should pay attention to our interests and to those
of our [Lebanese] friends.'[82]

Another arena over which Syria and Iran cooperated was Lebanon. Both
Syria and Iran had strong interests in Lebanon, though at times their
interests clashed. Iranian policy in Lebanon was largely determined
by its Islamic vision.[83] Iran wanted to obtain influence and a degree
of control over the Lebanese Shi'i community, something for which it
needed Syrian support.[84] Syria for its part viewed the Shi'i community
as a crucial element in its bid to dominate Lebanese politics.[85] Formal
bilateral consultations over Lebanon started in the aftermath of the
Israeli invasion of Lebanon in June 1982. Iran immediately pronounced
its support for Lebanon and Syria, and sent a high-ranking military
delegation to Damascus to offer help against Israel.[86] This assistance
took the form of around one thousand Revolutionary Guards that Iran
dispatched to the Beqa'a Valley in eastern Lebanon, with Syrian con-
sent. Agha and Khalidi suggest that while Syria did not favour an
independent Iranian military presence per se in Lebanon, it nevertheless
valued the Iranian involvement as reinforcement against Israel –
especially in light of Arab inaction following the Israeli invasion.[87]

Syria and Iran were involved in a number of issues in Lebanon over
the next six years, sometimes on opposing ends. The two countries were
implicated in the hostage taking of Western foreigners in Lebanon by
Hezbollah – both actively and as mediators – and used their partnership over Hezbollah activity as an instrument to obtain political
and economic concessions from Western governments.[88] In the early
phase after the Israeli invasion, the two countries cooperated in what
they perceived as the struggle against the Zionist regime and Western
influence, and to prevent the USA from foisting a Lebanese-Israeli
treaty on the region.[89] The two suicide truck explosions in front of the
US embassy and the US Marine compound in Beirut in 1983, as well
as the second attack on the US embassy in 1984, which were allegedly
supported or even executed by Iran with Syrian backing, were in both
governments' interest.[90] The Iranian Deputy Foreign Minister – and
head of the Revolutionary Guards – Sheikholeslam visited Damascus

immediately before both occasions in 1983.[91] Policies over Lebanon were closely discussed between the Syrian and Iranian leadership.

Whereas Syria had the upper hand in dealings with Lebanon, Iran being dependent on Syrian approval for its actions in the region, Iran nevertheless had influence amongst the Lebanese Shi'i community. This was particularly true for Lebanon's south.[92] Following the Israeli invasion and Iran's subsequent military presence in Lebanon, Tehran played a direct role in the creation of Hezbollah. After the summer of 1982, Hezbollah developed as a Shi'i resistance movement, with the initial goal of ending the Israeli occupation of Lebanon.[93] The group was ideologically inspired by Iran and strongly supported by the latter, not only financially and spiritually, but also militarily.[94] Syria used its alliance with Iran to mobilize the support and armed organisation of the Shi'i community against the Israeli military presence in southern Lebanon.[95]

However, the fact that Iran contributed to Hezbollah's growth at the expense of Syrian-backed Amal was a point of irritation for the Syrians.[96] Moreover, with Israel's partial withdrawal from the country completed in 1985, the two sides clashed over the direction of Lebanon's political future. The period between 1985 and 1988 was marked by a series of high-level bilateral exchanges to resolve their differences and mediate in the intra-Shi'a clashes throughout this period. These involved not only high representatives from the respective governments, but also members of Iran's clerical establishment. Thus Hojjatoleslam Mehdi Karrubi, Khomeini's representative and head of the powerful Iranian Martyr's Foundation, led an Iranian delegation to Syria and Lebanon in early May 1985, whilst Ayatollah Jannati, a prominent member of Iran's Guardian Council, travelled to the two countries later that year to discuss Lebanon's fate and promote Islamic unity.[97] This indicates the special interest Iran attached to Lebanon as a host to Iran's revolutionary ambitions. What is more, Ali Akbar Mohtashemipur, the Iranian ambassador to Syria since 1981 and a proponent of exporting Iran's revolution, was appointed Minister of the Interior in 1985.[98] He had been the chief coordinator of Iranian activities in Syria and Lebanon, and had played a key part in the founding of Hezbollah.[99] The fact that he was given the Ministry of Interior, a position of power in Iran, underlines the importance the Iranian regime ascribed to Syria and Lebanon.

Despite constant tensions in the Lebanese arena, Iran and Syria managed not only to preserve their alliance, but also eventually to arrange a truce between the Shi'i factions in 1988 – under threat of Syrian military intervention against Hezbollah. This followed intense diplomatic activity between the two partners.[100] In March 1987, for instance, following renewed clashes between Hezbollah and rival militias, Mohtashemipur made two trips to Syria to sort out Syrian-Iranian differences over Lebanon.[101] In July 1987, a month after the kidnapping of American journalist Charles Glass in Lebanon which reportedly led to further tensions in Syrian-Iranian relations, Syrian Foreign Minister Faruq al-Shara travelled to Tehran to reiterate Syria's support for Iran and express his country's wish to further strengthen the alliance.[102] The fact that the two sides managed to compromise and set their own interests aside in favour of their alliance, as demonstrated through their cooperation during the clashes between Hezbollah and Amal in May 1988, showed that their relationship had evolved into a stable alliance.[103] As Muhammad Ali Besharati, in his position as Deputy Foreign Minister and supervisor of the mediation team formed to end the Amal-Hezbollah clashes, stated during his visit to Beirut: 'We maintain the best of relations with the brothers in Syria. We also conduct the best of dialogues and maintain good understanding with them.'[104] Although Syrian-Iranian cooperation in Lebanon had been far from smooth throughout the decade, and had put the alliance to a real test, by the time the two sides managed to broker a truce between the Shi'i factions in mid-1988 relations had become consolidated.

Syrian-Iranian relations during the 1980s thus survived despite a series of crises and existential threats, which were partly created by regional developments and attitudes (such as in the Gulf conflict), partly by their conflicting views on certain issues (such as in Lebanon). These events and the fact that the two partners were able to resolve their differences through intense diplomatic activities only deepened their relationship and consolidated their alliance. Relations during this period were distinctly marked by the Iran-Iraq war, Syrian mediation to prevent the formation of an Arab-versus-Persian front in the region, Iran's revolutionary ambitions to widen its influence in receptive circles such as the Lebanese Shi'i community, and a general battle for control in Lebanon. Both sides' commitment to work out their differences through diplomacy is reflected in the number of visits of high-ranking officials during this period. This is not to say that each side was entirely content with the other side's conduct, and tensions certainly existed – in particular in the mid to late 1980s. However, both the Syrian and the Iranian regimes demonstrated their willingness to invest in a strengthened alliance.

Relations after Khomeini: 1989 until 2003

Whilst the 1970s had been important in establishing the framework for bilateral relations, the 1980s can be regarded as the formative years of the Syrian-Iranian alliance. Syrian-Iranian relations entered a new phase in 1989. Whilst cooperation over Iraq and Lebanon continued to play an important role in the relationship, the end of the Iran-Iraq war in July 1988 and the Ta'if Agreement of October 1989 – that started the process of setting an end to the Lebanese civil war – changed the nature of regional politics. By the time of Khomeini's death in June 1989, bilateral relations had become consolidated. Shortly after his death, the Iranian constitution was amended, abolishing the position of prime minister and placing more power in the hands of the president. Under the presidency of Hashemi Rafsanjani, the focus of Iranian policy was on economic reconstruction after the Iran-Iraq war, and its foreign policy was marked by pragmatism. Throughout the 1990s, Syria and Iran further strengthened their relationship, but not without ups and downs. The Kuwait crisis of 1990/91 was the first test in the alliance following the end of the Iran-Iraq war. The Arab-Israeli peace process and Syria's involvement in it dominated much of the 1990s; other matters of mutual concern continued to be regional security, Lebanon and Iraq. With the faltering of the peace process in the mid-1990s and the emergence of a Turkish-Israeli alliance, Syria and Iran grew closer together towards the end of the 1990s. High-level diplomatic exchanges continued throughout the decade, reaffirming bilateral relations.

The Second Gulf War: The Kuwait Crisis

The first regional crisis Syria and Iran encountered after the end of the Iran-Iraq war in 1988 and the death of Imam Khomeini was the Kuwait crisis of 1990/91. Both states took different positions on the crisis; whilst Syria joined the US-led coalition against Iraq, Iran remained neutral.[105] However, their different stances did not negatively affect their bilateral relations. On the contrary: increased regional diplomatic activity – including President Asad's first state visit to post-revolutionary Iran in September 1990 – led to the establishment of a Syrian-Iranian Higher Cooperation Committee, which further institutionalised their partnership.[106]

On 2 August 1990 Iraq invaded Kuwait. The ensuing second Gulf war changed the regional power balance, which both Syria and Iran used to reposition themselves after the first war. The fact that Iraq invaded another Arab country retrospectively justified Asad's support for Iran during the Iran-Iraq war.[107] Iran seized the opportunity to promote its role in the region: it condemned the Iraqi invasion, voiced its opposition to the presence of foreign forces in the region and called for regional cooperation in solving the crisis. President Rafsanjani accepted Saddam Hussein's offer to agree to all of Iran's conditions in implementing UN resolution 598, recognise the Algiers Accord and exchange prisoners of war, which put him in a position to mediate between Iraq and the Gulf Cooperation Council (GCC) as well as the international community, and play a more important role in the region.[108]

Both Syria and Iran condemned Iraq's invasion of Kuwait, but were against Western military intervention and the presence of foreign troops in the region, although Syria joined the US-led coalition against Iraq in the end. A number of high-ranking Syrian officials visited Iran shortly after the start of the crisis, in order to reaffirm their regional cooperation. In mid-August Syrian Vice President Khaddam met Rafsanjani in Tehran to deliver a message from Asad. According to an Iranian news agency, Khaddam expressed Syria's 'grave concern' over the Gulf crisis and stated that Syria was ready to cooperate with Iran in 'taking joint stances against foreign threats in the region'.[109]

In September Asad himself visited Tehran in order to discuss the crisis as well as developments in Lebanon. The two states announced a joint policy on the Gulf crisis and agreed to work towards an end to 'Iraqi aggression and the foreign presence in the Gulf'. The presidents issued a joint communiqué praising the alliance.[110]

One important outcome of Asad's visit to Iran was the creation of a Syrian-Iranian Higher Cooperation Committee in November 1990. Chaired by the respective Vice Presidents and Foreign Ministers, it was to meet at regular intervals for consultations.[111] Within the framework of these meetings, Rafsanjani returned Asad's visit in April 1991 at the head of a large delegation including the Foreign, Trade and Oil Ministers, the Secretary of the National Security Council, as well as parliament and Foreign Ministry officials.[112] In Damascus, the two presidents followed up on their discussions of regional affairs. Following this visit, the two sides issued a communiqué, which was released in Damascus and Tehran:

'On bilateral relations, the two presidents expressed satisfaction with the important, qualitative progress in Syrian-Iranian relations in the political field. They stressed the need to continue to consolidate these relations, which have proven their efficacy in spite of the events in the region, all the difficulties each country has faced and the constant pressures on both of them. The two presidents stressed the need to promote Syrian-Iranian relations to an exceptional level – especially in the economic, cultural and technical fields – in the interests of the two friendly countries and their people.'[113]

Regional Security: The 'Six-Plus-Two' Damascus Declaration

During Rafsanjani's Syria visit, the two presidents' discussions on regional security centred on the Damascus Declaration, which Asad explained to his Iranian counterpart. Iran opposed the Damascus Declaration, which called for an Arab regional security system between the six GCC countries – Saudi Arabia, Bahrain, Kuwait, Oman, Qatar and the United Arab Emirates – and Egypt and Syria, to the

exclusion of Iran. In March 1991, the GCC states, Syria and Egypt –
the 'six-plus-two' – had signed the Declaration, under which Syrian
and Egyptian troops were to be stationed in the Gulf in return for
$10 billion, to ensure post-war Gulf security. Iran was not pleased.
Shortly after the announcement, Ali Larijani, at that point a com-
mander of the Revolutionary Guards Corps, criticised the declaration,
complaining that neither Syria nor Egypt were Gulf powers and thus
should not take part in discussions about Persian Gulf security matters.
Whereas Egypt opposed an Iranian role in the regional security system,
Asad assured Iran's Foreign Minister that Iran would have a significant
role to play in the post-war order, and that the Damascus Declaration
would neither affect their alliance nor ignore Iran.[114] The USA, while
making some concessions to Iran, was keen on integrating Egypt into
the Gulf security system.[115] However, the Damascus Declaration soon
failed – the GCC preferred Western protection to a regional one, as
they probably distrusted Egypt and Syria and feared interference in
their internal affairs. In May 1991, Egypt began to withdraw its troops
from Saudi Arabia and Kuwait; in July the 'six-plus-two' Foreign
Ministers failed to reach an agreement on the formation of a joint
security force.[116] Judging by their record of cooperation and consultation in times of crises, had the initiative succeeded Syria and Iran
would in all probability have worked out their differences and found
an arrangement acceptable to both. In the long term Iran might have
preferred a Syrian-Egyptian military presence to a US one.

The Peace Process[117]

Vice President Khaddam, February 1996: 'Bilateral relations
are good. Over long years, these relations and confidence have
been entrenched between the two capitals. There is no problem
between the two sides, and we always discuss the best means for
developing and strengthening relations. There are several joint
interests between Syria and Iran, and between the Arab nation
and Iran. As for the rumours about differences on the peace process, this is incorrect. We have a clear position on peace, and the
Iranian leadership understands our position.'[118]

The Peace Process dominated regional relations for the better part of the 1990s. This was another arena over which Iran expressed its discontent with Syria's policies, although both sides tried to work out their differences. Between late 1990 and 1997, Syrian American and Israeli officials held a series of talks under US supervision to discuss the possibilities of a Syrian-Israeli agreement. Whilst the US and Israel were keen on breaking up the Syrian-Iranian alliance, Syria wanted to develop relations with the USA side by side to its alliance with Iran. It realised that the only way to exert pressure on Israel was through the United States, in view of the declining influence of the Eastern bloc after the break-up of the Soviet Union. Syria's participation in the anti-Iraq coalition alongside the United States brought Syria out of regional isolation and improved its position vis-à-vis the USA.[119] Talks soon reached a deadlock, however, as Syria insisted that Israel had to announce its readiness to withdraw to pre-1967 borders before negotiations could proceed, while Israel wanted Syria to outline clearly its definition of peace.[120]

In July 1991, following American mediation, Syria was the first country to accept US Secretary Baker's Arab-Israeli peace conference proposals, to the great irritation of Iran.[121] Iran's Foreign Minister Velayati reconfirmed in October that 'Iran [did] not accept the 1947 partition of Palestine and [believed] the whole of Palestine must be liberated'; several weeks later Tehran hosted an alternative Palestine conference in support of the 'Islamic revolution in Palestine'.[122] However, Iranian Interior Minister Hojjatoleslam Abdullah Nuri reiterated on a visit to Damascus in August that Syrian-Iranian relations remained strong despite the Syrian involvement in the peace efforts:

'The Syrian stance is not new. The Syrian brothers are reiterating a firm stance. Moreover, Syrian-Iranian relations are so strong and so deep that they cannot be affected by attempts to undermine them, regardless of events in the region. Furthermore, Syria is not a country that changes positions. It did not and will not change its principled positions.'[123]

In September 1993, after Israel and the PLO signed the Declaration of Principles in Washington, President Rafsanjani at once condemned the agreement and called it 'the biggest treason committed by the PLO against the Palestinian people'. Rafsanjani sent his Deputy Foreign Minister, Sheikholeslam, to Damascus to deliver a message to Asad and discuss the implications of the Israeli-PLO accords.[124] Iran, Syria and Lebanon opposed the UN resolution that endorsed the Declaration of Principles later in the year, with both Iran and Syria supporting each other's position regarding Palestine during Vice President Habibi's visit to Damascus in December. The latter's visit also served to coordinate policies vis-à-vis Hezbollah before Asad's meeting with Clinton in Geneva in January 1994.[125]

Washington wanted Asad to announce his readiness to establish diplomatic relations with Israel in return for the latter's readiness to withdraw. In order to achieve a new regional balance, the US wanted to push Syria to turn away from Iran and commit to peace negotiations with Israel. According to a senior American official in an interview with the Arab daily *al-Hayat* preceding the Geneva summit,

> '[the US] explained to the Syrians that their commitment to the peace process should be reflected in their relations with those who want to destroy it. [. . .] Iran was committed, in word and deed, to the destruction of the peace process [. . .]. He added that Iranian behaviour posed a threat to the interests of the US and all the states in the region that are committed to the peace process. It followed that if Syria was committed to the process, it must deal with this inconsistency.'[126]

To what extent Syrian-Iranian relations were in fact discussed during the summit was not clear, as apparently no statements regarding the alliance were made public.[127]

It is clear, however, that Syria continued its partnership with Iran. The fact that neither the peace process nor the development of Syrian-American relations went very far also prevented Syria from having to make a clear choice between Iran and the United States and Israel. Between 1993 and 1997 US Secretary of State Warren Christopher tried hard to persuade Asad to distance himself from Iran and sign a peace treaty with Israel, but in the end it all came to nothing.[128]

Syrian and Israeli officials did hold a number of direct talks in the United States, but never reached an agreement. And while Iran was unhappy about the Syrian-Israeli dialogue, both sides confirmed that their relations continued to be 'good and brotherly'.[129] Syria in fact denied any rumours about differences over the peace process, claiming that Iran understood its position on the peace process.[130] In February 1996, on the eve of a new round of talks between Syria and Israel, the Iranian vice president was in Damascus for meetings of the Syrian-Iranian Joint Cooperation Committee. In the news statement coming out of that meeting it was underlined that

> 'Syria is unequivocally confident that Syrian-Iranian relations are strong, solid and resting on sound foundations and principles, including mutual respect, close cooperation, a sincere under-standing of events, developments and new occurrences, and a genuine appreciation of the necessities and inclinations that each country may deem appropriate in the pursuit of its interests, objectives and independent policies.'[131]

By 1997 the peace process had stagnated, in particular after Netanyahu's rise to power in Israel in 1996 and Israel's security alliance with Turkey. Syria re-emphasised its ties with Iran and called for greater cooperation between Iran and the Arab world in general.[132]

Lebanon

In the Lebanese arena, Syria and Iran continued to cooperate while not always seeing eye-to-eye. The Iraqi involvement in Lebanon in support of General Michel Aoun brought the two sides closer together; Syrian-backed Amal and Iran-backed Hezbollah joined forces against Aoun and his allies in the summer of 1989. However, the Saudi sponsored Ta'if Agreement of October 1989, which granted Syria a prominent role in Lebanon's affairs while restricting Iranian access to Lebanon, upset the alliance. Syria accepted Ta'if, Iran rejected it. To preserve the alliance, however, Iran supported Syria as long as the latter supported the Islamic forces in Lebanon.[133] Yet in January 1990, renewed Amal and Hezbollah clashes occurred; later in the year Syrian military leaders met with the Hezbollah leadership to resolve differences with Amal.[134]

Most of the Syrian-Iranian dialogue on Lebanon in the 1990s focused on Hezbollah. Both Syria and Hezbollah emerged as winners at the end of the Lebanese civil war, the former establishing its hegemony over the country, the latter establishing itself as the main resistance buffer against the Israeli army in the south of Lebanon, and was thus the only Lebanese militia allowed to keep its arms. Syria and Hezbollah leaders were soon engaged in a working relationship. As Hinnebusch and Ehteshami explain:

'The end of Hizbollah's conflicts with Syria began with the death of Khomeini and the rise of the pragmatist Rafsanjani. As Syria's dominance in Lebanon was consolidated, mainstream Hizbollah leaders, encouraged by Rafsanjani, realized that they had to adapt to Syria's power and struck a working alliance with Damascus: in return for Syria's support for its unique role at the head of the Islamic resistance in the south, Hizbollah would tailor its activities to serve Syrian strategy in the conflict with Israel.'[135]

Iran under Rafsanjani acknowledged Syria's pre-eminence in Lebanon and accepted its conducting much of its Lebanon policies through its Damascus embassy. Thus when Iran was worried about a potential Lebanese-Israeli security agreement in 1993, for instance, it sent Foreign Minister Ali Akbar Velayati to Damascus in order to 'strengthen the Islamic Arab front [. . .] to prevent Israel and the United States from pressing the Arab side into making further concessions'.[136]

Another issue over which the two sides negotiated in the late 1980s and early 1990s was the fate of the remaining hostages in Lebanon, held by Iranian sponsored organisations.[137] Syria was pushing Iran to pressure the Hezbollah factions responsible to release the hostages. Iranians were divided. However, Rafsanjani as a pragmatist aligned himself with the Syrian position, which in the end prevailed. The last Western hostage was released.[138] While the hostage crisis of mid-1990 was an embarrassment to Syria, it in the end strengthened Syrian-Iranian cooperation as the two countries had to work out a solution together. Both sides agreed to adopt a 'joint strategy' aimed at freeing Western hostages, as proclaimed in a meeting between Syrian Vice President Khaddam and his Iranian counterpart Hassan Habibi.[139]

Iraq and Turkey

Despite differences during the Kuwait crisis, Syria and Iran continued to work together in the Iraqi arena over several issues, most importantly regarding the question of Kurdish nationalism. In January 1991 the Syrian and Iranian vice presidents met to affirm the need to protect the territorial integrity of Iraq.[140] Both countries reconfirmed their opposition to Saddam Hussein's regime on several occasions, while making clear that they could not be ignored in determining the future of Iraq.[141] Being both neighbours of Iraq and Turkey and having significant Kurdish minorities of their own, Syria and Iran shared vulnerabilities as far as the threat to territorial integrity was concerned. A series of tripartite meetings took place between the two regional allies and Turkey in the early to mid-1990s, to discuss the situation in Iraqi Kurdistan. The three Foreign Ministers met periodically in Damascus, Ankara and Tehran for talks on northern Iraq. All three were vehemently opposed to a fragmentation of Iraq, and the planned elections in 1995 in northern Iraq. Iran, Syria and Turkey also cooperated over challenges from Kurdish nationalism during this period, such as from the PKK.[142]

In the second half of the 1990s, the tides in Turkish-Syrian-Iranian cooperation had turned. Ankara accused Syria and Iran of supporting the PKK against the Turkish government. Turkish-Iranian relations were deteriorating amidst these accusations, not least following the emergence of an alliance between Turkey and Israel in 1996.[143] Turkish-Syrian relations were also at a low over continuing disputes over water issues. These developments led to closer cooperation between Iran and Syria. During Asad's visit to Tehran in August 1997, the Syrian president called on Iranians and Arabs to work together to hold up the territorial integrity of Iraq as well as regarding other regional issues.

Asad was particularly keen to ensure Iranian support against the perceived threat from Syria's neighbours, Turkey and Israel, following their military and security agreements. The emergent alliance between Turkey and Israel was supported by the US to isolate Iran, but only brought the latter closer to Syria.[144] As *al-Sharq al-Awsat* reported:

> 'The essence of Syria's thinking is that Israel's intransigence, the Turkish-Israeli alliance, Washington's failure to play the role of an honest and active sponsor in the peace process, and the key Arab players' loss of any hope of progress being made on the Arab-Israeli negotiating tracks towards the recovery of usurped Arab rights – be they in Jerusalem, the Golan or the other occupied territories – necessitates the creation of a strong Arab-Iranian axis to counter the Israeli-led and US-backed front aligned against the Arabs and Moslems.'[145]

Throughout the 1990s, Syria and Iran continued to cooperate and assist each other in diverse ways, both politically and militarily.[146] Relations during Rafsanjani's presidency were marked by pragmatism in an environment dominated by the peace process. Hafiz al-Asad's visit to Tehran in August 1997, on the eve of Khatami's assumption of the presidency, was meant to indicate to Iran 'that Syria [was] extremely keen to retain its close relationship with Iran and develop it as far as possible', even after Rafsanjani's successor had assumed his position.[147]

Syria sent a high-level delegation to take part in the Islamic Conference Organisation's meeting in Tehran in December 1997, including the Vice President, the Foreign Minister, and President Asad himself.[148] In May 1999, President Khatami visited Damascus to reaffirm his country's commitment to the Syrian-Iranian alliance.[149] Bilateral cooperation increased during this period in several fields, including economics, culture and the media. After assuming the Syrian presidency in July 2000, Bashar al-Asad visited Tehran in January 2001 to 'give a new boost to its relations with the Islamic Republic of Iran'. He affirmed his personal commitment to the Syrian-Iranian relationship and assured that he would 'spare no efforts to strengthen relations between the Arabs and Iran'.[150] Two months later, Iran's Foreign Minister visited Damascus.[151] Relations thus picked up at the end of the 1990s and early 2000s. Following the US-led invasion of Iraq and the fall of Saddam Hussein in 2003, the alliance became even stronger.[152]

Relations since 2003: Presenting a 'United Front'

al-Thawra, May 2003: 'Thanks to their strategic relations and cooperation, the two countries, which carry clout and play an important role in the region and the rest of the world, have redressed to a certain degree the balance of power tilted in favour of Israel thanks to US support for it. [...] [This] dictates the necessity of elevating their relations to face the pressing conditions resulting from the war on and occupation of Iraq [...] This is in view of the fact that Syria and Iran have intertwined interests and a joint responsibility towards Iraq [...] Syria and Iran are the two neighbouring countries of Iraq most affected by what is happening in that country. Iran, Syria and Lebanon have been targeted by threats against them recently.'[153]

The US-led invasion of Iraq and the fall of Saddam Hussein in 2003 changed the regional power balance and brought the two partners even closer together. The above statement was given in *al-Thawra* newspaper on the occasion of President Khatami's visit to Damascus in May 2003, in town to discuss regional issues with his Syrian counterpart Bashar al-Asad shortly after the fall of Baghdad. The idea of both Syria and Iran facing a common threat and having to stand together against foreign intervention became a recurrent theme in their bilateral discourse. During Syrian Prime Minister Naji al-'Atri's visit to Iran in February 2005, he declared that the two countries were presenting a 'united front' against the challenges they faced in the region.[154] On the occasion of President Ahmadinejad's visit to Damascus in January 2006, both sides reaffirmed their cooperation and coinciding visions. As the newspaper *Tishrin* reported, 'together, Syria and Iran represent the genuine resistance front against all programmes of elimination, divisions and occupation'.[155] The rhetoric of trying to break up the alliance between Syria and Iran – propagated largely by the United States – has only had the opposite effect, bringing the two allies closer together.[156] As will be outlined in the following, diplomatic exchanges have greatly increased in the years since the invasion of Iraq, and bilateral relations have expanded significantly on all levels, politically, economically and culturally.

Diplomatic Exchanges

While discussions about Iraq's future dominated meetings in the period directly before and after the invasion, Syria and Iran took the opportunity of renewed diplomatic engagement between the two sides to boost their cooperation. Preceding the invasion of Iraq, in October 2002 Syria and Iran held a meeting between their news agency directors in Tehran to discuss their coordination, in view of the Arab and Muslim world being targeted by 'the US and Zionist threats'.[157] In January 2003, Syrian Foreign Minister al-Shara met with Iranian president Khatami to discuss the imminent outbreak of war in the region and how to prevent it.[158] As mentioned above, Iranian President Khatami travelled to Damascus just after the fall of Baghdad to discuss the situation in Iraq and cooperation between Syria and Iran; important steps were also taken towards liberalising trade between the two countries.[159] While both sides had their own separate interests in Iraq, Vice President Khaddam went to Iran to try to establish a coordinated Iraq policy with the Iranian leadership in September 2003.[160]

While Syria and Iran made efforts to coordinate their Iraq policy, bilateral relations improved further. An Iranian industrial delegation visited Damascus in October 2003 in order to boost industrial cooperation between the two countries.[161] In the following months, further meetings took place between delegations of both sides to develop economic cooperation. In April 2004 the Syrian and Iranian Speakers of Parliament signed a memorandum of understanding to further increase coordination between the two sides.[162] A Syrian-Iranian parliamentary friendship society had been formed earlier.[163] Three months later, President Asad made a surprise visit to Tehran, accompanied by his

Vice President and Foreign Minister; President Khatami and his Foreign Minister reciprocated the visit in October 2004.[164] Naji 'Atri's 'united front' comment was made in the wake of Lebanese former Prime Minister Rafiq Hariri's assassination in February 2005, when Syria felt strong international pressure against it. 'Atri's visit to Tehran ended with a declaration by both sides that they had concluded a mutual defence pact.[165] Soon after, in April 2005, the Iranian Foreign Minister came to Damascus to discuss regional issues, high upon which ranked Lebanon – Syria being in the process of withdrawing its troops from there – and reaffirming the need for regular consultations between Syria and Iran.

In August 2005, Bashar al-Asad was the first foreign leader to visit President Ahmadinejad in Tehran after the latter assumed presidency.[166] *Tishrin* newspaper reported that

'the Iranian president has shown great concern for Syrian-Iranian relations, especially in these difficult circumstances the region is going through, thus confirming that the new Iranian leadership is the natural extension of the march of the Islamic revolution which has the same views and policies as Syria on all the issues that are fateful to the two friendly countries and people.'[167]

Ahmadinejad returned Bashar al-Asad's August visit and came to Damascus in January 2006, affirming bilateral relations were strong. He asserted that Syria and Iran had 'identical stances regarding the economic and cultural affairs and the regional issues', both being against foreign intervention in Middle Eastern affairs.[168] In an environment of growing international pressure against Iran and its nuclear programme, and efforts to break the two states apart, relations between Syria and Iran under the presidency of Ahmadinejad grew ever closer.[169] Ahmadinejad's strong support of the resistance against Israel was viewed positively in Syria, and he enjoyed popularity amongst the government as well as the people. While Iran firmly backed Syria over the UN inquiry into Hariri's assassination,[170] Syria consistently supported Iran's nuclear enrichment programme, which the two sides discussed in their bilateral talks.[171] Syria declared itself convinced of the peaceful nature of Iran's programme, and defended Iran's right to develop nuclear energy.[172] Throughout this period, bilateral relations further developed with scientific, academic, military, economic, industrial, telecommunications and cultural delegations going back and forth between Damascus and Tehran, and both presidents making several visits to the other country.[173]

Axis of Resistance

In July 2006, when war erupted in Lebanon between Hezbollah and Israel, Ahmadinejad assured Syria of his support. The two sides had just drafted a defensive military cooperation agreement the previous month.[174] Hezbollah's success to resist Israel in the 2006 war also boosted its external supporters, namely Syria and Iran. Posters of the triumvirate of Hezbollah leader Hassan Nasrallah, Mahmud Ahmadinejad and Bashar al-Asad could frequently be seen on walls and in shop windows in Damascus. Iran organised fireworks in Tehran

Poster above shop in Qaymariya depicting Ahmadinejad, Asad and Nasrallah, Damascus old town, 21 March 2008.

to celebrate Hezbollah's victory.[175] Iran continued to use its good relations with Syria to further support the anti-Israel resistance, using the frequent trips to Damascus of its high officials to meet also with Hamas leader Khaled Mashaal.[176] Iran started speaking of Syria and Iran as leaders of the 'Axis of Resistance', the latter comprising Iran, Syria, Hezbollah and (until 2012) Hamas.

During Syria's renewed efforts to reach an agreement with Israel that were made public in spring 2008, Tehran closely followed Damascus's indirect talks with Israel through Turkish mediation. Syria was quick to reassure its ally that these talks would in no way affect their bilateral relationship. Bashar al-Asad visited Tehran in early August 2008 to calm down the Iranians and stress that nothing would change between them. Syrian spokesperson Buthaina Sha'ban reaffirmed that Iran was not worried at all about Syria's indirect talks. 'I was there with the president on that trip, relations with Iran are very good. Relations with Iran are great on all levels, they have never been as good', she proclaimed several weeks later when asked about her country's relationship with Iran.[177] *Etemaad* – one of the Iranian dailies – at the end of August ran a front-page interview with the Syrian ambassador to Iran entitled 'Syrian ambassador: We won't sell Iran to Israel'.[178] To preserve a united front, Foreign Minister Mottaki also gave a statement saying that it was Syria's right to demand the return of the Golan Heights.[179] As during the peace process of the 1990s, Iran officially stood firmly behind Syria regarding the latter's actions vis-à-vis Israel. However, the initial 2008 round of talks between Syria and Israel broke off following Israel's attack on Gaza in January 2009 and the ensuing blockade against it, which both Syria and Iran strongly condemned.[180]

Fostering solidarity among resistance groups is one of the priorities of the Islamic Republic, an issue repeatedly emphasized during bilateral visits. Iran's Supreme National Security Council deputy secretary Ali Baqeri named Iran and Syria as strong pillars of resistance in the region during his visit to Damascus in late 2010,[181] and Ahmadinejad awarded Asad the 'Grand National Order of the Islamic Republic of Iran for his resistance against arrogant powers, his defense of the rights of the Palestinian and Lebanese nations, his key role in the stability and tranquillity of regional countries, and his great efforts to

In solidarity with Gaza, Israeli flags were put on Damascene streets for people to walk over. This picture was taken in January 2009 in Qaymariya, a popular street in the middle of Damascus old town. Flags of Syria, Hezbollah, Lebanon, Iran, Palestine and Iraq are hanging above.

strengthen brotherly ties between Iran and Syria' during his visit to Tehran in October 2010.[182]

Economic Relations

Economic cooperation has developed extensively over the last years, expressed in particular through Iranian investments in Syria.[183] The two sides cooperate in the fields of trade, agriculture, construction of power plants, oil and gas, silos and cement production factories.[184] In October

2006, Iran, Venezuela and Syria signed a memorandum of understanding for a Syrian oil refinery project, further expanding economic cooperation.[185] In early 2011 an agreement was endorsed to construct a gas pipeline from Iran through Iraq to Syria and the Mediterranean, to send Iranian gas to Europe.[186] The Iranian car manufacturer Iran Khodro produces the Samand Sham car in Syria, the result of a joint car production venture between the two countries. Another Iranian carmaker, SAIPA, has also launched a joint venture with Syria.[187] Iran's Minister of Housing and Urban Development, Ali Nikzad, put the volume of bilateral trade exchange at $336 million in January 2010, up from $14 million in 1997. Another source valued Syrian exports to Iran in 2010 at $29 million (mainly olive oil, plastics, textile yarn, and iron and copper), and Iran's exports to Syria in the same year at $389 million (mainly engineering services).[188] The aim is to reach an annual trade volume of $5 billion in the future.[189] While economic relations are still modest in comparison to political and military relations, something acknowledged by the two sides, they are nevertheless developing.[190] In May 2010 Syria and Iran signed an agreement to create a joint bank, a further sign of both sides commitment to strengthen economic cooperation; in October 2010 two memoranda of understanding were signed on free trade and industrial cooperation.[191] An Iranian high-technology exhibition was held in Damascus in February 2011, with 147 Iranian companies and 313 Iranian experts taking part, an Iranian trade fair took place in Damascus in May 2011, and Tehran hosted a Syrian trade fair in April 2012 where over 300 Syrian companies showcased their latest products in the fields of textile, food, agriculture, medicine, cosmetics and car industries. The latter marked the beginning of the free trade agreement between the two sides, signed in December 2011 and which started to be implemented in April 2012.[192]

Relations since the Beginning of the Syrian Uprising, 2011

Deputy Foreign Minister for Arab and African Affairs Hossein Amir-Abdollahian in April 2012: 'Iran's approach toward the Syrian crisis centres around a cessation of violence and killings in Syria, no foreign political and military intervention, the

protection of the Bashar al-Assad government, and the necessity
of conducting national reforms.'[193]

In March 2011, the wave of popular uprisings in the Arab world that
had swept the Tunisian and Egyptian leaders off their feet earlier that
year reached Syria. Iran at first ignored growing tensions in Syria,
believing that only those countries supporting the United States and
Israel were prone to what Iran termed 'Islamic Awakening'. Syria did
not fit into the Islamic Republic's rebranding of the Arab Spring. Once
the on-going crisis in Syria could no longer be denied, Iran adopted
Syrian official rhetoric of blaming armed insurgents and terrorists for
the unrest.

Iran has stood by its ally throughout, supporting the Syrian regime's
so-called reform initiatives and stressing the need to look for a political
(as opposed to military) solution to the crisis, accusing the USA and its
allies of foreign meddling in Syrian affairs and in turn rejecting claims
it was helping Syria quell the protests. Asked about the difference
between events in Bahrain and in Syria, an Iranian official responded
that 'part of the events in Syria is real, such as people's demands and
their need for reforms. Like all other Arab states, Syria needs reforms
and democracy. Yet, a greater part of the so-called events in Syria is
artificial – initiated by foreign intervention, by flooding the country
with weapons, manipulating regional change to weaken an important,
resistant state.'[194] The new Iranian ambassador to Syria, appointed
in October 2011 after his predecessor's departure, went further and
described the on-going confrontations in the region as a war between
the 'resistance and anti-resistant fronts'.[195]

Britain and the United States accused Iran as early as April 2011 of
secretly helping the Syrian government suppress protests, in particular
providing technical assistance to monitor online communications.
Iranian officials repeatedly rejected these claims, stressing their belief
that Syria was capable of resolving their internal problems independently, and accused both countries of pursuing 'double-standard policies'
in the region. Regional nations will not 'overlook US support for the
Egyptian and Tunisian dictatorships and its silence on the massacre
of the defenceless Bahraini people', a Foreign Ministry spokesman

proclaimed.[196] Moving from the defensive to the offensive, Iran
condemned 'foreign meddling' in Syria, claiming it had information
that 'Arab countries have sent weapons and fighters to Syria with help
and financing from the US and Israel'.[197] Whenever an opportunity
arose, Iranian officials stressed the need to prevent any foreign interference in Syria, accusing Israel, the United States and its allies of trying
their best to lead the country into chaos.

Iran insists the Syrian crisis needs to be resolved through dialogue,
with the Iranian media lauding Syrian reforms and steps such as the
referendum on the new constitution held in February 2012.[198] The
Islamic Republic was supporting UN special envoy Kofi Annan's six-
point peace plan for Syria as long as it did not call for Asad to step
down. Annan had travelled to Tehran in April 2012 in order to gather
support for the plan from Syria's allies, believing that Iran could be part
of the solution.[199] Asad's private emails leaked to *The Guardian* and
published in March 2012 also showed that advisors to the Syrian president were consulting with the Iranians on what issues to include in the
president's speech, demonstrating just how far cooperation went.[200]

However, while the Iranian government has pledged its full support
to 'the Syrian government and people', popular sentiments on both
sides are divided – often along the lines of support for their own
governments.[201] Many Iranians critical of their own government sym-
pathise with the Syrian people, and feel they are going through the
same process the Iranians went through during the Green movement
in Iran following the 2009 presidential elections, when many Iranians
were arrested and tortured after contesting the election results. In
Syria, pro-government Syrian youth has held demonstrations in front
of the Iranian embassy in Damascus to support Iran's policy in Syria,
while members of the opposition kidnapped several groups of Iranians
in Syria to put pressure on the Islamic Republic to change its stance
on Syria.[202] Five Iranian engineers were kidnapped in December 2011
on their way to work at the Jandar power plant in Homs Governorate,
and two further Iranians who had gone to search for the missing five
were also taken hostage. In January 2012 two groups of 11 Iranian
pilgrims were abducted en route from Damascus to Aleppo.[203] While
the Iranian hostages were still held captive in May 2012, Iran managed

to help Turkey in negotiations over two Turkish journalists held hostage in Syria by pro-government forces. The two were released in May following Iranian mediation, and flown to Tehran.[204]

While Syria and Iran have their differences, points of agreement outweigh points of disagreement, as Syria's former ambassador to Iran Turki Saqr asserted.[205] Throughout the last decade, Syria and Iran have consistently developed and expanded their bilateral relations through countless delegations going back and forth between the two countries. In 2010 alone, officials of the two countries exchanged up to 400 visits 'with the aim of enhancing bilateral relations in various fields'.[206] The efforts made by the United States to separate the two allies have failed and had the reverse effect, causing Syria and Iran to present a joint stand against Western interference in regional affairs. Both sides have supported each other during challenging times.

Conclusion

Relations between Syria and Iran developed in different stages throughout the second half of the twentieth century. Diplomatic relations between Syria and the Iranian monarchy were established in 1946, but were marked by tensions and remained limited despite a brief rapprochement between the two states in the mid-1970s. Following the Islamic revolution in 1979 and a shift in Iran's foreign policy, diplomatic relations expanded rapidly and turned into an alliance. The focus of this chapter has been on the diplomatic exchange between the two countries, to demonstrate how Syria and Iran have managed to establish a strong relationship and consolidate their alliance through cooperation over points of differences. Frequent meetings of high-ranking officials in times of crises were perceived crucial by the two sides to work out their differences.

The foundations for a close alliance between the Syrian Arab Republic and the Islamic Republic of Iran were laid in the 1970s, when Syria played host to and cooperated with Iranian oppositional activists in Syria and Lebanon. The establishment of personal links between the Syrian regime and Iranians who were to play important roles in the early revolutionary regime cannot be underestimated.

People like Yazdi, Ghotbzadeh and Tabataba'i were amongst the first post-revolutionary Iranian officials to visit Syria to discuss the future of bilateral relations; Mohtashemipur played a crucial role in the alliance, first in his position as Iranian ambassador to Damascus, then as Minister of Interior. These links provided a good platform on which to build an alliance.

In terms of content, the alliance was built on several issues of mutual concern. These included a common stance on Israel and the United States; both sides' animosity towards neighbouring Iraq and the prevention of turning the Iran-Iraq war into an Arab-versus-Persian affair through Syria's support of Iran during the war, of which Syria reaped economic benefits; both sides' (at times divergent) interests in Lebanon; and their mutual need for a regional partner. Both Syria and Iran realised that an alliance could prove useful in the long term, which made them overcome short-term differences. Whilst the 1970s had been important in establishing the framework for bilateral relations, the 1980s can be regarded as the formative years of the Syrian-Iranian alliance.

Throughout the 1990s, bilateral relations between the two states intensified and survived tests such as the Kuwait crisis and Syria's participation in the peace process. Syria and Iran maintained their cooperation over Lebanon and Iraq, and met regularly to discuss issues of mutual concern. Against the background of an emerging Turkish-Israeli alliance and the failure of the peace process to bear fruits, the two partners grew closer together towards the end of the decade.

Bilateral relations since the invasion of Iraq in 2003 have picked up on all levels, political, military, economic and cultural. International pressure on both Syria and Iran – the former following Hariri's assassination in Lebanon, the latter largely over its nuclear programme, and both countries over their support for Hezbollah and Hamas – have only brought them closer together. Lebanon, Iraq and Palestine/Israel have continued to be high up on the list of issues of mutual concern. Economic cooperation has increased significantly over the last years. While popular support for the alliance is divided broadly reflecting support for one's own system, the two allies have stood by each other in times of crises.

CHAPTER 2

POLICY AND VALUES

This chapter provides an insight into policy formulation in Iran and Syria in order to understand better the role and place of cultural diplomacy in both countries. To what extent there exist shared values between the two allies will also be discussed. We will first look at foreign policy formulation in post-revolutionary Iran before examining the evolution of Iran's cultural diplomacy practice, by introducing the main institutions involved in the process. It will become clear that the Islamic Republic has placed a high value on culture since its inception, but has become more organised about promoting its culture abroad through cultural diplomacy practices since the mid-1990s, when it established the Islamic Culture and Relations Organisation. Syria lacked Iran's motivation to promote its culture, which it still considered as part of a wider Arab culture. Unsurprisingly, it has not institutionalised its cultural foreign policy to the same degree as Iran. Run by the Syrian Ministry of Culture, Syria maintains few cultural centres abroad, the one in Tehran being one of the recent additions.

Moving from policy to values, this chapter will look at shared values and cultural themes promoted between the two allies. Officials on both sides often refer back to a common Islamic heritage and the sense of a shared cultural history between the two nations. One period frequently cited is the rule of Sayf al-Dawla in Aleppo in the tenth century, when poets and writers moved back and forth between Persian and Syrian lands. Common values such as anti-Zionism and anti-imperialism contributed to Syria and Iran forming a close relationship, as this common ground allowed them to phrase their partnership in terms of those values.

Iran's Foreign Policy Formulation

The complex power structure of the Islamic Republic of Iran makes the origins of policy formulation at times difficult to ascertain.[1] Policy is formulated through an interplay of formal and informal power centres, the former rooted in the constitution and visible through institutions of the state, the latter often associated with religious bodies. The president, while head of the state executive and in charge of managing daily political affairs, neither controls the informal power centres, nor determines the general guidelines of Iranian domestic and foreign policy. It is the Supreme Leader who is in charge of setting the directions, and being in command of the armed forces and security services.[2] This division between formal and informal power structures in the foreign policy making process could at times lead to political disorder; the decision for the American hostage-taking for example was taken unofficially and only later officially endorsed.[3] All power centres, during the first decade, were controlled by an Islamic-revolutionary leadership elite, that – while not unified – was bound by loyalty to the person and the political and religious teachings of Ayatollah Khomeini.[4]

Khomeini's guidelines for Iran's foreign policy were expressed through specific slogans, such as 'Neither East nor West', 'Export the revolution and the Islamic Republic', 'War, war until victory', 'War against international superpower' and denouncing the United States as 'the great Satan'.[5] At the early stage of the revolution, some of the right-wing informal power centres within the clerical establishment influenced foreign policy. They were intent on export of the revolution and forming alliances with Islamist movements in the region.[6] Their influence had declined by the time of Khomeini's death in June 1989. Khomeini had taken the self-conferred role of spiritual leader and spokesman for the Muslim world seriously, feeling a transnational Islamic responsibility.[7] Under Khomeini's successor, Hojjatoleslam Ali Khamene'i – who received the title of Ayatollah with his assumption of the Supreme Leader's office – Iran's foreign policy was determined more by its geo-strategic, national and economic interests rather than revolutionary, pan-Islamic ambitions.[8] The years of war with Iraq had weakened Iran's revolutionary optimism to install its Islamic goals abroad, and replaced it with more pragmatic foreign policy goals.[9]

Since the constitutional reforms of August 1989, the president had assumed those responsibilities formerly in the hands of the prime minister, conferring some of these to his first vice president, who was accountable to him.[10] While the president chaired the National Security Council – formed following the reforms – where foreign policy was debated, and while the foreign minister reported directly to the president, his influence on foreign policy was limited. The president could not enforce any foreign policy decision without the support of the Supreme Leader. Other power centres within the state system played a role too. Members of parliament could seek clarifications from ministers and influence public opinion; by constitution the government moreover required the parliament's approval for entering into any international treaties, memoranda of understanding or agreements with other states and parties. The Guardian Council's role was to ensure that the government's foreign policy decisions were in line with the constitution. The foreign minister had a say in setting the policy directions of the foreign ministry and in some appointments. However, particularly at times of crisis and regarding key ambassadorial appointments – like the ones to Syria – he had to follow directives coming out of other power centres in the system.[11]

The Supreme Leader's office has always played an important role in Iranian foreign policy formulation towards Syria, with increasing influence from the Revolutionary Guards. Following the 2009 presidential election, Karim Sadjadpour of the Carnegie Endowment for International Peace suggests:

'In terms of how Iranian foreign policy is going to be carried out, what has transpired again in the last four months is that the institution of the Revolutionary Guards has been further empowered; they are essentially running Iranian foreign policy in places like Iraq, Afghanistan, Lebanon and Syria, and the institution of the foreign ministry has been further relegated.

I think amongst the professionals at the foreign ministry morale is very low; and I would describe the current Foreign Minister Mottaki as basically an apparatchik, someone who is more of a spokesperson than someone who is actually deciding policy.'[12]

Iran's ambassadors to Syria have generally been closer to the leader's office than to the foreign ministry. The two appointments under Khatami were the exception: Husayn Sheikholeslam, ambassador from 1998 to 2003, had been Deputy Foreign Minister for Arab-Iranian affairs in Iran for nearly two decades prior to his appointment, his successor Muhammad Reza Baqeri became Deputy Foreign Minister for Arab and African affairs after his departure from Syria in 2005.[13] The previous ambassadors clearly showed close links to the Supreme Leader. Ali Akbar Mohtashemipur, the Islamic Republic's envoy to Syria from 1981 to 1985, was a student and confidant of Ayatollah Khomeini, and assumed the position of Minister of Interior in 1985.[14] His successor, Muhammad Hassan Akhtari, held the post twice, from 1986 to 1997 and between 2005 and 2008. After his first posting to Damascus he joined the leader's office, dealing with international relations. Before and after his second posting he was head of the World Assembly of the ahl al-bayt (al-majm'a al-'alami li-ahl al-bayt; for short: ahl al-bayt Assembly) in Iran, a Shi'i institution aiming to revive the thoughts of the prophet Muhammad, study the lives and work of the family of the prophet, and strengthen Islamic unity.[15] Ahmad Mousavi, ambassador from 2008 until 2011, had been Iran's Vice President for Legal and Parliamentary Affairs prior to assuming his position in Syria.[16] The current ambassador, Muhammad Reza Raouf Shaybani, resembles his Khatami-era colleagues, having been Deputy Foreign Minister for Middle East and Commonwealth Affairs before being appointed to succeed Mousavi in August 2011.[17]

Iran's Supreme Leader also has his own representative (nemayande-ye rahbar) in Syria, Ayatollah Mojtaba Hosseini. According to Buchta, the leader has representatives – usually clerics – in every important state ministry and institution, and in revolutionary organisations, amounting to a total of around 2,000. In terms of foreign relations, they ultimately oversee the work of Iranian cultural centres and Islamic organisations. Their main function is to enforce the authority of the Supreme Leader, being more powerful than other government functionaries and even ministers, having the authority to intervene in any matter of state.[18] Political scientist Schirazi explains:

> 'The Representatives of the Imam are one of the most important institutions of supervision and propaganda. They act as a kind of extended arm of the leader in all chief educational, administrative and security agencies and other state institutions, and use their considerable power to intervene in the running of those organisations.'[19]

In many cases, they were appointed by Khomeini himself and remained after his death to represent Khamene'i.[20] Ayatollah Mojtaba Hosseini has his own office in the Damascus suburbs, close to the shrine of Sayida Zaynab, where he also overlooks the hawza (Shi'i religious school) of Imam Khomeini.

It is thus the Supreme Leader and his entourage who ultimately direct Iran's foreign policy decisions towards Syria. Having looked at Iran's foreign policy formulation more generally, we will examine how its cultural foreign policy was generated, on what principles the latter was based, and how it was organised.

Iranian Cultural Foreign Policy [21]

Principles of Iran's Cultural Foreign Policy

The Supreme Council of the Cultural Revolution: 'Upon the victory of the Islamic Revolution in Iran, which was indeed a Cultural Revolution, Islamic Iran took up its historic mission to promote and deepen the cultural ties with other nations as well as presenting to the world the true Iranian and Islamic culture.'[22]

From the outset, the revolutionary administration emphasised the need to promote its culture abroad, stressing the Islamic character of the revolution. At home, it set out to Islamicise Iranian society by attempting to eliminate any non- and anti-Islamic elements from Iran's national culture and making the teaching of the Arabic language, the original agent of Islam, mandatory in secondary school education.[23] Khomeini believed that the world was divided into oppressors and oppressed, and that Iran, as the only truly Islamic and non-aligned country, had the duty to lead the revolutionary movement and help Muslim and other oppressed nations to reach real independence.[24] To this end, an Iranian cultural official explained the change of goals in Iranian policy:

> 'The Islamic revolution is known to be a genuine revolution with the aim of freeing the oppressed in the world from the burden of the oppressors. It is a revolution with unifying and humane goals, wishing to defend Muslim identity, strengthening unity and fighting against any kind of division among Muslims. Its basic goal is to give a picture of genuine Islam.'[25]

One of the main aims of Iran's foreign policy during the first decade – at least in theory – was to export its revolution in order to achieve Muslim unity, to confront the oppressor nations and gain Muslim sovereignty. In Khomeini's world view, the source of the Muslim world's problem lay in its drifting apart from the divine path of Islam, the adoption of the corrupt ways of either the East or West, and its disunity. To solve their problems, Muslims had to return to Islam and divisions had to be overcome to achieve unity.[26] To this end, Khomeini called upon Muslims to rely on Islamic culture, resist Western influence and to be independent.[27] The export of the revolution required the breaking down of Persian-Arab barriers, for which the notion of Islamic unity was an important instrument. It was based on the idea that all Muslims share a set of basic convictions as well as facing the same enemy – namely the 'militarily, economically and culturally expansive West, which threatens the political independence and cultural and religious identity of the Islamic world'.[28] As such, the revolution was publicly characterised as being neither Iranian nor Shi'i, but rather Islamic and universal – Khomeini did not advertise the fact that associates of the Islamic revolution abroad were generally Shi'i figures connected to the Iranian clergy.[29]

The means by which the revolution should be exported were not clearly specified, and Khomeini's view on the issue of exporting the revolution by force was ambiguous,[30] but it is clear that the Islamic Republic recognised the importance of communication in spreading its revolutionary message. As Khomeini stated in 1980, 'the greatest means by which the revolution can succeed here and be exported is *tablighat* [propagation, communication, and proselytisation], in its proper form'.[31] It has been explained that *tabligh* means 'propagation', but that 'its Islamic connotation derives from the word *balagha*, meaning "to reach", "to get", or "to affect", [and] also means "proselytizing".'[32] The Islamic Propagation Organisation (sazeman-e tablighat-e eslami) was set up in 1981 to promote the teaching of Islam, enhance people's Islamic knowledge, coordinate public propagation activities and explain the Islamic revolution.[33]

Khomeini apparently told a group of diplomats who had been recalled to Tehran for consultation:

> 'It does not take swords to export this ideology. The export of ideas by force is no export. We shall have exported Islam only when we have helped Islam and Islamic ethics grow in those countries. This is your responsibility and it is a task which you must fulfill. You should promote this idea by adopting a conduct conducive to the propagation of Islam and by publishing the necessary publications in your countries of assignment. This is a must. You must have publications. You must publish journals. Such journals should be promotive and their contents and pictures should be consistent with the Islamic Republic, so that by proper publicity campaigns you may pave the way for the spread of Islam in those areas.'[34]

Iran's cultural politics in the first revolutionary decade showed many characteristics of Nye's concept of soft power. Recognising the importance of culture and values, trying to set an example and introducing one's culture abroad are all components of soft power. However, soft power and cultural diplomacy depend on legitimacy and how policies are perceived. The Islamic Republic's revolutionary propaganda in the early years was not successful in winning over followers. As long as Iran was still calling for an export of its revolution, regional neighbours in particular were extremely wary of Iran's intentions. Syria was an exception in the sense that due to its close political relations with the Islamic Republic and absence of competing ideologies there was less fear of the latter wanting to replace the former. Even in the early revolutionary period, Iran was able to engage in cultural diplomacy within the framework of the Syrian-Iranian alliance. This is not to say that relations were free from tensions, and Syria was not always happy with Iranian activities on its soil, but the two partners found a way to keep their relationship intact.

Cultural Foreign Policy Formulation and the Islamic Culture and Relations Organisation (ICRO)

On the institutional level, Iran's cultural movement in the first revolutionary decade lacked coherence and central organisation. While the department of international affairs of the Ministry of Culture and Higher Education was theoretically responsible for conducting bilateral cultural relations with foreign countries, following the revolution a rising number of Iranian institutions and public organisations started to develop cultural activities abroad. These included established institutions such as branches of ministries that were reorganised under the new administration, as well as newly formed bodies such as the Islamic Propagation Organisation, which fell under the supervision of the Ministry of Culture. These institutions acted independently from each other, and with an increase in numbers, Iran's cultural movement abroad soon became fragmented. As there was no centralised policy or directive, every institution managed its activities at will. Money did not seem to be difficult to obtain; according to a senior cultural official, the government at the beginning of the revolution allocated budgets for revolutionary propaganda to all ministries.[35] Efforts mainly targeted Muslim communities, and aimed at spreading the principles of the revolution.

The Ministry of Culture and Islamic Guidance evolved throughout this period by integrating several ministries. In March 1978, the

Ministry of Culture and Higher Education was formed by merging the Ministry of Culture and Art with the Ministry of Science and Higher Education. In May 1979, the Ministry of Information and Tourism was renamed Ministry of National Guidance, which was in turn renamed Ministry of Islamic Guidance in 1980, acquiring a more religious character at a time when the factions around Khomeini secured their positions. A number of the departments of the Ministry of Culture and Higher Education were subsequently integrated into this ministry, until it was renamed the Ministry of Culture and Islamic Guidance in March 1987.[36]

By the time of the death of Imam Khomeini in 1989, in particular after it had become clear during the course of the Iran-Iraq war that most Arab countries were more interested in Arab than Islamic unity, the revolutionary zeal of the early period had ebbed away. The attempts to disseminate revolutionary propaganda transformed over time into a more subtle and organised effort to introduce Iran's culture and values abroad. To reassure Iran's regional neighbours, Khamene'i proclaimed the end of an active revolutionary export as part of Iran's policy, which President Rafsanjani confirmed.[37]

To have an integrated policy, the Islamic Republic on the initiative of a group of cultural personalities set up the ICRO in 1995 to merge the main institutions. The latter included the international affairs departments of the Ministry of Culture and Islamic Guidance and the Islamic Propagation Organisation, the World Assembly for the Rapprochement between the Islamic Schools of Thought (al-majm'a al-'alami lil-taqrib bayna al-madhdhahib al-islamiya; for short: taqrib Assembly), the ahl al-bayt Assembly,[38] and the Council for the Dissemination of the Persian Language and Literature (shura-ye gostaresh-e zaban va adabiyat-e farsi). Having been approved by the leader, ICRO had the sole responsibility of coordinating Iran's cultural foreign policies. It was established as an independent organisation affiliated to the Ministry of Culture and Islamic Guidance, under the ultimate guidance of the Supreme Leader, and to work in cooperation with the Foreign Ministry. A higher council (shura-ye 'ali) – to include three cultural figures selected by the Supreme Leader, as well as the Foreign Minister, the head of national radio and television, the directors of the above-mentioned institutions and a representative of the foreign affairs office of the leader – was to oversee its policies under the leadership of the Minister of Culture and Islamic Guidance.[39]

ICRO's mission was to introduce the foundations of the Islamic revolution and the ideas of Imam Khomeini, in particular in the Islamic world, realising Islamic unity by strengthening cultural relations among Muslim states. According to its constitution, Islamic thought and learning should be revived and spread in the world with the objective of 'awakening Muslims and communicating the message of the true Islam to the inhabitants of the world'. ICRO was to strengthen and organize the cultural facilities of the Islamic Republic abroad, and to present Iran's culture and civilization. One goal was to spread the Persian language and its literature. Strengthening a sense of national and cultural identity amongst Iranians living abroad was another concern. The school of the ahl al-bayt – the Shiite school of thought – was to be introduced as the 'school of glory and perfection' (madrasat al-'azza wa al-kamal). Promoting and reforming the cultural, political, economic and social situation of Muslims in the world – especially the followers of the ahl al-bayt – was another goal.[40] Looking at ICRO's objectives, one can clearly discern a focus on Islam in the direction of Iran's cultural diplomacy.

ICRO, as the main organ supervising the Islamic Republic's cultural foreign policy, was from now on in charge of directing the content and reach of Iran's cultural diplomacy. It coordinated Iran's bilateral cultural programmes with foreign countries, provided the necessary background information for setting up cultural agreements and treaties, undertook and supported research in Islamic and Iranian studies, interacted with cultural and religious personalities and institutions in foreign countries, sought to increase Persian language teaching and strengthen chairs of Persian language at universities, organised cultural festivals and exhibitions, and was to be active in the field of writing, translating and distributing books and publications with the object of introducing Islamic and Iranian science, philosophy, culture and civilisation. ICRO published over 20 journals in different languages inside Iran, to be distributed in the representations outside Iran; and over 30 of its cultural centres abroad have their own publications. This is clearly in line with Khomeini's urge to Iranian diplomats to encourage publications. The constitution also specified that ICRO was to help establish and support the activities of hawzahs and universities outside Iran. Moreover, ICRO was to establish and administer Iran's cultural representations abroad and appoint cultural and propaganda representatives, whose duties it supervised.[41]

ICRO's work aimed at co-opting people rather than coercing them. Its activities were in line with the main goals of cultural diplomacy, namely increasing familiarity, increasing appreciation, engaging people and influencing people's behaviour. The guidelines for Iran's cultural policies and programmes were set by the organisation's head office in Tehran. The Iranian public was informed about its policies by the department for public relations and conferences, which also interacted with the media to hold news conferences, the idea being that having an informed domestic public opinion helps towards maintaining a unified picture to the outside. In practice, it is questionable to what extent the public followed ICRO's policies.

Whilst no figures regarding the organisation's budget are available, it does not seem to lack funds to organise and implement its cultural policies abroad. ICRO's budget has several sources. The government allocates yearly budgets from the public treasury for the organisation and each country in which ICRO is active. Additional sources include income raised by cultural activities carried out by ICRO abroad, assistance from people and places of religious legal funds. The remaining income's sources have to be approved by the higher council of ICRO.[42]

Iranian Cultural Centres

Iranian cultural centres abroad (raizani-ye farhangi-e jomhuri-ye eslami-ye Iran) actively implement the official policies by promoting the Islamic Republic's ideas and values, building up relationships and teaching Persian language and literature. ICRO set up these cultural centres across the world, in particular in countries with a Muslim majority. In case the Ministry of Culture and Islamic Guidance had previously established a centre somewhere, ICRO took over responsibility for it. These centres, of which there exist over 60 worldwide,[43] are formally attached to the Iranian embassy or consulate in each country. However, they have separate budgets administered by ICRO, and refer back to ICRO in Iran rather than the foreign ministry.[44] Cultural councillors (raizan-e farhangi), as the directors of the cultural centres are called, are appointed through ICRO. They often have an academic background or constitute a cultural figure in Iran; they can but do not necessarily come from inside the organisation. They are subordinated to the Supreme Leader's office or his representatives rather than the ambassadors. Other than the directors, the centres generally employ a cultural attaché, a public relations officer, an IT manager and a librarian, depending on the size of the centre.[45]

The means by which the cultural centres abroad try to accomplish their aims are manifold. Activities include exhibitions (books, Quran, photos, handicrafts), organising cultural weeks, conferences and seminars, teaching Persian language and literature, cooperating with intellectuals and cultural institutions of the host country, and organising events for Iranian residents abroad. The cultural centres in non-Islamic countries moreover aim to introduce the principles of Islamic thought through a programme of 'dialogue between religions'.

Brenda Shaffer in her edited volume on *The Limits of Culture: Islam and Foreign Policy* argues that the Islamic Republic rarely promotes cultural and ideological goals at significant expense to the material interests of the state.[46] It is true that while ICRO in theory considers all countries to hold the same status, in practice the organisation is much more active in countries with which it has strong bilateral relations, and where there is a sizable Muslim community. Indonesia, Malaysia and Syria have been cited as countries where ICRO is particularly effective.[47] Within the context of Arab-Iranian relations, Iranian cultural officials often refer to Iran's cultural relations with Syria as a model (namudhaj).[48]

While individual institutions such as those represented in ICRO, like the ahl al-bayt Assembly or taqrib Assembly, still carry out separate cultural activities abroad, they do so in cooperation with ICRO and do not act independently as they did before the creation of the latter. The taqrib Assembly for instance is involved in organising a conference on Islamic unity in Damascus, together with ICRO and the Syrian Ministry of Awqaf (religious endowments).[49]

It has become clear that the Islamic Republic of Iran clearly believes in the power of culture and spreading its values abroad. Like Britain and Germany, it has set up its own institution for dealing with its cultural diplomacy, ICRO. Unlike in Britain and Germany, the latter is not responsible to the Foreign Ministry, but attached to the Ministry of Culture and Islamic Guidance and ultimately responsible to the Supreme Leader. In that respect it fits in well with Iranian foreign policy making, in particular with regards to Syria, which is also directed by the leader's office.

Syria's Foreign Policy Formulation

In Syria under Hafiz al-Asad, the key decision-maker in policy formulation – whether foreign or domestic – was the president himself. While Asad appeared to be a consensual leader who took decisions within a circle of top foreign policy and military elites – including long-serving Vice President Abd al-Halim Khaddam, Defence Minister Mustafa Tlas, Chief of Staff Hikmat al-Shihabi and Foreign Minister Faruq al-Shara – in the end it was Asad himself who took the main decisions. As Ehteshami and Hinnebusch state:

> 'It is likely that, if Asad feels strongly about a decision, a coalescence of other elites against him is extremely unlikely, that the choice of those to be included in the consultation unit is his and that he stands above and arbitrates among a typically divided elite. There is certainly no evidence that any elite actor has contested Asad's role as final arbiter and survived politically. It appears that [. . .] foreign policy became virtually the "reserved sphere" of the presidency.'[50]

What happened to those who tried seriously to challenge Asad's decisions can be seen in the case of his brother, Rif'at, who was banished from Syria following a protracted power struggle between the two brothers after Hafiz had fallen ill in late 1983. In a showdown shortly before Rif'at had to leave the country, Hafiz allegedly told him: 'You want to overthrow the regime? Here I am. I *am* the regime.'[51]

As the president ultimately was the one who decided, foreign policy could be implemented without major institutional restrictions. Because of his grip on power, Asad managed to impose foreign policy initiatives that were not necessarily popular amongst the Ba'th party base or in public opinion, the alliance with Iran being one of them. As long as unpopular decisions could be justified in terms of the struggle with Israel, Asad felt that opposition could be contained.[52] Foreign policy in Syria was thus made within a small elite, dominated by the president.

This structure largely continued under Bashar al-Asad. Bashar had secured his power base after assuming presidency in 2000, building up support in Syria and the region by keeping the country together despite external pressures and instability in Iraq and Lebanon. To keep this support base, however, he had to 'reach consensus, negotiate, bargain, and manipulate the system'.[53] As Middle East Historian David Lesch maintains:

> 'The decision-making process remains a rather ad hoc response to challenges and threats, without long term strategic thinking and reliant therefore on traditional modus operandi. There is no national security council-like mechanism coordinating policy; instead, there seem to be informal committees that focus on various foreign policy issues.'[54]

While the president does not have absolute authority over all domestic policy matters, he has control over foreign policy decisions. An International Crisis Group Interview with a Syrian official on Syrian foreign policy formulation reaches similar conclusions:

> 'Overall objectives are set by the president with input from those around him. Then, it's up to others to suggest how to achieve them. For instance, if the minister of foreign affairs makes an

interesting proposal, the president will give him some leeway –
but only up to a point, because he still has to contend with other
tendencies. Moreover, the leadership tends to maintain multiple,
parallel channels on any given issue. But, in the end, the president always remains in a position to arbitrate and distribute
roles. The balancing and real decision-making takes place at the
top. No one else is even fully in the picture.'[55]

This has held true until the start of the Syrian uprising in March 2011.

As for Syria's embassy in Tehran, Damascus has generally appointed
loyal career diplomats to the role of ambassador. The two long-term
ambassadors of the recent past – Ahmad Hassan who was in Tehran
for all of the 1990s, and Hamid Hassan, who has been ambassador
since May 2003 – were Alawis. Ahmad Hassan briefly served as Information Minister upon his return to Syria. Hamid Hassan started his
professional life as a university professor of Arabic literature before
joining the Foreign Ministry. A career diplomat, he served as Syria's
ambassador to Armenia before being appointed to Tehran. Until Syria
set up a cultural centre in Tehran, it conducted its (minimal) cultural
diplomacy through the Ministries of Culture, Education and Foreign
Affairs, and its embassy in Tehran.[56]

Syrian Cultural Foreign Policy

Unlike Iran, Syria has no tradition of propagating its culture abroad.
Its foreign policy has always been more narrowly security-driven; culture has not played a major role in its foreign policy formulation. In
that respect Syria is no exception in the Arab world. As Syrian analyst Samir Altaqi asserted, Syrian cultural diplomacy was weak and
not very effective.[57] Syria analyst and former Israeli negotiator Itamar
Rabinovich explained Syria's stance on public diplomacy in connection
with Syrian-Israeli negotiations in the mid-1990s:

'Asad's negotiators were quite clear in explaining his position in
this matter. Public diplomacy as such had no value. Substance
alone had value, and the one substantive issue was Israel's

withdrawal from the Golan. Israel should begin by commit-
ting to Syria to withdraw from the Golan. On this basis peace
could be made. When the Syrian public finds out that Israel is
withdrawing from the Golan it will support the motion of
peace.'[58]

Syria's cultural foreign policy initiative lacked an institutional body.
It was organised by the Department of International Relations of the
Ministry of Culture. The ministry was established in 1958, during
Syria's union with Egypt, and has played a dominant role in patronis-
ing culture ever since, being resistant to relinquish control over any
cultural activities. Its department for coordinating cultural relations
abroad supervises artistic and cultural exchanges, initiates cultural
weeks, programmes, film screenings, exhibitions and theatre performances for foreign artists and intellectuals in Syria, and oversees Syria's
cultural centres abroad.[59] Syria currently has five cultural centres
abroad, in Madrid, Paris, Sana'a, Sao Paolo and Tehran, and is planning
to open centres in Berlin and Moscow. The cultural centres operate
under the supervision of the Ministry of Culture, which also finances
them. The centres mainly offer language classes, host libraries and
organise exhibitions and film shows.[60] Overall, Syria's international
cultural relations are not based on a strategic vision but are rather
impulsive, taking place as a result of specific political events such as
official visits or political statements from friendly countries. Therefore
cultural relations are not based on local needs but rather on political agendas, and often represent only the official culture of all sides
concerned. Cultural relations between Syria and other countries generally reflect the level of bilateral relations.[61]

Syria's motivation for propagating its culture abroad was minimal
compared to that of the Islamic Republic. It neither wanted to promote
a revolutionary ideology nor did it have various institutions and power
factions pushing for cultural relations with other states. Syria instead
had ideologically always seen itself as being at the centre of Arabism –
the 'beating heart of Arabism'.[62] Arab nationalism was at the roots
of Syrian foreign policy and at the core of its Ba'thist ideology; Syria
claimed to be defending Arab and not just Syrian interests through its

foreign policy choices.[63] Michel Aflaq, one of the founders of the Ba'th party, stated in 1955:

> 'Culture is the whole Arab cultural heritage; it is a communal view of the feeling for the future. The Arabs are bound together by language and history, and culture has validity for them only if it is an expression of Arabness and expressed in Arabic. The development of Arab culture is the mission and duty of every Arab. It has to be freed from the shackles imposed on it by its past colonial history. Every Arab will share the cultural awakening.'[64]

While this was written at the height of the Arab nationalist ideology, the theory of having a common Arab culture remained. Promoting one's national culture abroad would act against this principal pan-Arab vision. In that sense, the cultural centres that the Syrian Ministry of Culture set up abroad were more expressions of political relations between Syria and the country under concern than of a genuine Syrian desire to disseminate its culture in other countries. Emphasizing that Syria was but a representative of the wider Arab nation publicising Arab culture, the few cultural centres it had were called 'Arab-Syrian cultural centres'. A study on Syrian cultural policies identified two of the most common uses of culture in Syrian official rhetoric as 'resistance culture' and 'pan-Arab culture'.[65] In line with Syria's ideology, the activities of the Syrian cultural centres focused on the themes of resistance and anti-imperialism, and promoting Arab culture mainly through language teaching.

Shared Values: Cultural Themes Between the Two Allies

'Why does Jerusalem – the first qibla of Muslims – remain under the oppression of Zionism? How could this regime [in Iraq], which is an aide to the Zionist entity, follow the Imperialists and attack the Islamic Republic in Iran, and impose on it the oppressive war? Why do conditions like poverty, hunger, Westernisation, ignorance, corruption and backwardness prevail in Islamic countries, whilst these countries possess riches and resources? Why do many Islamic states and peoples tend to be obsessed with nationalism and forget basic Islamic values?'[66]

These are some of the questions raised by the Iranian cultural attaché to Damascus in his 1986 editorial in the Iranian cultural centre's *Islamic Culture* Journal. They hint at those issues that have dominated the Arab-Iranian dialogue promoted between Iran and Syria, namely anti-Zionism, anti-imperialism, the need for Muslim sovereignty and Islamic unity. Although the Syrian-Iranian alliance has been referred to as a 'marriage of convenience' or an 'odd couple',[67] there existed common ground between the two countries in terms of shared history and values, which both sides could draw upon to justify their relationship. While the Syrian-Iranian relationship is largely based on pragmatic foreign policy considerations, it was this common ground that enabled them to form a close alliance.

Syria's main ideological concerns since the latter half of the twentieth century have been pan-Arabism, anti-Zionism and anti-imperialism. Whilst pan-Arabism was a secular, Arab nationalist ideology and thus indeed at odds with Iran's pan-Islamic ideology, both countries' shared anti-Zionist and anti-imperialist ideologies facilitated their alignment.[68] Iran's change of strategy towards Israel, expressed through its commitment to the Palestinian cause and anti-Zionism, brought Iran ideologically closer to Syria. Their ideologies clashed mainly in the early period following the revolution, over Iran's attempts to export an Islamic state to its neighbouring countries. However, as Iran gave up on its export of the revolution and the importance of pan-Arabism declined over time, the common ideological ground between the two sides increased – revolving around their shared anti-Western world-view and the desire to preserve their cultural heritage in the face of globalisation and Western influence.

Islamic Heritage and Cultural History

'Political relations between Syria and Iran may be new and have developed in their present form after the Islamic revolution. Cultural relations, however, go back a long time in history.'

Ali Ansarian, Director of the Iranian cultural centre, Damascus, April 2008.[69]

'Cultural relations between Syria and Iran are old. Links between the two date back to Abbasid times in particular. There are certainly commonalities between the two cultures – Syria and Iran are both Eastern countries.' Bassel Neyazi, Syrian cultural attaché, Tehran, September 2008.[70]

When it was suggested to the director of the Iranian cultural centre in Damascus that Syrian-Iranian cultural relations appeared to exist to a large extent on the official level, as it was the two governments promoting relations rather than an exchange existing on the popular level – in contrast to Lebanon where the opposite seemed to be the case – he protested vehemently. Relations between Bilad al-Sham (Greater Syria) and Iran date back a long time, he argued, and used to be much stronger on the popular level. There existed an avid exchange of scholars and intellectuals at times when there were no borders. He admitted that the situation had changed today, but stressed that the two countries were trying to promote an exchange based on their common history.[71]

This common history between Iran and Bilad al-Sham propagated by the two sides revolves to a large extent around writers and scholars moving between Bilad al-Fars and Bilad al-Sham, during a time when 'there were no borders and the lands were united by one religion, one language – which non-Arabic speakers learned for the sake of religion – and one culture', as Syrian scholar Abdulhamid Murad put it.[72] Scholars travelling between the east and west of the Islamic lands played a real role in fostering a cultural unity throughout the first six Islamic centuries; they 'travelled from country to country, inquiring about each country's scholars, writing about them, reading about them'.[73] Muhammad Ali Azarshab, previous director of the Iranian cultural centre in Damascus, highlighted the avid cultural exchange between Iranian and Arab lands during the Hamdanid period, when the Shi'i amir Sayf al-Dawla was ruling from Aleppo and fostered literary activities. Sayf al-Dawla reigned in Aleppo from 947 until 967, where he gained fame both for his military victories and his cultural influence, attaching gifted poets and prose-writers to his court. These poets dealt with religious, historical, philosophical, astronomical and literary topics, with poetical contests frequently held.[74] Philosophers like al-Farabi (d.950), who moved from Bukhara to Baghdad to Aleppo to Damascus, were exemplary for this cultural exchange across the lands.[75]

Prominent examples from the sixth century are Ali Ibn Asakir (1105–1176), who travelled from Sham to Khurasan – and wrote tarikh madinat dimashq (History of Damascus), a book about important personalities who have visited Damascus – and Abu Sa'd al-Sam'ani (1113–1166) who travelled from Khurasan to Sham. Together the two went to Nishapur and Herat.[76] Sufi figures like Ibn al-Arabi (1165–1240), Jalal al-Din Rumi (1207–1273), Shahab al-Din Suhrawardi (1154–1191), Sa'di (c.1213–1292) and Hafiz al-Shirazi (c.1320–1390) hold a special place in bilateral cultural exchange.[77] As part of their cultural exchange, Syria and Iran have organised conferences discussing the lives and works of these scholars and philosophers, and the Iranian cultural centre in Damascus has published a number of books on them.[78] Another feature of Syria and Iran's shared history is both sides' interest in reviving their common heritage, for instance through a renewed interest in historical manuscripts. To this end the two sides cooperate in organising conferences on and exchanges of manuscripts.[79]

Syria hosts the shrines of important figures of the ahl al-bayt, the family of the prophet Muhammad, such as that of Sayida Zaynab and Ruqayya, as well as allegedly the head of Imam Husayn at the Umayyad mosque. While the presence of these figures in Damascus evokes the days of the Umayyad dynasty that is anything but revered by the Shi'a – the Umayyad caliph Yazid being responsible for Imam Husayn's death at Karbala – it nevertheless provides for a huge number of Iranian pilgrims visiting Syria every year, and Iranian investments into the upkeep of these shrines. The issue of Iranian religious tourism to Syria will be treated in detail in Chapter 7. Suffice it to say here that the shared history between Bilad al-Fars and Bilad al-Sham has contributed to continued exchanges between Syria and Iran.

Whereas the shared Islamic history plays a role in determining the content of dialogue between Syria and Iran today, as it provides for a common ground on which to base the discourse for their cultural relations, it is the more politically motivated shared values like anti-Zionism and anti-imperialism that allow for a close relationship. Following the Islamic revolution, these concepts became firmly entrenched into Iran's foreign policy motivations. Of Iran's foreign policy principles, Syria agreed on several, including the fight against Zionism, the liberation of Jerusalem and opposition to pro-Israeli states, and anti-imperialism.[80]

Anti-Zionism and Anti-Imperialism

Opposition to Israel and the occupation of Palestine is one of the main tenets of Syria's foreign policy. The Islamic revolution in Iran changed the country's stance on Israel and called for the liberation of Jerusalem. The closure of the Israeli embassy in Tehran and the opening of a Palestinian one in its place clearly demonstrated this change of strategy.[81] During Arafat's visit to Iran shortly after the revolution, Khomeini proclaimed 'imruz iran, farda felestin' – 'today Iran, tomorrow Palestine' – implying that the liberation of Palestine would come next. Khomeini declared the last Friday of the month of Ramadan as 'Jersualem (Quds) Day', and called on all Muslims to celebrate this day. Jerusalem is the third holy city for Muslims, after Mecca and Medina. According to the long-serving Palestinian ambassador to Iran, the rationale behind introducing this day was to remind people of the occupation of Jerusalem, and not to forget the importance of the city and the al-Aqsa Mosque.[82] Syrian Member of Parliament Muhammad al-Habash, a liberal pro-regime cleric who sometimes appears as the government's unofficial public relations officer,[83] affirmed on a visit to Tehran in October 2006 that the designation of the last Friday of Ramadan as World Quds Day was a memorable legacy of Imam Khomeini.[84] Iranian diplomatic representations abroad put on events to commemorate Jerusalem Day; the Iranian cultural centre in Damascus, for instance, organises a seminar on Jerusalem and at times other activities such as a competition for young artists to represent Jerusalem through art and literature.[85]

The issue of Palestine is certainly a point of convergence in official Syrian and Iranian values and outlook. Both see themselves as
part of the resistance front – the 'Axis of Resistance' – and are against
the occupation of Arab land. When American journalist Charlie Rose
made the comment to Bashar al-Asad that some found it interesting
that Syria's allies were Islamists (Hezbollah and Hamas), in one case a
theocracy (Iran), and yet Syria was a secular state, Bashar replied that

> 'that's true. [...] This is one of the things that they don't under-
> stand in the West, especially in the United States. Because, if I
> support you, doesn't mean I am like you, or I agree with you.
> It means I believe in your cause. That's the difference. Maybe if
> we don't have this cause, maybe we have a different debate with
> them, or a different relation.'[86]

Casting Syria's relationship with Iran in the mould of resistance to
Israel was useful to Damascus in justifying the alliance to its public,
which supported the resistance. In Iran, the public was more divided
on the issue. As one taxi driver complained in the summer of 2006, at
the end of the war between Hezbollah and Israel: 'Why do we have to
give money to them? It's not our problem, it's an Arab problem, what
do we have to do with it? We have our own problems.'[87] Another taxi
driver gave a similar statement, in the run up to the 2009 presidential election. 'It might be true that Ahmadinejad does not put money
into his own pocket. But he gives all our money away to Lebanon, and
Syria, and Palestine. What good is that to us?'[88] Unlike in Syria, there
was little popular support for the Palestinian cause and the anti-Israeli
resistance in Iran outside the government and clerical circles.

The idea that Syria and Iran should stand together against
imperialism is one of the foundations of their alliance. The anti-
imperialist rhetoric has not changed much in the last three decades. It
is mostly concerned with calling for confrontation with Zionism and
imperialism; the discourse on the latter has turned mainly into an
aversion to US intervention in regional and international issues since
2001 and the need to preserve a united front. The common ideological

ground between the two allies, revolving around their shared anti-Western worldview and the desire to preserve their cultural heritage in the face of globalisation and Western influence, has increased over time following Iran scaling down its goal of exporting its revolution after the death of Khomeini. In September 1998, the Syrian and Iranian Ministers of Culture discussed in Damascus 'the ongoing attempts in the West to distort the image of Islam and to depict it as a symbol of violence and terrorism. They called for confronting those attempts through cultural cooperation among Islamic states to promote the true image of Islam as a religion of love and tolerance.'[89] Whilst this notion of a perceived threat to Islamic identity had started before 11 September 2001, it has only intensified since.

Islamic Unity and Muslim Sovereignty

The themes of Islamic unity and Muslim sovereignty are main tenets of revolutionary Iran's foreign policy. The two associations set up in the 1990s under Khamene'i's leadership, the taqrib Assembly and the ahl al-bayt Assembly, institutionalised Iran's approach to these subjects. The former was formed in 1990, picking up the work of the Dar al-Taqrib that had frozen its activities following the Islamic revolution in Iran.[90] The Dar al-Taqrib movement had been an ecumenical movement founded in Cairo in 1947 by Iranian cleric Muhammad Taqi Qumi in cooperation with the al-Azhar university, aiming at rapprochement between Sunnis and Shi'a.[91] The ahl al-bayt Assembly, formed at the same time as the taqrib Assembly, had a different motivation. While it supported the idea of Islamic unity and considered it crucial in the struggle against the 'world arrogance', the ahl al-bayt Assembly saw the Shi'i community at the forefront of this struggle.[92]

Overall, Iran's calls for Islamic unity had lost their revolutionary vigour of the 1980s, and became more relevant on a national rather than transnational level under Khamene'i – while remaining very much part of the Islamic rhetoric.[93] In practice, even in the early phase of the revolution ideological concerns did not take precedence over pragmatic foreign policy decisions, as evident in the fact that the Islamic Republic sided with the Syrian government against the Syrian

Muslim Brotherhood in the early 1980s – Tehran did not want to lose its only ally amongst the Arab governments.[94]

Syria had never officially promoted Islamic unity. However, in its dialogue with Iran there existed a notion of having to stick together faced with foreign intervention and an outside threat. In view of their good political relationship, the Syrian government tended to tolerate activities organised by Iran in Syria to promote Islamic unity. The Syrian Ministry of Awqaf actively engaged in these, as did some Syrian religious organisations close to the government, such as the Abu Nur foundation, now known as the Sheikh Ahmad Kaftaru Academy.[95] The latter was founded by the late Sheikh Ahmad Kaftaru, long-serving grand mufti of Syria who worked in close cooperation with the Syrian government.[96] He was moreover a proponent of Islamic unity and rapprochement between the Islamic schools of thought. On his first visit to Iran in 1972, he emphasised that 'the most important thing was for the Sunni and Shi'a to work together. If Shi'a meant love for the house of the prophet, then we are all Shi'a.'[97]

The concept of Islamic unity was useful for the Syrian government in the sense that it played down confessional divisions, the latter being a taboo subject in Syria that considered itself a secular state. Hafiz al-Asad had not even wanted to include in Syria's 1973 constitution a clause stipulating that the president of the republic had to be Muslim, only conceding after public pressure pushed him to do so.[98] To the Alawi regime, Islamic unity was preferable to the exclusionist stance of the conservative Sunni circles.[99] It has been maintained, in fact, that rapprochement between the Islamic schools of law, or taqrib, has been used to prove that Alawis are Muslims, as taqrib underlines common traits between the Twelver Shi'a and the Alawis.[100]

Conclusion

This chapter has provided an insight into the process of foreign policy and cultural foreign policy formulation in Iran and Syria. In both countries foreign policy has been dominated by a leader acting in consultation with his advisors, in the Iranian case the Supreme Leader being the final authority, in the Syrian case the president. Iran's cultural foreign policy was conducted in an uncoordinated manner by several institutions during the first revolutionary decade, before becoming unified in a single institution, ICRO. Iranian cultural centres abroad implement Iran's cultural diplomacy by promoting the Islamic Republic's ideas and values, building up relationships and teaching Persian language and literature. In Syria, cultural diplomacy has been conducted largely through its Ministry of Culture, in cooperation with the Education and Foreign Ministry, and based on Syria's Arab identity. Syria only has a very limited number of cultural centres abroad, and lacks motivation to expand its cultural diplomacy efforts.

The Syrian-Iranian cultural dialogue draws largely on those values perceived to be shared between the two, namely a common history, anti-Zionism, anti-imperialism and to some extent Islamic unity. While their bilateral relationship is largely based on pragmatic foreign policy considerations, this common ground enabled the two countries to form a close alliance. Officials on both sides often refer back to these conceptual issues as a basis of the Syrian-Iranian relationship. How cultural diplomacy between Syria and Iran has evolved, and plays out in practice, will be examined next.

CHAPTER 3

PRE-1979 CULTURAL DIPLOMACY AND FOUNDATIONS FOR POST-REVOLUTIONARY CULTURAL EXCHANGE

Cultural diplomacy is one of the pillars of foreign policy, and more often than not reflects the state of bilateral relations. The case of Syria and Iran is no exception. The development of cultural diplomacy between Syria and Iran was closely connected to the two countries' diplomatic relationship. As relations before the Islamic revolution in Iran were limited, bilateral cultural diplomacy was minimal before the 1980s. However, at times when diplomatic relations were stable, there were attempts to work out frameworks for developing cultural relations between the two countries. In 1953 a friendship treaty was signed between the two sides, and in 1975 Syria and Iran concluded a cultural agreement. Although these were real attempts at setting up a cultural programme between the two countries, the agreements remained mostly on paper, as a true motivation for implementation was lacking. Thus the agreement of 1975 for instance provided a comprehensive plan for cultural cooperation, and in fact resembled the post-revolutionary agreement of 1984 – but it was never ratified or put into practice. The 1984 agreement laid the foundations for post-revolutionary cultural diplomacy. However, it was not until the mid-1990s – when bilateral relations became further institutionalised – that detailed programmes were drafted to implement the 1984 cultural agreement, setting out clearly how to cooperate in the cultural field.

In the following, the development of cultural diplomacy between Syria and Iran from Syrian independence in 1946 until the Islamic revolution in Iran in 1979 will be examined based on an extensive survey of documents from the Iranian embassy in Damascus of the period under concern. Because the analysis is based on correspondence between Imperial Iran's embassy with Syrian authorities and Iranian ministries, the focus is on Iran's cultural diplomacy in Syria. It transpires from the correspondence, however, that Syria's cultural activities in Iran were limited to sporadic academic exchanges. We will then turn to the 1984 cultural agreement, analysing the text and comparing it with the 1975 agreement, before looking at the subsequent implementation programmes, all of which laid the foundations for cultural diplomacy between Syria and post-revolutionary Iran.

Pre-Revolutionary Attempts and Constraints

Looking at the state of cultural diplomacy from Syria's independence in 1946 until the Islamic revolution in Iran in 1979, it becomes clear that attempts at building up cultural relations between the two states were half-hearted and dependent on enthused individuals. There was a dichotomy between what Iran's cultural officers in Syria would have liked to achieve and what means and support they were given by their ministries in Iran. However, Iran's cultural movement at the time of the Shah was more diversified than the proponents of post-revolutionary Iranian cultural diplomacy liked to portray it. Imperial Iran's limited attempt at cultural work in Syria did not simply revolve around the three cores mentioned by one of the Islamic Republic's cultural attachés in Damascus, namely suppressing Islam from Iranian culture, reviving the traditional cultural heritage of Iranian history before Islam, and laying the foundations for Western culture.[1] While part of the message propagated by Imperial Iran was indeed to promote the Shah and his glory, there were nevertheless some genuine efforts at developing bilateral cultural relations between Syria and Iran.

The 1950s and 1960s: Cautious Beginnings

After Syria gained independence in 1946, Iran recognised Syria's independence and proceeded to open a consulate in Damascus, which was upgraded to full embassy status in December 1949 with the appointment of Moshfegh Kazemi as ambassador.[2] In view of strengthening bilateral ties, the Syrian and Iranian governments started discussions about concluding a friendship treaty between the two countries in 1951, a draft of which was ready to be signed by January 1952. The text comprised five articles, in which they reaffirmed their will to maintain peace and fraternity between the two sides, to treat each other's diplomatic representatives in accordance with international principles, to start negotiations to conclude agreements concerning cultural, consular, trade and customs matters, and to resolve disputes between them peacefully.[3] Although the treaty was straightforward and rather non-committing seeing that its content was general, the Shah's government was hesitant to sign. This worried the Syrians. The Iranian embassy in Damascus was put in an embarrassing situation, as it had no clear directions from its Foreign Ministry as to what reasons to give the Syrian side for the delay. It emerged that the Iranians were uneasy about the unstable nature of the Syrian governments since the late 1940s, and preferred the agreement not to be linked to the current government in particular, but to the Syrian state as such.[4] The Iranians seemed eventually to overcome their anxiety – the friendship treaty was signed in Damascus on 24 May 1953, the wording of the 1952 draft text unchanged, and ratified in January 1955.[5] In the speeches accompanying the signing ceremony, both sides pointed out their joy of entering a new stage of friendship, and that relations between Arab and Iranian lands went back 2,000 years.[6] It has to be noted, however, that Syria was by far not the first Arab country with which Iran set up friendly relations, the latter having previously established agreements with Egypt, Iraq, Jordan and Lebanon.[7]

Friendly relations between Iran and Syria did not translate into an interest in a cultural exchange between the two sides. The May 1957 correspondence between the Iranian embassy in Damascus and the Foreign Ministry shows the lack of real motivation on the part of the Iranian government to expand its cultural efforts towards Syria. In it, the Iranian ambassador to Syria elaborated on the poor state of Iran's cultural relations with Syria due to lack of initiatives and sufficient funds coming from Iran, and suggested a number of ways to change this. The easiest way to improve cultural relations in Arab countries, he explained, was to focus on universities – that is, to facilitate entry of Arab students to Iranian universities, or to send Persian teachers to Syrian universities. He pointed out that Damascus University had complained to the Iranian embassy in 1955 about the lack of lecturers to teach Persian language and literature at the Faculty of Literature, but unfortunately this opportunity had not been taken up by Iran. Another effective method of introducing Persian language and litera-ture was to send books to Syrian universities and libraries.[8] While the Iranian ambassador in Syria saw a potential for strengthening relations on the cultural level, the ministries in Tehran were not responsive to his suggestions. Promotion of culture did not yet hold a prominent place in Iranian foreign policy making.[9]

It seems that cultural diplomacy in the 1950s went only as far as enthused individuals could drive it. One of these was Ahmad Aram, who was despatched as cultural attaché to the Iranian embassy in Damascus in the early 1950s. A scholar and intellectual fluent in a number of languages including Arabic, Ahmad Aram was keen to be in touch with the Shi'i community of Damascus. He started teaching Persian to pupils at the Muhsiniya school in the Shi'i Amin quarter of old Damascus in 1951, in agreement with the Iranian embassy. There he taught classes once a week on a voluntary basis. However, accord-ing to one of his former students, Labib Beidun, interest amongst the Syrian pupils was limited and numbers soon dwindled from around twenty to one dedicated pupil.[10] Besides Aram, Mustafa Ali Abadi was sent from Iran to teach Persian at the school. According to Beidun, Aram's successor as cultural attaché also offered to teach Persian at the embassy to the interested few.[11] In July 1958, the Iranian embassy in

Damascus was closed and reduced to a consulate general in response to the creation of the United Arab Republic. When the ambassadors were recalled and bilateral relations downgraded, Iran stopped sending teachers to the Muhsiniya school, and Persian teaching was undertaken by local Syrian scholars such as Rashid Murtada who came from a Syrian Shi'i family.[12]

The embassy reopened after the union between Syria and Egypt fell apart in 1961, and an ambassador was dispatched in March 1962. Persian language teaching tentatively started as an option for first and second year undergraduates at the faculty of literature of Damascus University in autumn 1962.[13] In autumn 1965 the Iranian government recalled its ambassador and diplomats from Damascus in protest at the statements pronounced in parliament by the Syrian Prime Minister Yusuf Zu'ayyin.[14] Following this incident, relations that had been friendly since Syrian independence came to a virtual standstill. They picked up again after the 1967 Arab-Israeli war, and returned to ambassadorial level after the October war in 1973, in which Iran condemned Israel's aerial bombardment of Damascus that killed and injured civilians. To show its support to Syria, Iran decided to appoint an ambassador to Damascus again.[15] Cultural relations picked up at the same time.

The 1970s and Muhammad Javad Mashkur:
Attempts and Constraints

As bilateral relations warmed up in the mid-1970s, the situation of cultural interaction between Syria and Iran improved, albeit still dependent on the efforts of some motivated few. At the forefront of these was Muhammad Javad Mashkur. A professor of Persian language and literature, historian and scholar of Iranian and Islamic studies, he was sent to Damascus in 1974 as Iran's cultural attaché. He started to teach Islamic sciences and history at Damascus University, as well as Persian language, and worked towards establishing chairs of Persian language and literature at Damascus and Aleppo University.[16] During the time of Mashkur, a number of important steps were taken towards setting up an organised cultural exchange between the two countries.

This came at a moment of high-level exchanges between Syria and Iran, starting with the signing of an economic agreement in May 1974.[17] Discussions started on drafting a cultural agreement between the two countries, a cultural centre was attached to the Iranian embassy in Damascus, and a number of cultural activities were organised in the Syrian capital and beyond.

The cultural agreement, which was signed between the two sides in Tehran in November 1975, followed classical methods of cultural diplomacy, namely calling for cooperation in the fields of education, culture and arts, travel and sports. It was based on the draft of the September 1958 agreement between Iran and the United Arab Republic, which had been ratified by Iran and Egypt in April 1971.[18] What is notable is its similarity in terms of methodology and wording to the post-revolutionary cultural agreement of 1984, which suggests continuity in the framework for cultural diplomacy – the thematic content of which differed markedly. The 1975 agreement laid out a comprehensive programme to consolidate and develop bilateral cultural relations between Syria and Iran, including a call for setting up chairs for Persian language in Syrian universities and chairs for Arabic in Iranian universities, as well as facilitating the establishment of cultural centres in each other's country.[19] Whilst the agreement provided a detailed framework for expanding cultural relations, neither side seemed particularly pressed to ratify the agreement and put it into practice. Mashkur complained frequently to his superiors at the Ministry of Culture in Tehran about the lack of cooperation and interest of the ministry in providing the necessary facilities for him to proceed with his work. It is also clear that the Syrian case received less attention from the ministry than for instance Egypt, with which Imperial Iran had much closer ties.[20]

Nevertheless, a cultural centre was gradually set up, Persian classes were given at the Arabic literature faculties of Damascus University and later on Aleppo University, film shows and photo exhibitions were put on, a number of book exchanges took place and some cultural festivals celebrating philosophers linking the two cultures, like al-Farabi and Suhrawardi, were organised in the mid-1970s. Persian classes at Damascus University were given mainly by Mashkur himself, while the Iranian embassy worked with the faculty of literature at Aleppo University towards enabling Syrian students who had gained their PhDs from Iranian universities to teach there, namely Muhammad al-Tounji.[21] The Iranian cultural centre in Damascus started off in October 1974 based at the embassy, and later moved to an independent building.[22] Persian classes started at the centre in December of the same year; a library – named after Suhrawardi – was gradually set up through donations from the Iranian Ministry of Culture and local cultural bodies such as the majma' al-lugha al-'arabiya (Arabic Language Academy).[23]

Iranian cultural activities thus were more wide-ranging than post-revolutionary literature suggests, but the content was indeed mixed. Whilst some actions focused on underlining the shared heritage between Iran and the Arab world and were thus in line with creating a bilateral cultural dialogue, other actions were there mainly to celebrate the Shah and his past achievements. Thus the Shah's birthday was an annual occasion for festivities, and the cultural developments Iran achieved in the 1960s and 1970s were highlighted when occasions arose.[24] The cultural centre worked together with the Syrian ministries of culture, education and higher education, the majma' al-lugha al-'arabiya, the Zahiriya Library (which held a collection of Persian manuscripts), Damascus University as well as other foreign cultural centres. The Syrian point of contact for the Iranian cultural attaché was the director of the cultural department of the Syrian Foreign Ministry. In the late-1970s, this happened to be Ali Mohsen Zifa, who had just returned from his posting as Syrian ambassador to Iran, which might have facilitated Muhammad Javad Mashkur's work from the Syrian side.[25] The latest pre-revolutionary cultural report I managed to obtain dates back to March 1978, in which Mashkur continues to describe the centre's efforts despite lack of sufficient means.[26]

Parallel to these constrained endeavours to set up a cultural dialogue between Syria and Iran by means of education and introduction of each other's cultures, a number of actions were also undertaken to renovate and rebuild the shrines of members of the ahl al-bayt located in Syria, in particular the shrines of Sayida Zaynab and Ruqayya, in view of facilitating the visit of these sites by Iranian pilgrims. While individual Iranians gave donations to the endowments of the shrines via the Iranian embassy in Damascus throughout the years, an agreement was concluded between the two governments in 1973 to cooperate in renovating the shrine of Sayida Zaynab.[27] We will discuss the development of cooperation over these shrines and religious tourism in detail in Chapter 7.

We have little evidence of Syrian efforts to promote its culture in Iran during the period under concern. From independence in 1946 until the beginning of the Asad era, Syrian governments changed frequently and subsequent leaders were preoccupied with domestic politics and Arab nationalism, which was at its height in the 1950s and 1960s. Syrian foreign policy in general was more concerned with hard power than propagating ideas, especially considering the continuous enmity with Israel and the recurrence of Arab-Israeli wars. As Syrian foreign policy was thus truncated, the Syrian side cooperated with the Iranian government in theory, mainly by agreeing to the cultural treaties and the idea of expanding cultural ties, but did little actively to introduce its culture in Iran, let alone to establish a cultural centre in Tehran. The correspondence confirms that at least one Syrian student did obtain a scholarship to study in Iranian universities as part of the cultural exchange, and several Syrian students and professors visited Iran and took part in conferences there.[28] In 1957, for example, Tehran University invited Damascus University to send one student representative to its conference on 'Cultural Freedom', to present a paper in English or French on either 'Traditional values and modern civilisation', 'International cultural relations' or 'Problems of freedom of culture', and in the 1970s a delegation from Damascus University visited Iran and Tehran University.[29] Overall, however, interest in the other country seemed limited.

There were a number of Syrian intellectuals specialised in Persian literature and language, who set about translating some of the major Iranian literary works into Arabic. Most notable amongst these may have been Muhammad al-Furati, a Syrian from Dayr al-Zur in the east of Syria. The Ministry of Culture appointed him as translator from Persian to Arabic, which he practised from 1959 until 1973. His translations included works by Sa'di, Hafiz and Rumi, as well as some of the Rubayat of Omar Khayam.[30] However, people like al-Furati were Syrians interested in Iranian culture, not Syrians trying to promote their own culture in Iran.

Cultural diplomacy between Iran and Syria in the period between 1946 and 1979 was thus largely limited to attempts to expand cultural relations on paper at times when diplomatic relations were improving. It was tightly linked to the state of political relations between the two sides, and Syria certainly was not the main Arab country Iran tried to develop closer ties with. Whilst the framework for an extensive cultural programme between Iran and Syria was worked out and put on paper in the 1975 cultural agreement, lack of serious motivation on both sides led to it never being ratified or fully implemented. The Syrian presence in Iran seemed to have been confined to not more than a handful of students studying at Iranian universities as well as some visits by Syrian intellectuals, who had little impact on bilateral policy at home. The Iranian cultural presence in Syria was more pronounced, but more as a result of the endeavours of motivated individuals like Ahmad Aram and Muhammad Javad Mashkur than due to Iranian government efforts.

The similarity between the 1975 cultural agreement and the post-revolutionary agreement of 1984 suggests that the pre- and post-revolutionary media for cultural exchange followed a similar framework. The difference lay in the will for implementation as well as the message to be propagated. The 1984 agreement and the subsequent cultural implementation programmes between Syria and Iran will be discussed in the following as foundations for cultural exchange following the Islamic revolution.

Foundations for Post-Revolutionary Exchange

The 1984 Cultural Agreement

Bilateral relations between Syria and Iran changed course following the Islamic revolution in Iran. Officials from both sides were soon involved in drafting a cultural agreement to further strengthen the 'bonds of friendship' between the two countries. Culture held a prominent place in the Iranian revolutionary administration. While the

Cultural agreements, their contents and implementation. Table by author.

Cultural Agreement	Content	Implementation
1953 Friendship Treaty Signed: 24 May 1953	1. Establish peace and friendship between the two countries and people 2. Treat each other's diplomatic representatives in accordance with international principles 3. Start negotiations to conclude agreements concerning cultural, trade, and customs matters 4. Resolve disputes between them peacefully	Ratified by the Chamber of Deputies on 22 January 1955
1975 Cultural Agreement Signed: 8 November 1975	1. Develop cultural and scientific relations a) Exchange of teachers, scholars, experts, students b) Cooperation between universities and teaching institutions c) Facilitate establishment of teaching institutions and cultural centres of the other side 2. Introduce the art and culture of the other country a) Exchange of books and publications, translations b) Exchange of films and documentaries, radio and television; possible co-production c) Organise musical and theatre events d) Organise sport meetings and exchange visits e) Organise art and scientific exhibitions 3. Develop mutual understanding 4. Encourage granting scholarships to students of the other country 5. Collaborate in fighting against illiteracy 6. Create and maintain cultural institutions of the other country in one's country 7. Create Persian language chairs in Syrian universities and Arabic language chairs in Iranian universities 8. Recognise each other's diplomas and certificates 9. Set up joint commission to implement this agreement	Did not seem to be ratified or implemented, although first steps were taken (e.g. Persian language classes started in Damascus and Aleppo University although no chair was set up; an Iranian cultural centre opened in Damascus)

| 1984 Cultural Agreement Signed: 21 February 1984 (Numbers in brackets: comparison with 1975 agreement) | 1. Cooperate in the development of curricula and the educational system 2. Develop cultural and scientific relations (1/1975) 3. Encourage granting scholarships to students of the other country (4/1975) 4. Present the other side with experts and specialists in various fields 5. Create Persian language chairs in Syrian universities and Arabic language chairs in Iranian universities (7/1975) 6. Recognise each other's diplomas and certificates (8/1975) 7. Invite the other side to participate in international conferences and seminars 8. Cooperation between national councils of UNESCO 9. Provide facilities to the other side to open a school in one's country (1c/1975) 10. Increase mutual understanding through choice of texts in school books 11. Introducing the art and culture of the other country (2/1975) 12. Facilitate cooperation between scholars with the aim of reviving shared civilisation and cultural heritage 13. Develop mutual understanding (3/1975) 14. Provide the necessary facilities for setting up cultural centres in the other country (1c/1975) 15. Exchange films produced in each country; work towards co-producing films (2b/1975) 16. Cooperate in radio, television and news agencies; exchange radio and television programmes (2b/1975) 17. Encourage cooperation in sports and organise visits of sport and youth institutions (2d/1975) 18. Encourage cooperation between student organisations 19. Set up joint commission to supervise implementation of this agreement (9/1975) | Partly implemented in the 1980s. Implementation programmes drafted and implemented since the mid-1990s. |

(*Sources*: 1953 friendship treaty, 1975 cultural agreement, 1984 cultural agreement.)

Islamic Republic in the early 1980s did not have a unified cultural foreign policy, it was the international department of the Ministry of Culture that was in charge of liaising with governmental cultural authorities abroad, and thus to establish Iran's cultural diplomacy with foreign countries. While the message of post-revolutionary Iran's cultural policies differed clearly from that of Imperial Iran, the framework the Islamic Republic's Ministry of Culture used to strengthen ties with other nations seemed to be the same as the pre-revolutionary one. This becomes clear by looking at the text of the 1984 cultural agreement between the governments of the Islamic Republic of Iran and the Syrian Arab Republic, which closely resembled the 1975 agreement between the latter and Imperial Iran – suggesting that the Islamic Republic followed traditional methods of cultural diplomacy.

The Syrian Minister of Education and the Iranian Minister of Culture and Higher Education signed this cultural agreement in Tehran in February 1984; it called for partnership between the ministries of education, culture and higher education.[31] Just like the 1975 agreement, the 1984 agreement laid down the structure for cooperation in the fields of education, culture and arts, travel, sports and media. In fact, the only difference between the two agreements was that the 1984 one was more detailed than the pre-revolutionary one, in particular in the field of education and higher education; it also added a small section on cooperation between student organisations of the two countries. One additional article for instance called for encouraging cooperation between scholars of both countries with the specific aim of reviving the shared civilisation and cultural heritage of Syria and Iran (Article 12).[32] The Islamic Republic had more incentive than the Shah to stress its shared cultural history with the Arab world, considering that Islam emerged there. Apart from these additions, the agreement incorporated all articles of the 1975 agreement, bar one article that called for cooperation to combat illiteracy (Article 5).

Both pre- and post-revolutionary Iran's cultural diplomacy followed similar methods; the content of what values to promote as such was not laid down in the texts. The opening paragraph of the agreement set the ideological tone, however, indicating that the two governments drafted the agreement in order to 'strengthen the bonds of friendship and fraternity between their two peoples, starting with their belief in what they share of cultural heritage and civilisation, which represents an important part of the history of the struggle of the two peoples, and from that expand the development of cultural relations, in line with the politics of resistance to Imperialism and Zionism, and develop friendly relations between the two brotherly peoples.'[33]

Establishing cultural relations was officially based on Syria and Iran's shared heritage, and the concepts of anti-imperialism and anti-Zionism.

The 1984 cultural agreement marked the beginning of official cultural diplomacy directed by the two governments, and provided the basis for all subsequent cultural implementation programmes between the two sides.[34] Whereas cultural relations were thus formalised with the signing of the agreement, a number of its articles were only gradually implemented at a later stage. The cultural agreement had to be renewed every five years. While the cultural agreement of 1984 established the general fields of cooperation and formed the foundation for the cultural work, it was the cultural implementation programmes subsequently drafted between the two sides that instructed both countries on more concrete steps.

The Cultural Implementation Programmes

Syria and Iran first agreed upon drafting an implementation programme for their 1984 cultural agreement in 1991, during the Syrian Minister of Culture's visit to Tehran. During the latter's subsequent visit in the summer of 1994, the two sides signed the programme, which set out clear directions on how to further consolidate cultural relations. The programme was initially valid for three years, for the period 1995–1997.[35] Subsequent implementation programmes have been drafted and authorised every three years. The reason why the first implementation programme was put together as late as 1994, a decade after the cultural agreement was initially signed, could lie in the fact that only in the early 1990s Iran's cultural diplomacy became institutionalised. What is more, after Syrian-Iranian relations survived the ups and downs of the 1980s, the two sides further consolidated their relationship in the 1990s, with the creation of institutions such as the Syrian-Iranian Higher Cooperation Committee.

The cultural implementation programmes clearly laid out steps to increase cultural cooperation. The programme for the years 2003–2005, signed in Tehran in December 2002 by the Syrian and Iranian Ministers of Education, showed the main concerns of cultural diplomacy between the two sides, in particular that a large emphasis was put on cooperation in the field of education, which filled the first and second section of the programme, the former dealing with primary and secondary education, the latter with higher education. The third section dealt with cooperation in the field of culture and art, being subdivided into matters of cinema, antiquities and museums, music, theatre and art, performances and exhibitions, revival and promotion of Arab and Iranian heritage, and the national libraries (al-Asad library and the Iranian national library). The fourth section focused on media cooperation, the fifth on sport and youth. The sixth section outlined financial conditions, namely which side was to pay for what in terms of covering expenses for their exchanges of people, granting of scholarships, university chairs and setting up exhibitions. All in all, the programme contained 70 articles stipulating how to implement cultural cooperation between the two countries.[36] Whereas not all articles were put into practice, bilateral cultural diplomacy intensified during the last decade.

Conclusion

Cultural diplomacy between Syria and Iran had tentatively started in the pre-revolutionary period, mainly through the efforts of motivated Iranian cultural officials but with little support from the Iranian Imperial ministries. It was more diversified than post-revolutionary reports suggest, but had little reach and neither money nor human resources seemed to have been invested in cultural diplomacy. Following the revolution and the start of extensive bilateral exchange between Syria and the Islamic Republic, cooperation in the cultural field picked up. Cultural diplomacy started gradually in the wake of the 1984 cultural agreement, and was invigorated in the second half of the 1990s, with the drafting of the first implementation programmes at a time when bilateral relations became more institutionalised.

In line with Iran and Syria's different motivations for cultural diplomacy, the vast majority of cultural activities were undertaken by Iran in Syria. Only recently has Syria started to become more actively engaged in Iran, which will be elaborated in Chapter 5. Shortly before the 1984 agreement was signed, Iran set up a cultural centre in Damascus, through which it subsequently applied its cultural diplomacy principles. The work of this centre, which became the main coordinator of Iran's soft power efforts and hence the public face of its cultural diplomacy, will be looked at in detail in Chapter 4.

CHAPTER 4*

IRAN'S CULTURAL DIPLOMACY IN SYRIA: THE IRANIAN CULTURAL CENTRE IN DAMASCUS

Starting in the early 1980s, cultural diplomacy between Syria and revolutionary Iran developed parallel to the formation of close political relations between the two countries. It was Iran who drove the institutionalisation of bilateral cultural relations between the two allies forward. In this chapter, I will set out how the Islamic Republic's cultural diplomacy played out in practice, by looking at the case of the Iranian cultural centre in Damascus. The state of foreign cultural centres in Syria in general and the establishment of the Iranian cultural centre in particular will be discussed before examining the objectives and organisation, activities and reach, and limits of the Iranian cultural centre in Damascus, to discern how Iran went about propagating its ideas in Syria on the official level.

The Islamic Republic understands the importance of cultural diplomacy in advancing its ideas and establishing lasting links with Syria. Iran finds an audience in Syria, albeit to a large extent one that is already sympathetic to its ideas. Iran's cultural diplomacy in Syria is largely confined to the official cultural sphere and has to be seen very much within the context of the Syrian-Iranian alliance. As such, Iran's reach is limited, however, as many Syrians – in particular of the Sunni majority background – regard the relationship as an alliance between the Syrian leadership and the Shi'i Islamic Republic and are wary of Iran's intentions.

Setting the Scene: Foreign Cultural Centres in Damascus and the Establishment of the Iranian Cultural Centre

Damascus hosts a number of foreign cultural centres. Pioneers of cultural diplomacy, the French have the longest cultural presence in Syria, not least due to their particular historical connection to Syria dating back to the French Mandate period. The Institut français d'Etudes Arabes de Damas (formally attached to the regional Institut français du Proche Orient in 2000) was set up in 1928 as a research institution to provide a base for Arabists to deepen their knowledge of Arab-Muslim culture.[1] Later on, in 1977, the French set up their Centre culturel français to offer a separate forum for their cultural activities and French language classes.[2] Other countries followed suit. The British Council opened in Damascus in 1942,[3] the German Goethe-Institut in the mid-1950s,[4] the Russian cultural centre in the mid-1960s,[5] the Spanish Instituto Cervantes in 1991 and the current Italian cultural centre in 2000.[6] The Americans have a cultural centre attached to their embassy. Imperial Iran's cultural attaché attended the opening of the American centre in 1977, and was impressed by the centre's library of 8,000 books and the space they had, which included a cinema.[7] Turkey, while not having a cultural centre as such, had been active in strengthening bilateral cultural cooperation with Syria in recent years, to reflect their growing interaction until 2011. There was a project under way to establish a joint Syrian-Turkish Museum of Ottoman history in the historic Tekkiye Sulaymaniya Mosque complex in Damascus.[8] However, all cultural cooperation came to a halt after Turkey changed its position on Syria following the start of the Syria crisis in 2011 and started supporting the Syrian opposition.

Imperial Iran had begun to develop a cultural centre in the mid-1970s as a result of the efforts of the cultural attaché, Muhammad Javad Mashkur. Following the revolution and the ensuing focus on culture, the Islamic Republic embarked upon its cultural work in Syria soon after diplomatic relations kicked off. Even before the cultural agreement was signed in February 1984, an Iranian cultural centre opened in Damascus in 1983. As stated by Shafi'ai, former cultural attaché to Damascus, Iran considered the establishment of an Iranian cultural centre in Damascus a necessity, as the Islamic Republic gave a special importance to the Arab world in view of the presence of many cultural commonalities between the two.[9] Accordingly, the Minister of Culture and Islamic Guidance – at the time Muhammad Khatami, later to be president – opened Iran's cultural centres in Damascus and Beirut on a trip to the region.[10]

The Syrian government cooperates with foreign cultural centres and is open to foreign cultural activities within a certain framework. The scope and activities of the cultural centres generally reflect the state of bilateral diplomatic relations between Syria and the country under concern. The Goethe-Institut for instance closed in 1967 over differences between Syria and Germany regarding the latter's position on Israel and the Arab-Israeli war, and only opened again in 1979.[11] The American cultural centre has been closed down at times of strained political relations. Many European cultural centres have temporarily closed or stopped their activities following the beginning of the Syrian uprising in 2011. All activities have to be authorised by the Department of International Relations of the Syrian Ministry of Culture, which is also responsible for Syria's cultural activities abroad. Cultural and political relations go hand-in-hand.[12] The Syrian-Iranian relationship is based on the two governments' strong political relationship – all cultural activities organised by the cultural centre are seen within the framework of this relationship.

The Iranian cultural centre observed other foreign cultural centres in Damascus. After the fall of the Soviet Union, the Iranians closely followed the cultural activities of the Americans in particular. They perceived a competition with the United States over whose ideology was to fill the vacuum left behind by the break-up of the 'leftist ideology'. Being afraid that 'Western atheism' would take the place of 'Eastern atheism' in the young generation, the Iranians strove to instil their Islamic ideology instead.[13] They carefully assessed how the Americans were reaching out to the Syrians and whom they were reaching – taking into consideration factors such as the location of the American cultural centre. The latter was situated in an area of Damascus where most of Syria's political elite lived; other than that it was a wealthy quarter. The Iranian cultural attaché concluded that it was the children of this neighbourhood that the Americans could reach out to, and that they were the ones frequenting the centre.[14] The Iranians were thus assessing what access the Americans had in promoting their culture, and how to compete with them. The Iranian cultural centre itself was first located in Mazzeh, close to the Iranian embassy. Mazzeh was a well-to-do neighbourhood, but less central than the one of the Americans. The current cultural centre is situated in the heart of Damascus, right next to Martyr Square and in walking distance to the shrines of Sayida Ruqayya and the Umayyad Mosque in the old town. Its central location makes it very accessible to anyone.

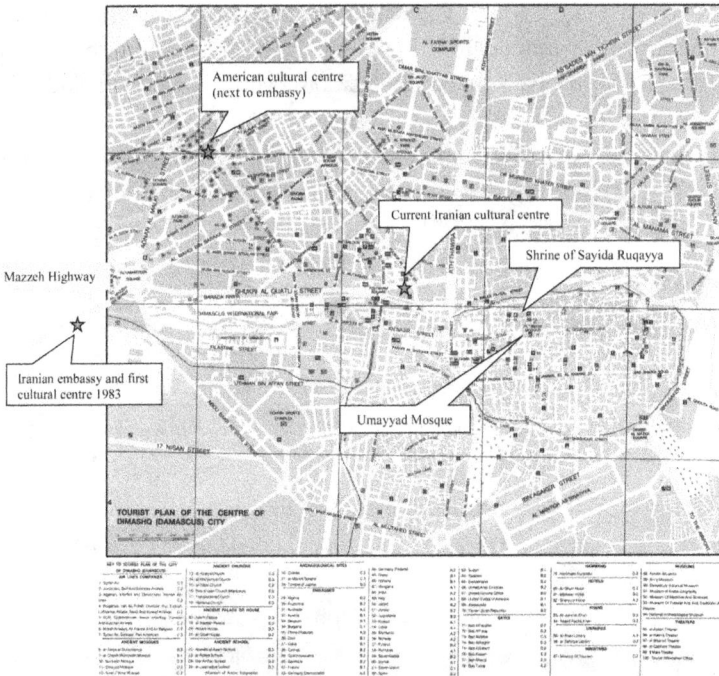

Map of central Damascus with the Iranian and American cultural centres marked.[15]

The Centre's Objectives and Organisation

In accordance with Iran's cultural diplomacy practice, the centre is officially placed under the supervision of the Iranian embassy in Damascus; the two bodies cooperate closely with each other.[16] The director of the centre, also referred to as cultural councillor, is sent directly from Iran. Ali Ansarian, director from 2002 to 2010, came from inside the ICRO, having been cultural attaché in Syria in the 1980s, expert on Middle East affairs at the Ministry of Culture and Islamic Guidance and ICRO in the 1990s, and director of Iran's cultural centre in Abu Dhabi before coming to Damascus in 2002. His predecessor came from an academic background; he was professor of Arabic literature at Tehran University before and after he took up his post in Damascus from 1998 to 2002.[17]

Cultural councillors to Damascus have included clerics and laypersons; no noticeable difference in policies has been observed between one group and the other. The cultural councillor is representing Iran's interests to its partners in the Syrian cultural sphere; like the ambassador, he is involved in public relations work. Partners include the ministries of culture, education, higher education, tourism, information and awqaf, academics, clerics from religious schools, writers, newspaper editors, governmental and non-governmental cultural officials, and intellectuals.[18]

Directors of the Iranian cultural centre in Damascus.[19]

Year	Director (Cultural Councillor)	Professional background
1981/3–1987	Dr Sadegh Aynevand	Academic
1987–1991	Hojjatoleslam Muhammad Salar	Writer and ICRO
1991–1994	Hojjatoleslam Muhammad Shariati	ICRO
1995–1998	Sayyed Morteza No'amatzadeh	Society for the Defence of Palestine
1998–2002	Dr Muhammad Ali Azarshab	Academic
2002–2010	Ali Ansarian	ICRO
2010–present	Hojjatoleslam Dr Ali Khayat	Academic (Quranic studies)

So what does the Iranian cultural centre in Damascus try to achieve? Its goals revolve around expanding cultural, scientific, religious and artistic relations between the two countries, following the principles of ICRO.[20] Introducing Iranian Islamic culture, stressing the importance of Islamic unity and promoting Persian language and literature feature strongly, as does the need to increase academic interaction by organising university exchanges on the student and teacher level. These goals follow the guidelines set out in the 1984 bilateral cultural agreement, and are clearly in line with the basic aims of the concepts of cultural diplomacy. They aim at building lasting relationships between the people and bringing Islamic Iran's culture and values closer to the Syrian people.

One of the first steps towards introducing revolutionary Iran's ideas to Syrians after the opening of the cultural centre was the establishment of a quarterly journal – *Islamic Culture* – in 1985, published in Arabic until 2006.[21] The journal was published with the permission of the Syrian Ministry of Information; each edition had 2,000 copies. According to Iranian officials the journal had a following amongst Syrians, and was even sent abroad to some other Islamic countries.[22] It is highly questionable, however, whether the journal managed to reach out to Syrians outside a particular circle of people who were already involved in Islamic thought or had an interest in Iran in one way or another – such as a limited number of clerics, academics and intellectuals. Nevertheless, by looking at the subjects treated in this journal, we can discern what themes and values were at the forefront of the Islamic Republic's cultural foreign policy in Syria.

Of the over 1,500 articles written between 1985 and 2006, around two-thirds deal explicitly with Islamic matters, be it by writing about Islamic studies, the thoughts of Imam Khomeini, the Quran, Islamic heritage, the ahl al-bayt, or the Islamic revolution. The remaining third of the articles revolves around topics such as poetry and literature, social affairs, Palestine, and cultural dialogue. However, all in all, a large amount of the articles on poetry and literature equally deals with religious literature, such as poetry about Imam Khomeini and the Islamic revolution, about the Prophet Muhammad and the ahl al-bayt. Islam indirectly plays a role in most topics; articles about women deal

Number of articles by subject in *Islamic Culture* journal, 1–100 (1985–2006).[23]

Subject	Number of articles
1. Islamic Studies (including topics such as the Prophet, Justice, the holy month of Ramadan, Islamic Law, Philosophy)	201
2. Poetry and Literature	146
3. The ahl al-bayt School	143
4. Personalities and translations	130
5. Islamic matters and concepts (including topics such as 'Islamic Awakening', 'Global Imperialism', and various concepts in Islam)	121
6. Imam Khomeini	116
7. About the Islamic revolution and Republic	91
8. The Quran	84
9. Subjects in Islamic Unity	79
10. Social affairs, women and family affairs	57
11. Arab-Persian cultural relations	57
12. Introducing Iran and the Islamic world	39
13. Palestine and the crimes of Zionism and imperialism	35
14. Cultural dialogue between civilisations	34
15. Publications, books and libraries	34
16. The life of Prophet Muhammad	33
17. Book reviews	29
18. Imam Khamene'i	28
19. Islamic heritage and literature	25
20. Islamic economy	22
21. Rights and freedoms in Islam	20
22. Globalisation and cultural invasion	17
23. Sciences from an Islamic viewpoint	15
24. *Ijtihad – Marja'iya – Velayat-e faqih*	9

with subjects like the role of women in the Quran and Islamic society; many of the articles on Palestine look at the issue from an Islamic point of view – e.g. 'Jerusalem is the primary concern of Muslims'.[24] In the editorial of the journal's first issue, the editor states:

> 'The "Islamic Culture" of the Iranian Islamic cultural centre in Damascus is concerned with unveiling the genius of the Islamic civilisation by way of researching about early scholars, precious books and fine arts, in order to ease the way for the sake of [. . .] Islamic sciences.'[25]

In the early period of publication Islamic themes were particularly dominant, with the first issue of *Islamic Culture* dedicated to Islamic unity, and following issues focusing on historical personalities of the Islamic world. While the journal was the Iranian cultural centre's first step towards introducing Iran's ideas to the Syrian public in an organised manner, its importance to us lies more in the fact that it reveals what subjects the Iranians wanted to promote in Syria than in the extent of its reach.

Iran gradually established several departments within the centre, each in charge of coordinating a range of activities to reach out to Syrians. Currently, the centre has two libraries, one general library for the centre's staff with books about Syria, Arab-Iranian relations, Islamic history and religious studies, and one public library as part of the Arab-Iranian Cultural Studies Centre. The centre has its own bookshop, the Islamic culture bookstore, located next to the entrance of the building. It has a publishing department, one for cultural activities in Syrian provinces – in charge of organising cultural weeks across Syria – a public relations department and a women's department.[26] Language teaching forms an integral part of the centre's programme.

Activities and Reach

The Iranian cultural centre in Damascus seeks to build lasting relationships between the Syrian and Iranian people and introduce Islamic Iran's culture and values through a range of activities it organizes,

The Iranian cultural centre in Bahsa. Damascus, 20 December 2005.

coordinates and supervises. These include research activities and publishing, conferences and seminars, cultural art weeks and exhibitions, activities in the field of Islamic unity and rapprochement between the Islamic schools of thought, educational and university activities. In what follows, some of the centre's activities will be examined in order to discern how the Islamic Republic has been communicating its ideas and values in Syria. It will become clear that Iran employs conventional methods of cultural diplomacy to foster relations with its ally, and is being supported in its efforts by the Syrian authorities. It reaches mainly those that already have an interest in Iran, or those that have an interest in cooperating with Iran due to professional circumstances.

Publications and Book Fairs

The centre's publishing department has been active in publishing material promoting Islamic culture, thought and unity. In addition to the *Islamic Culture* journal, the centre has been publishing books as well as pamphlets dealing with a similar range of issues as the journal, emphasising the shared Islamic heritage between Iran and the Arab world, defending the Islamic Republic's ideology and promoting its revolution. Since 2003 a cultural publication – *Gahnameh Farhangi (Occasional Cultural Diary)* – has been produced in Persian, observing the cultural movement in Syria and recording the centre's activities. Both the journal and the cultural publication were stopped in early 2006, when the centre's website started playing a more prominent role. Since then, a quarterly publication – *Faslnameh Farhangi (Quarterly Cultural Diary)* – can be found online.[27] The latter is directed more at Iranians themselves, both in Iran and in Syria, in order to give them a better idea about the centre's activities, in particular students.[28] In 2011, the Iranian cultural centre resumed publishing the *Islamic Culture* journal. The website is well organised, and accessible in Persian and Arabic. While ICRO headquarters designs the website, which is uniform for all countries where it has a presence, the Iranian cultural centre in Damascus has an internal webmaster in charge of updating the information. The cultural centre's homepage seems to get several hundred hits per day, suggesting that a certain number of people keep up with the centre's activities. By May 2012, the centre's website had a total of 337,967 visitors to its Persian homepage and 145,165 visitors to its Arabic homepage since its launch in 2006.[29]

Every three months the centre produces a brochure in Arabic and Persian introducing a number of intellectuals or religious personalities, presenting one of Iran's provinces, and most importantly laying out the centre's cultural programme and activities for the coming quarter. The brochure provides an accessible way of introducing information about Iran.[30] It is available in print and can also be downloaded from the website. The centre's publications are distributed to subscribers and sold in the centre's own bookshop, which also sells Persian literature, religious and political writings in Persian and Arabic, Persian language books, guide books and films.

In addition to its publications, the centre organises annual book fairs in Damascus: one in February as part of the celebrations honouring the anniversary of the Islamic revolution, held in the entrance hall of the centre, and one in June commemorating the death of Imam Khomeini, held next to the shrine of Sayida Zaynab outside Damascus and lasting for three months.[31] The collections on offer are comprehensive; books include displays from the centre's own bookshop, as well as a wide array of books brought mostly from a Lebanese publishing house invited by the Iranians to participate in their book fairs. There is a choice of books on the family of the prophet, religious books, books on morals, family and education, Arabic novels, books on Zionism and Hezbollah, as well as books on sciences.[32]

These book fairs mainly advertise Iran's own cultural ambitions, but also provide a forum for promoting culture in the wider sense – by including sciences, moral education and secular Arabic literature. Although having thus the potential to attract Syrians from all backgrounds, they generally attract specific crowds. The February book fair is frequented by the regulars of the cultural centre, the summer one by the religious community around the shrine of Sayida Zaynab, including many foreign (mostly Shi'i) visitors in particular from the Gulf region and Iraq. No Syrians without a connection to one or the other would generally visit these fairs.

The book fairs that form part of the cultural weeks held in various Syrian provinces throughout the year to familiarise the Syrian population with Iran's history and culture are more effective in gathering a broader base of people, as they are less linked to locations with a specific Iranian or religious character. The same applies to the annual Damascus International Book Fair, in which Iran participates. At the 2008 book fair, the Iranian cultural centre was among four cultural centres represented (Iran, Russia, Spain and the United States).[33] At the 2010 International Book Fair, Iran was one of eight non-Arab countries participating, alongside North Korea, Russia, Spain, Italy, India, Turkey and the United States. At these international book fairs, the Iranian cultural centre exhibits books from its own bookstore as well as from partner organisations such as the taqrib Assembly and the ahl al-bayt Assembly.[34]

Cultural Weeks and Film Festivals

Iranian cultural weeks in Syria were first introduced in 1994, at the time of the signing of the first implementation programme for the

Book exhibition next to the shrine of Sayida Zaynab. Sayida Zaynab, 1 July 2008.

cultural agreement, in order to raise Iran's profile in the country and increase awareness of Islamic culture. During these weeks, Islamic art and calligraphy, Iranian handicrafts, miniatures and drawings are exhibited, and poetry evenings, film shows and seminars organised, in addition to the book fairs. The weeks aim at introducing Syrians to the Islamic revolution and Iranian culture, and are viewed as a means to strengthen Islamic cultural identity.[35] In this vein, the Iranian ambassador to Syria stated at the opening of the cultural week in Damascus, held at the national museum in September 2004 in the presence of the Ministers of Culture of both countries, Muslim and Christian religious men, and members of the diplomatic corps, that the cultural week was 'a meeting place for the intellectual elites and a starting point for dialogue, literary cooperation and civilisational intermingling'; it furthermore 'put light on the enlightenment of Islamic civilisation'.[36] At the same time, the weeks are a means for Iranian cultural officials to become familiar with the specific culture and society of the Syrian provinces, and their intellectuals, and establish links to the universities (in Aleppo, Latakia and Homs) and educational centres in the provinces.[37]

These weeks are also seen as a way to face up to the challenges presented to the Islamic world in the age of globalisation, particularly after 11 September and the invasion of Iraq, by reviving Islamic civilisation and presenting a united front. Syrian president Bashar al-Asad noted in a meeting with the Iranian Minister of Culture and Islamic Guidance in 2004 that 'Islamic states have consistently been targeted – through cultural invasions by other countries – and said that Damascus was ready to cooperate with Tehran in all cultural fields, including cinema, music, traditional and contemporary arts as well as theatre'.[38] Likewise, on the occasion of the Iranian cultural week in Idlib (Northern Syria) in August 2005, the Idlib governor stated that 'the two countries' officials are cooperating to establish a united cultural front in an effort to confront the West's cultural invasion'.[39] In the same vein, Mir Mas'ud Husaynian of the Iranian embassy in Damascus declared at the opening of the Iranian cultural week in Safita (Western Syria) in June 2008 that 'in view of the West's cultural invasion, Islamic countries had to have joint efforts in their cultural relations to neutralise the adversaries' conspiracies against them'.[40] These cultural weeks strive to underline how deeply embedded culture is in Iranian and Islamic civilisation. Exhibits include not only items with an Islamic character, but also non-Islamic elements such as exhibits from the Iranian national museum that incorporate pre-Islamic history.

The cultural weeks are arranged by the centre's department for cultural activities in Syrian provinces, in cooperation with local institutions in the various provinces. Up to eight cultural weeks are organised each year.[41] They usually take place either at a regional Arab cultural centre, university or the national museum (in the case of Damascus), and are advertised in the national newspapers and by posters in the cities under concern, to reach out to the broader population.[42] The Iranian cultural centre carefully plans its cultural weeks. In preparation, the centre draws up biographies of cultural figures of the particular province, such as poets and writers. It examines the facilities of the location and does a background study of the society make-up, including the political and religious profile of the people of the targeted area, in order to tailor its activities accordingly. To facilitate their work, the Iranian cultural officials establish links with political and cultural public figures and officials of the province.[43]

The Iranian cultural week in Aleppo in March 2008 for instance took place at Aleppo University, and was well advertised across town, including on the main gate of the citadel, one of the most prominent historic destinations of the city. The seminar on the role of Aleppo in Arab and Iranian culture, held under the auspices of the cultural week, was well attended – the large lecture hall was full to the last seat. It seems, however, that a large part of the audience was made up of history students who had been strongly encouraged to attend by their professors. The head of the newly opened Persian department called on all history students to remain seated after the lecture until their names had been called out.[44] In this way, whilst interest in Iran's efforts to promote its culture remains limited amongst the Syrian general public, Iran tries to reach out to specific target groups – in this case students.

The cultural weeks are successful in the sense that they introduce Syrians without prior connection to Iran to the country; the fact that they take place in public places without a specific Iranian character helps in attracting those who might otherwise be put off. While many Syrians would not go to an event held at the Iranian cultural centre itself, they do not hold the same reservations about those public places at which the cultural weeks are held. Although Syrian cultural centres are often associated with the Syrian administration and considered places for state-produced rather than independent culture, they are nevertheless public places open to all.

The same holds true for Iranian film weeks. While films have been regularly shown at the Iranian cultural centre, the centre also organises Iranian film weeks in Syrian cinemas, which have a wider reach. In May 2010, an Iranian cinema festival took place in Damascus's al-Kindi Cinema, one of the old Syrian cinemas. For the opening night of the festival, a Syrian-Iranian co-production was screened. The film, called *Al-Ghuraba (Strangers)*, was directed by an Iranian and starred Syrian actors. Several welcome speeches were given, focusing mainly on resistance against Israel. Speakers included an official from the Iranian cultural centre, the Iranian ambassador, the head of the Syrian Cinema Association as well as a spokesperson for the Iranian television channel al-Kawthar that co-sponsored the event. The synopsis of the film demonstrates further the content of Syrian-Iranian cooperation:

> Setting: Present-day Damascus. A Syrian university student falls in love with a girl. He starts working for the girl's neighbour, an old Palestinian man in a wheelchair, to get to know the girl and earn some money. One day while arranging papers in the old man's office, the student finds his diary, which tells the story of how the old man fell in love with a girl called Leila in the 1940s. At that time he was still living in Palestine. He last saw her in 1948 when everyone had to board a ship in Haifa to leave – Leila missed the boat by seconds. He shows the young man some of his old possessions, the most treasured of which is his Palestinian passport with a Palestinian stamp on it – showing that once upon a time Palestine had its own administration. His saddest souvenir is the one earring he has left and hadn't had a chance to give to Leila – he had given her the first earring on

the night he asked for her hand, when he secretly came to see her. Just when he wanted to give her the second one, they were discovered by her mother and he ran back home, but was beaten up by the Israelis on his way and put into prison. In the end it turns out that the girl the boy had fallen in love with, also called Leila, knows the old Leila as she is working in the Palestinian refugee camp in Damascus. They get reunited in the end and the old man gives his Leila the other earring. The young man tells the young Leila that he loves her, but we only see this as a flashback after we have learned that the young Leila blew herself up as a suicide bomber.[45]

The film thus clearly fed into the discourse on resistance, anti-Zionism and anti-imperialism. It even managed to bring in the massacre at the Sabra refugee camp in Lebanon in 1982 – in a flashback we see the old man going to the camp to find his Leila, who was taking care of orphans there, but he was hit by a bomb and taken to a nurse before he could talk to her.

It was interesting to see the reactions of the audience to the film. The cinema was completely full, with mostly Syrians attending and some Iranians; the Syrian actors were present as well. Talking to an Iranian student after the film, she said she was disappointed by it. While she had not had great expectations – seeing that it was a governmental production – after the opening shot she thought it might be a good film, an artistic film, but then it turned out it was just an ideological film – which she did not care for much. A number of Iranian academics and their families, sitting in the row behind me, left halfway through the film – apparently they were not too impressed by it either. A number of Syrian students liked the film and thought it was well done, although they did not comment on the ideological content of it. Asked to explain the divergence in views about the film amongst the Syrian and Iranian audience, the Iranian student explained that many Syrians cared about Palestine and the resistance; Israel was close to their borders and a real enemy, occupying part of their own land. For Iranians, Palestine was far and most of the support for it came out of government circles, not from the population.[46] Again, the discourse

al-Kindi Cinema on the night of the Iranian cinema festival opening (top), and a poster advertising the festival (bottom). Damascus, 23 May 2010.

on Palestine did not appeal to the Iranian people, but was propagated by the Islamic Republic.

Seminars and Conferences

Seminars and conferences form an important part of the work of the Iranian cultural centre. Since its establishment in the 1980s, the centre has organised nearly a thousand seminars and conferences. According to a former cultural attaché to Damascus, these seminars and conferences have the aim to 'defend the Islamic faith, answer the doubts of the enemies, and introduce the true Islamic culture'.[47] Hence the majority of these events revolve around religious issues, although a number of conferences about cultural relations and literary themes have also been organised. In addition to the seminars held as part of the cultural weeks, the centre holds a monthly seminar series, a special Ramadan seminar series taking place every other day during the month of Ramadan, and seminars and conferences on special occasions such as the World Quds Day.

On the occasion of the anniversary of the Islamic revolution, an annual seminar was organised for several years entitled 'The revolution and cultural elites', during which three Syrian personalities were honoured for their role in fostering Syrian-Iranian relations – one political, one academic and one cultural figure.[48] These included ministers, intellectuals, and Sunni and Shi'i religious personalities. The fact that these Syrians accepted being honoured by the Iranians suggests their acquiescence with the latter's efforts. It has to be added, however, that most of the personalities honoured by the Iranians had some sort of personal link to Iran, and were part of or close to the Syrian government. The Minister of Information honoured in 2004, Ahmad Hassan, had recently returned from a ten-year posting as Syria's ambassador to Tehran; the Minister of Higher Education in 2005 was Hani Murtada, a Syrian Shi'a whose family has been guardian of the waqf of Sayida Zaynab for centuries.[49] Salah al-Din Kaftaru, who heads the Sheikh Ahmad Kaftaru Academy, a prominent (Sunni) Islamic school in Syria endorsed by the government, was honoured the same year.[50] His father had been Grand Mufti of Syria for decades, and one of the few Syrian ulama promoting a rapprochement between the Islamic schools of thought.[51] Religious figures included Hojjatoleslam Abdullah Nizam from the Muhsiniya association (2006), Sheikh Nabil Halabawi, Imam of the Mosque of Sayida Ruqayya (2007), and Sheikh Ahmad Hassun, Grand Mufti of Syria (2008).[52] By their choice of recipients for the awards, the Iranians were thus cultivating their links with Syrians influential in the political and religious sphere who were predisposed to work together with Iran – be it through their official positions or through personal circumstances.[53]

Syrian religious associations actively cooperate with the Iranian cultural centre at the annual conference on Islamic unity, which the centre organises in line with the Islamic Republic's strive for unity. This conference takes place in Damascus in collaboration with the Syrian Ministry of Awqaf and the Iran-based taqrib Assembly, under the patronage of the Syrian Minister for Awqaf. The rhetoric during the 2008 conference was very much dominated by the idea that Muslims should unite and stand together in the face of challenges the Muslim community at large faces by the West, in particular the United States and Western media, as these challenges were seen as a result of disunity amongst Muslim ranks.[54] It thus has not diverged much from the thoughts of Imam Khomeini, and is in line with the political discourse between the two partners. The concept of Islamic unity is more attractive to the Syrian government than the promotion of separate Islamic identities.

The issue of religion is sensitive in Syria, a secular republic where any discussion of religion is kept under tight control. An event such as the conference on Islamic unity is organised in view of the close relationship between the two states and does not stray far from the official religious rhetoric. The Syrian Sunni participants are all part of the religious community close to the Syrian government, promoting what Böttcher calls 'official Sunni Islam'.[55] While there is no fully official Islam in Syria due to the lack of a prestigious national institution of religious learning, like al-Azhar in Egypt for example, and the subsequent lack of a unified religious elite, the state has always depended on co-opting popular clerics willing to work closely with the government – like the Kaftaru family and current Grand Mufti Hassun.[56]

It is these same religious scholars who take part in events organised by the Iranian cultural centre. The Sheikh Ahmad Kaftaru Academy also cooperates with the Iranian centre in organising Qur'an recitation competitions. As Böttcher explains:

'Syrian Sunnis are reluctant to accept Iranian Shi'i presence in Syria, which for them only serves strategic purposes. Only the [Sheikh Ahmad Kaftaru Academy] agrees to cooperate with the Iranian Shi'is. Iranian and Iraqi Shi'is are frequent visitors in the [Academy]. They attend the Friday prayer and participate in some of the [Academy's] activities.'[57]

The Iranian activities thus fall within the parameters of the official religious discourse.

Since 2003, a monthly women's seminar has been introduced, treating issues such as the role of women in society and environmental questions.[58] Delegations from Tehran's all female al-Zahra University are regularly invited for academic exchanges, and to take part in conferences and seminars.[59] The centre set up a women's department to coordinate the seminars and other activities connected to the role of women in society. The centre's women's committee consists of Iranian, Syrian, Palestinian, Iraqi and Egyptian women, and includes university teachers, women active in Palestinian organisations, from the Sheikh Ahmad Kaftaru Academy, Shi'i institutions from the Amin quarter in old Damascus, and Radio Quds.[60] The range of nationalities and professional backgrounds suggests that the women's committee constitutes a meeting place for female intellectuals with a religious orientation.

The seminars and conferences organised by the Iranian cultural centre are generally well attended and reach either those Syrians who are involved in one of the partner organisations – such as the universities and the official religious institutes – or those that spend time at the Iranian cultural centre. The seminars taking place on particular occasions and conferences such as the one on Islamic unity as discussed above are able to draw in a more diverse audience as they are well advertised, often take place in public places such as the national library, and work in close cooperation with Syrian institutions. The monthly seminar series usually only attracts those students and intellectuals who regularly frequent the cultural centre. This series was launched to provide a forum for Syrian and Iranian intellectuals to exchange their views on topics of mutual interest, often connected to Islam and philosophy, and takes place at the Centre for Iranian-Arab Cultural Studies at the Iranian cultural centre.

The Centre for Iranian-Arab Cultural Studies

The Centre for Iranian-Arab Cultural Studies officially opened in the basement of the cultural centre in May 2005.[61] It states three main objectives: one is to introduce Iran's Islamic and cultural civilisation to the Arab world through seminars, publications and translations, and by setting up Persian language and literature departments at Syrian universities. The second is to foster cooperation in the field of translation, by encouraging academic research projects and supporting translations of poetry, novels and film scripts from Persian into Arabic. The third is to increase cooperation between Syrian and Iranian research centres and universities, by way of implementing agreements between both sides, equipping Syrian universities with Persian language books and literature, as well as securing scholarships for Arab intellectuals to go to Iran.[62] The centre thus focuses on implementing intellectual exchange between the two countries in the cultural centre within the framework of the bilateral cultural implementation programmes.

The Studies Centre presents itself as Iranian-Arab rather than Iranian-Syrian, considering itself a bridge between Iranian and Arab culture and their shared heritage. At the heart of the Centre is a library hosting around 10,000 references for Iranian studies in Persian and around 4,000 in Arabic, in addition to journals, magazines and university theses. This library is indeed a meeting place for Syrian, Iranian and Arab students and researchers by providing a forum for interaction on a daily basis. Iranian students studying at Syrian universities use the Persian references for comparative literary studies and exchange advice on how best to live in Syria. Syrian students used to frequent it less regularly, coming only for specific requests or to use some of the Arabic sources in the fields of Islamic law and rhetoric, but since the establishment of the Persian department at Damascus University the number of Syrians using the library has gradually increased as students studying Persian literature come to the Studies Centre to use Persian language sources.

The Story of Fatima Zahra

In March 2008 I met Fatima Zahra at the Centre for Iranian-Arab Cultural Studies of the Iranian cultural centre in Damascus. Fatima was a Japanese girl in her mid-twenties, fully covered (even wearing gloves and sunglasses), and expressed her love for Imam Husayn. A beautiful girl with a broad smile, she had converted to Islam several years ago in Syria and then went to Egypt to study Arabic. She was visiting the Iranian cultural centre to obtain information about an Iranian university planning to open a branch in Sudan, since she wanted to study Islamic mysticism there. She was very attracted to Iran's scholarship on the topic. The centre's librarian called someone to ask about this university, but when he received no answer he gave Fatima the link to the main university's website. Both the librarian and I persuaded her to try to go to the main branch of the university in Iran, rather than the planned subsidiary in Sudan. She had only chosen the latter as she did not speak Persian, so was easily persuaded to change her plans. We chatted a little and she revealed her knowledge about Imam Ali's, Fatima al-Zahra's and Sayida Zaynab's sayings that she had memorized in Japanese translation, and then she had to leave. When I last heard from her by email a few months later, she was indeed preparing her trip to Iran. I have often thought about her since. The Japanese Fatima Zahra was the perfect ambassador for Iran's soft power, since she truly believed in the values the Islamic Republic was trying to promote abroad, without being connected to the official apparatus.

The Centre for Iranian-Arab Cultural Studies is a showpiece of the cultural centre – Iranian delegations to Syria are generally shown around the library to demonstrate the work the centre is involved in. The

university theses displayed at the centre often receive particular attention, as they indicate the existence of a Syrian interest in Arab-Iranian
studies. These theses treat subjects such as Syrian-Iranian relations,
Arab-Iranian relations today and in the Middle Ages, comparative literary studies, studies on contemporary and ancient Iran, and Persian
literature, and were completed by students at Syrian universities in
cooperation with the centre.[63] Facilitating cooperation between higher
education institutions in Syria and Iran is one of the most important
missions of the Iranian cultural centre, as it cultivates lasting relationships between the intellectual elites of both countries and fosters ties
between the two peoples.

The Iranian Cultural Centre in Latakia

According to a study undertaken by ICRO, Syrians from the coastal
region and the mountains surrounding it – areas mostly associated with
Alawis – are more open to Iran's cultural efforts than in other parts of
Syria, which is why Iran concentrates a large amount of its regional
activities in those areas.[64] Taking this into account, in 2006 the Iranian
cultural centre opened an outlet in Latakia. Since it was not in Iran's
interest to underline an Iranian-Alawi bond, the director of the Iranian
cultural centre in Latakia at the time, Ali Hosseini, denied that it was
mostly Alawis frequenting the centre – 'all kinds of Syrians come to us',
he asserted, 'we also have Christians coming here for instance'.[65]

The centre organised mostly language classes, which Hosseini
taught himself with the help of a Syrian girl who had recently returned
from her undergraduate studies at Isfahan University. In addition to
language teaching, the centre arranged lectures and poetry evenings.
Events were announced in the regional newspaper *al-Wahda* – which
also covered the centre's activities – and on the last page of the quarterly
programme distributed by the Iranian cultural centre in Damascus.
The centre moreover sent invitations to local cultural centres and university professors to spread the news about events taking place.

The cultural centre is currently located in a rented apartment in the
city centre, but the Iranians have obtained a piece of land where they
are planning to build a new centre in the future. Activities take place

The Iranian cultural centre in Latakia (top), and announcement of a literary seminar at the centre in *al-Wahda* newspaper (bottom). Latakia, 10 August 2010.

either at the centre itself, or at the Arab cultural centre in Latakia, and seemed to find an audience – the lecture theatre was packed when I attended a lecture on Arab-Iranian cultural relations in 2008, and one Iranian doctoral student who had given a lecture at the Iranian centre also confirmed that it had been well attended.[66] Most students who attend language classes at the centre learn Persian because they like the language and are interested in Persian literature. Unlike in Damascus, students do not learn it because they believe it enhances their work opportunities. There is no Iranian community in Latakia; a few Iranians study medicine at Tishrin University but have no connection to the cultural centre.[67]

The atmosphere at the centre seemed more relaxed than at the centre in Damascus. While talking to the director, several people came and went. One who identified herself as a poetess came to ask Hosseini whether he could indicate Iranian poetesses who had written about Jerusalem and the resistance; she had been searching but had not been able to find any. My Iranian friend, a literature student at Damascus University, whispered to me that she would not find any, as none of the intellectuals in Iran wrote about these issues other than government officials. Hosseini could not think of anyone either but told her to do some research. Another one passed by to ask the director something. She was a language student at the centre and learned the language because she liked it. She was an engineer and worked in a large company; Persian was not useful for her career, she learnt it for herself. She had never been to Iran but hoped to go. She would like to go to Mashhad to visit the shrine of Imam Reza, for instance. In the meantime, a journalist had arrived to introduce himself to Hosseini and ask him about the centre's activities. He had just started working for the *Ba'th* newspaper, he explained to the director, and was very interested in attending the centre's events. He took a brochure and said he would certainly come to the forthcoming events. He inquired about the Quran recital competition held at the Iranian cultural centre in Damascus during the month of Ramadan, and applied to take part in it. When I observed that it was a busy morning, Hosseini replied that it was always like that, people came and went, and afternoons were even busier when they had the language classes.[68] The Iranian cultural centre in Latakia thus seemed to be appreciated as a place to study Persian and inquire about subjects connected to Iran.

Activities for Iranians Resident in Syria

The Iranian cultural centre in Damascus also has a unit that deals specifically with Iranians resident in Syria, who are to a large extent Syrians of Iranian origin. These Iranians have migrated to Syria over the last 300 years, mostly for financial reasons. Official figures show their number at 7,000 to 8,000, but seeing that many have taken Syrian nationality, correct estimates are difficult to obtain. According to official Iranian data, most Iranian residents live in Damascus and Aleppo; in Damascus, they are concentrated in the Shi'i quarters of the city such as Zayn al-Abidayn (55 per cent), the Amin and al-Jura quarters (35 per cent) and the area around Sayida Zaynab (10 per cent). The majority have a low income and low education. In 1996, the Iranian embassy established a committee for the Iranian residents in cooperation with the cultural centre. This committee keeps statistical data and provides assistance to families in need, organises cultural activities and tries to advance economic relations between Syria and Iran. The Iranian cultural centre attempts to strengthen the religious identity of these Iranian residents and to develop a sense of Iranian identity amongst them. The Iranian cultural officials are well aware that any sense of patriotism for Iran amongst those of Iranian origin resident in Syria is very weak, and will take time to build up, as many have resided in Syria for generations. However, they are trying to instil in them some sense of bond with Iran by organising Persian language courses specifically for them, distributing copies of the Arabic language Iranian newspaper *Kayhan Arabi* and a number of magazines on a weekly basis, teaching them about Iranian culture and civilisation, including tourist, pilgrimage and archaeological sites, and assisting them with any problems they might have.[69] To what extent the Iranian cultural centre's efforts have an impact on the Iranian residents is not clear.

Limits of the Centre's Reach

Iranian officials regard their cultural centre in Damascus and its activities as a model for Iranian-Arab cultural cooperation. Unlike in pre-revolutionary cultural diplomacy efforts, the centre has no shortage of funds and institutional support from ICRO in Iran. The Syrian authorities cooperate with the centre and approve its activities within the framework of the bilateral cultural agreement of 1984 and the subsequent cultural implementation programmes. According to one of its former directors, the Iranian cultural centre in Damascus never faced problems with the Syrian authorities and the government always supported it. However, the Iranians also knew which sensitive issues to avoid in their dialogue – they stayed clear of sectarian and ethnic questions in their official discourse for instance.[70] The centre is accessible and most of its activities are free of charge – the language classes offered are affordable and thus attractive.[71] Syrians have no language barrier to making use of the Iranian cultural centre as all staff are bilingual (Arabic and Persian), the vast majority of the centre's publications are published in Arabic, and most lectures and seminars offered are held in Arabic. The centre advertises its events on Syrian radio channels and newspapers, and by printing posters that are then distributed. For this purpose the centre's officials keep up good relations with the Syrian media.[72] Activities are also advertised in a monthly brochure issued by the Syrian Ministry of Tourism, in which cultural activities in Damascus are advertised in Arabic and English.

However, the centre's reach has limits. The centre used to attract only a specific crowd, generally with a particular interest in Iran or Shi'ism, who frequented the centre mostly for religious reasons – they wanted to learn Persian as they considered it the second language of Islam, and were interested in the discourses propagated by the Islamic Republic. In the years just before 2011, this crowd had become more diversified as interest in Iran was growing, especially amongst the young generation who saw work opportunities in the bilateral field. The centre has also become more 'user-friendly' for non-religious visitors – until recently for instance all girls had to wear a veil inside the centre, which might have put some Syrians off.[73] This has changed now, and visitors are free to dress the way they like – which they do.

One big limitation of Iran's cultural work in Syria is its close association with the two governments. Iran's activities are always seen within the framework of the Syrian-Iranian alliance that facilitates them. This limits Iran's appeal in particular amongst the Sunni majority, as they regard the relationship partly as an alliance between the Alawi dominated Syrian government and the Shi'i Iranian Islamic Republic. Syrian Sunnis mainly are wary of Iran's activities in Syria, and generally stay clear of the cultural centre. The exception are those that in some ways work with the Syrian government, be it through the Ministry of Awqaf or one of the officially sanctioned religious institutes. In that respect, Iran's activities that take place outside the centre and religious places like the Sayida Zaynab area are more successful in reaching a wider Syrian public. However, the official and religious character of Iran's cultural work in Syria keeps cultural players and intellectuals – who are in fact interested in Iran's independent culture – away from the cultural centre.

Conclusion

Having looked at Iran's cultural diplomacy efforts in Syria, it can be said that the Islamic Republic of Iran understands the importance of introducing its ideas and values abroad and establishing lasting relationships. The Syrian regime cooperates with the Iranians in expanding bilateral cultural relations, whilst the drive for developments in the cultural field has come from Iran. For Iran, cultural diplomacy certainly is an instrument of foreign policy. It has to be underlined that Iran's cultural work in Syria is facilitated by the two countries' close political relationship, and thus dependent on the latter. Moves and decisions are taken at the governmental level. The activities that come out of the cultural agreements reach down to the people only in a limited sphere. While the Iranian cultural centre's publications, organisation of cultural weeks, seminars and conferences, and the setting up of a centre for Iranian-Arab Cultural Studies are all steps to foster relations between the Syrian and Iranian peoples, it appears that with the exception of the language teaching and university activities (which will be discussed in Chapter 6) and the cultural weeks, most of Iran's efforts reach an audience that already has an interest in Iran – in most cases for religious reasons or out of professional opportunism – and are thus limited.

ICRO regards its cultural diplomacy work in Syria as exemplary. It is proud that the Iranian cultural centre in Damascus is amongst the largest and most active centres of ICRO. Whilst the organisation regards it as important to reach out to other countries in general, it is a lot more active in countries that have good relations with Iran and have a large Muslim population. Iran's cultural diplomacy work in Syria thus has to be seen within the specific framework of the Syrian-Iranian alliance. Here we can see a weakness of Iran's cultural foreign policy. The fact that the Islamic Republic in practice directs its cultural diplomacy efforts mainly towards countries with which it already has good political relations limits its ability to be effective as a soft power in a wider sense.

CHAPTER 5

SYRIA'S CULTURAL DIPLOMACY IN IRAN: THE ARAB-SYRIAN CULTURAL CENTRE IN TEHRAN

While Iran had started early on to set up an Iranian cultural presence in Syria with a particular motivation to do so, Syria had neither an institutional drive nor great interest in promoting its culture in Iran. Whereas the Syrian Ministry of Culture supported Iranian cultural activities in Syria, and called for greater cultural cooperation in theory, in practice it did little to advance its own cultural diplomacy activities in Iran. This only changed as late as the early 2000s, when Syria stepped up its work on the cultural front in response to the region being targeted by the West following 11 September and the ensuing US-led 'War on Terror'. In this atmosphere, where the United States called for a break-up of the Syrian-Iranian alliance, Syria and Iran grew closer together and increased their cooperation in all fields. This resulted in Syria, a country without a tradition of cultural diplomacy, opening a cultural centre in Tehran in the spring of 2005. Not surprisingly, one of the main themes promoted by the centre has been resistance and anti-imperialism.

In the following, the case of the Arab-Syrian cultural centre in Tehran will be analysed to discern the motivations of Syria's cultural diplomacy towards its partner and to what extent Syria in fact has a presence in Iran. The feat of opening a cultural centre in Tehran will be discussed against the background of the situation of foreign cultural centres in Iran, before turning to the establishment of the Syrian centre, its objectives and organisation. This will be followed by an examination of the Syrian centre's activities and reach, as well as the limits thereof. It will be argued that the Syrian centre is interesting more on a symbolic level than for what it actually does. While it does have a role in furthering the Arabic language in Iran, its presence is primarily an expression of the strengthening of the Syrian-Iranian alliance in the face of external challenges.

Setting the Scene: Foreign Cultural Centres in Tehran and the Establishment of the Arab-Syrian Cultural Centre

'Imam Khomeini regarded the cultural dominance of the foreigners as the crucial element of political economic dependence and he believed: If the minds are dependent and the culture of a nation not independent, not only that one cannot be hopeful of ensuring the future, but also the dominance of the world-devourers over the nation will be consolidated. "This West or East has become dominant over all Muslim countries, the most important of which has been the cultural dominance".'[1]

In the spirit of 'Neither East nor West, only the Islamic Republic', Iran has been averse to foreign cultural influences since the first revolutionary decade. Considering the importance the Islamic Republic has given to the power of culture, this is not surprising. This aversion is reflected in the restrictions imposed upon foreign cultural activities in Iran. Cultural attachés in European embassies complain about the lack of possibilities to organise cultural exchanges between Iran and their respective countries. Tehran currently hosts only two foreign cultural centres, the Austrian Kulturforum and the Syrian cultural centre. In addition, the Chinese have recently opened a Confucius Institute at the University of Tehran, as a result of China's expansive cultural diplomacy initiative launched in 2004. None of the conventional European cultural institutions are able to operate in Iran, with cultural attachés struggling to coordinate cultural exchanges through their embassies. European cultural centres have been closed down one after the other during the last three decades.

The German Goethe-Institut for instance was closed down in February 1987. A German satire TV show had made fun of Ayatollah Khomeini: dressed as an Iranian news presenter, the show's host announced that 'this week, the eighth anniversary of the Islamic revolution was celebrated – Ayatollah Khomeini is being celebrated by the people and presented with gifts' while showing a photo montage that suggested female fans were throwing bras and slips at Khomeini. Whilst the TV show was a private enterprise independent from the German state, the episode resulted in strained diplomatic relations for a period to come. What is more, it proved a welcome pretext for the hardliners at the Ministry of Culture and Islamic Guidance to get rid of the institute. 'As an institution that allowed a glimpse into the outside world, we were a thorn in the mullahs' side, as they feared an influence especially on young spirits,' stated the head of the Goethe-Institut at the time.[2] Germany has tried in vain to reopen the institute. As a compromise, the embassy opened a German language institute in 1995 that has been very popular with young Iranians, with over 5,000 language students each year. The language institute faces problems every now and then, including accusations by neighbours that its female language students dress in un-Islamic fashion. However, the institute has managed to survive.[3] The cultural attaché at the German embassy complained how frustrating it was to organise any cultural event in Iran, as official permission often came either last minute, which made advertising events impossible, or not at all, which left projects suspended in the air with no clear rejection. Censorship was also common, and visiting artists were closely watched by the Iranian Ministry of Culture and Islamic Guidance.[4] Considering the restrictions imposed on Germany's cultural work in Iran, one outlet for cultural activities has been the German Protestant church in Tehran. The church has been host to a number of concerts and cultural events, which have been tolerated by the Iranian authorities – but certainly not encouraged.[5]

In a bid to improve British-Iranian ties during the Khatami administration, Iranian authorities invited the British to reopen the British Council in Tehran in 2001. However, they subsequently made the Council's work increasingly difficult, leading to it being closed down again in early 2009.[6] The authorities had denied British employees visas to Iran for the last two years before the closure, and pressed the Council's Iranian employees to hand in their resignations. With their staff being intimidated, the British Council decided it could no longer operate under these circumstances.[7] The Council's work in recent years had already been confined to teaching training courses and assisting in scholarship exchanges. Cultural activities in the wider sense, such as language teaching and artists' visits, had not even been on the British Council's agenda knowing the Iranian state's sensitivity concerning foreign cultural activities.

The French have not had a Centre culturel français in Tehran since 1980. Their cultural work is carried out by a sub-section of the embassy, le Service de Cooperation et d'Action Culturelle, which focuses on French-Iranian relations in the fields of culture, languages, science and technology. Their partners include the ministries of culture and Islamic guidance, higher education, education, the main universities and language centres in Iran, and the national museums.[8]

The European cultural attachés in Tehran meet regularly with each other. To increase visibility of the European Union, it is standard practice among European cultural attachés to meet once or twice during each six-month term of the rotating European presidency in order to organise a joint event, such as a film week. In Iran, there have been repeated attempts at organising a joint European cultural week, but in vain – the Iranian authorities prefer European countries to have dispersed events rather than a joint effort on a larger scale.[9]

The only fully operating European cultural centre in Tehran is the Austrian Österreichisches Kulturforum. Set up in 1959, the Austrians are proud that their cultural forum has been running without interruption until today. While they started off organising mainly cultural events such as concerts and lectures, they have run a popular language programme since 1989. The cultural centre operates under the umbrella – and protection – of the embassy, although located in an independent building. Within the forum's grounds, they are free to organise events without asking for prior permission from Ershad; girls can decide for themselves whether they want to follow Islamic dress code inside the centre. While the Iranian authorities are unable to influence the activities within the centre, they can harass Iranians frequenting the centre as soon as they leave the grounds, which is why the Austrians are careful not to provoke the authorities too much. They refrain from organising events during mourning periods like Ashura, for instance, and have completely banned alcohol on the centre's premises.[10] The Forum offers talented Iranian musicians a space to perform, and has its own choir and orchestra; music plays an important part of its programme. Whilst the institute has proven a popular cultural outlet, organising events outside its own premises has proved more complicated – in public places, the Austrians face the same constraints as other European cultural attachés.[11] The fact that the Austrian cultural forum has been able to operate without interruption may also be explained by Austria neither having a history of interference in Iranian domestic affairs (unlike Britain), nor having provided an excuse for the Iranians to close down their forum (unlike Germany).

The latest addition to the limited cultural scene is the Chinese Confucius Institute in Tehran. Established in August 2008 based at the University of Tehran, the institute is a collaborative effort between the latter and a university in southern China, Yunnan University, in line with the infrastructure of China's cultural diplomacy. The institute mainly aims to teach Chinese, ancient, modern as well as business Chinese, and literature. Other than that, it is trying to set up Confucius classrooms in other Iranian universities and private language schools, and has organised a number of cultural activities to date, including a Chinese cultural week.[12] As Europe and the United States were trying to isolate Iran, the Islamic Republic seemed to welcome initiatives from other players – China was welcome in particular due to its economic potential.

Against this backdrop, Syria established an Arab-Syrian cultural centre in Tehran. Syria had decided in 2004 to set up a centre in Iran's capital, at a time of heightened diplomatic interaction between the two countries. The official aim was to reciprocate Iranian cultural activities

in Syria and fulfil the stipulation of the cultural implementation programme based on Article 14 of the 1984 cultural agreement that called
for cooperation between the two countries to set up cultural centres
in each other's country.[13] According to Nazih Khoury, responsible for
Syrian cultural centres abroad, Syria felt it should have a cultural presence in Tehran, seeing that Iran had many cultural activities in Syria.
If these had been the only reasons, Syria could have set up a centre
in the Iranian capital at any time after 1984. As bilateral relations
picked up in the late 1990s and early 2000s, however, and the alliance was 'reinvigorated' after 2003, cooperation on the cultural level
also intensified. To present a 'united front' through actions as much as
words, the Syrians asked the Iranian Ministry of Culture and Islamic
Guidance for permission to open a centre, which was granted. The
head of ICRO welcomed the idea of opening a Syrian cultural centre in
Tehran, expressing his belief that this step would further strengthen
cultural relations between the two 'brotherly countries'.[14] The centre
opened its doors in the spring of 2005.[15]

In the three years prior to the opening of the centre, Syria had
started organising an annual Syrian cultural week in Tehran, as an
initiative to boost Syrian-Iranian relations on the cultural level. To
open the first such week and discuss stepping up bilateral cultural
ties, a large Syrian delegation came to Iran in spring 2002, including
Vice President Zuhayr Mashariqa, Minister of Culture Najwa Qassab
Hassan, and Su'ad Bakur, president of the Syrian Women's Union. The
Syrian cultural week was held in a cultural centre in Tehran, where
paintings from the collection of the Syrian Ministry of Culture, tourism posters and books were exhibited, films screened and presentations
given by representatives of the Syrian Ministry of Education and the
Women's Union. The Syrian delegation visited sights such as the shrine
of Imam Khomeini as well as his houses in Tehran and Qom, and
held a number of separate official meetings with the Iranian political
elite, including with the Supreme Leader Ali Khamene'i, Chairman of
the Expediency Council Hashemi Rafsanjani,[16] President at the time
Muhammad Khatami, Minister of Culture Ahmad Masjed-Jame'i,
and Muhammad Araqi, head of ICRO. In each meeting, the need to
strengthen cultural relations between the two countries was further

emphasized.[17] The opening of the Arab-Syrian cultural centre in Tehran constituted one concrete step in that direction.

The Centre's Objectives and Organisation

The Arab-Syrian cultural centre in Tehran is an interesting project, bearing in mind both the general lack of Syrian cultural diplomacy and the difficulties foreign cultural centres have experienced in Iran. The centre's objectives are less clear-cut than the ones of the Iranian centre in Damascus. It has been established primarily for political reasons, to underline the alliance between the Syrian and Iranian states

The Syrian-Arab cultural centre in Tehran, off Africa (Jordan) Street. Tehran, 5 November 2008.

at a time of increased international pressure against them, and secondarily in order to respond to Iranian cultural activities in Syria by providing an outlet for cultural cooperation in Tehran. Ibrahim Zarur, interim Syrian ambassador to Iran in 2003 and dean of the history faculty at Damascus University, explained that when Syria opened a cultural centre abroad it generally reflected a strengthening of bilateral relations with the country under concern.[18] In the case of Syria and Iran, the step-up of bilateral relations since the beginning of the US-led military intervention in Iraq in 2003 triggered the discussions on establishing a cultural centre. The existence of a Syrian cultural centre in Tehran serves the purpose of highlighting the excellent state of the political relationship, and to present a united cultural front. What the centre does in practice comes second, but is in line with these aims. In terms of reach, more important than its general cultural activities has been Arabic language teaching.

The official objective of the centre is to bring Arab culture and Syria closer to 'Syria's Iranian friends' and strengthen cultural relations.[19] Mahmud al-Sayyed, Syrian Minister of Culture at the time, affirmed one month before the centre's opening that it was to play an important role in strengthening cooperation between the Arab and Persian cultures.[20] The first director of the centre, Musa al-Gharir, states to this end that the establishment of the Arab-Syrian cultural centre was a natural development considering the expansion of bilateral relations. Opening a centre in Tehran was a necessary step to widen cultural relations and strengthen the common ground between the two peoples. Al-Gharir added that the centre was to unite Syrian and Iranian efforts in opposing all attempts that try to separate them, in line with cultural policies in Syria that worked towards spreading culture and establishing cultural institutions, encouraging dialogue and respecting the opinion of the other, similar to what the Syrians believed Iranian cultural policies to be.[21]

Al-Gharir had no prior connection to either Iran or Syrian cultural diplomacy, having been professor of economics at Damascus University prior to his appointment.[22] He periodically gave lectures at Iranian universities in different cities, speaking about topics ranging from current affairs to the challenges the two countries faced.[23] Unlike the directors of the Iranian cultural centre in Damascus, who were generally fluent in Arabic, al-Gharir spoke no Persian, which limited his access to those Iranians who did not speak Arabic. However, many of the Iranians who frequented the centre were either learning Arabic or spoke it already. One Syrian professor of Persian literature was not very impressed with the appointments at the centre: 'While the Iranians at least succeed in appointing Iranians to their centre who speak Persian and Arabic, the Syrians have appointed people to the Syrian cultural centre who know neither Persian nor Arabic [literature] – they just appointed people because of their activity in the [Ba'th] party.'[24] Al-Gharir's successor as director was Afif Haydar, another economics professor from Damascus University.

According to al-Gharir, the Syrian centre faced no problems with the Iranian authorities in organising events. Most activities took place on the centre's own premises unless they were co-hosted by other institutions, such as Iranian language institutes or local cultural centres. The centre was located in a villa in the northern part of Tehran, in a residential area close to the Syrian embassy. It contained classrooms for language teaching, a library holding Arabic literature and reference books in Arabic, an exhibition hall and offices. The director, his deputy and the librarian were sent to Iran from Syria; other employees were Iranians who were bilingual in Persian and Arabic, and Syrian students who studied in Tehran and taught Arabic at the centre.[25]

The Syrian cultural centre in Tehran organised Arabic language classes and a number of cultural activities in the centre's grounds, including poetry nights, lectures, book fairs and art exhibitions. The Syrian Ministry of Culture set the annual programme at the beginning of each year, in terms of numbers of lectures and types of activities. The content was decided later between the centre and the Syrian ministry.[26]

Activities and Reach

The Syrian cultural centre in Tehran has the stated aim to introduce Arab-Syrian culture to Iranians and consolidate bilateral relations on the cultural level. Looking at the activities it undertakes, one can discern that while the centre stresses Syria's history and heritage, it essentially emphasizes Syrian culture as a culture of resistance, as many of the events revolve around anti-imperialism and standing firm against Western cultural hegemony. One of the first events of the centre, a poetry night in March 2005, illustrates this point. A number of Iranian poets participated in the event, which was attended by a crowd of Iranian intellectuals and academics, as well as university students. While the Iranian poets in their poems confirmed the significance of Damascus and Syria's cultural role in history and civilisation, and the necessity to continue cultural cooperation between the two countries, the centre's director used the opportunity to underline the importance of increasing cooperation between Syrian and Iranian intellectuals and academics in order to confront the Western cultural invasion that targets the civilisation, identity and culture of the region.[27]

The Syrian cultural centre generally groups its activities around an occasion, and organises several events under a specific theme. One such annual occasion is Syria's independence day on 17 April, 'aid al-jala', in which Syria's independence from the French is commemorated. The centre usually puts on a poetry night as part of the celebrations, a photo or art exhibition in the centre's exhibition hall, and at times holds a public lecture. In the 2006 lecture held at the Shahid Beheshti University in Tehran, the Syrian lecturer spoke about how the 'Project for the Greater Middle East' was a Zionist project by the United States, which aimed at serving Zionism and its interests in the region, and to ensure American hegemony over the oil wells.[28] On the occasion of the anniversary of the 1973 Arab-Israeli war the Syrian centre also undertakes a number of activities, such as setting up a picture exhibition, lecture and film screening. The film in 2009 was a Syrian film about the Golan Heights.[29] It is clear that anti-imperialism and resistance against Israel are recurrent themes of the activities of the Syrian centre.

Following the 33-day war in the summer of 2006 between Israel and Hezbollah, the Syrian cultural centre organised a poetry evening lauding the resistance and condemning American support of Israel. It opened a photo exhibition entitled 'The True Promise', showing images of the aftermath of Israeli attacks against Lebanon.[30]

In a seminar on 'The historic and strategic dimensions of the victory of the resistance in Southern Lebanon', participants discussed the implications of the July war for the region. They underlined how the event boosted the strength of the resistance; the realisation that Israel was no longer regarded as invincible was considered one of the most important results of the war. Participants included representatives of the Iran offices of Hezbollah and Hamas, as well as officials from ICRO; they emphasised the need for unity and closed ranks vis-à-vis the 'Zionist entity'.[31] In December 2008, on the Iranian Minister of Culture's visit to Damascus – in town for an Iranian cultural week – his Syrian counterpart called for the production of a joint Iranian-Syrian film on the 33-day war and the Lebanese resistance, saying the film would be 'an eternal work of art'. The Iranian minister welcomed the proposal and invited him to select a Syrian filmmaker to visit Iran for the project.[32]

In the context of the Syrian uprising that started in March 2011, the Syrian cultural centre organised a number of activities dealing with 'the conspiracy against Syria and Zionist-American plans and their tools in the region' in April 2012, in cooperation with Tehran University's Faculty of Law and Political Science. By showing films and photo exhibitions about the 'crimes of criminal gangs who practised terrorism and murder at the expense of Syrians and hit the infrastructure as well as public and private property', in addition to pictures of the large pro-government demonstrations staged in Syria, the Syrian centre projects the official message of the state. The latter is wrapped in the overall rhetoric of the role Syria and Iran have in 'foiling the Zionist-American plans targeting the region'.[33]

The Syrian cultural centre serves as a forum for discussion about topics of mutual interest between the Iranian and the Arab side, predominantly on an official level. The centre is not on the radar of independent cultural players unconnected to an official body. Whereas the subjects of the seminars at the Iranian cultural centre in Damascus revolve more around religious themes, the Syrian centre in Tehran focuses on anti-imperialist ones – in line with Syria's ideology and foreign policy principles. Some of the Iranians frequenting the centre, in particular students, overlook the ideological component and mainly appreciate the fact that it offers a good environment for studying Arabic.[34] One former student of the centre wonders:

> 'I am not sure what impression the Syrian cultural centre left for the students who attended the course: most students merely considered it a place to learn Arabic and were not particularly concerned with Syria as a specific Arab neighbouring country, or even aware of Syrian political and cultural affairs. I assume that the centre was not attempting to leave an impression on this issue seriously either.'[35]

While many activities of the Syrian cultural centre are ideological in nature, it also organises a number of cultural events to promote Syrian art and literature, such as a celebration of the life and works of Nizar Qabbani, one of Syria's most famous poets of the twentieth century. The festivities revolved around a photo exhibition, the screening of a documentary film portraying the writer's life, and a book fair. Qabbani apparently enjoyed popularity amongst the Iranian readership, which a seminar discussion about Qabbani's works amongst Iranian researchers, critics and translators attested to.[36] As the centre serves as a meeting place for Iranian academics from the Arabic language and literature faculties in and around Tehran, literary activities met with real interests amongst those teachers and professors. One former Iranian language student at the Syrian cultural centre recalls the following about lectures at the Syrian cultural centre, which she attended in 2007:

> 'As far as I remember, the Syrian cultural centre held lectures where they invited speakers from Iran and Syria, and discussed issues related to literature in Syria and Iran, and how the works of the writers from the two countries were inspired by each other. They had lectures where they invited novelists from Iran and Syria, and would exchange ideas on fiction writing in both countries. I also recall an event where the head of the cultural centre talked about the cultural impact, mutual relations, and exchanges between Syria and Iran, inviting his Iranian

counterpart and also university professors who worked on Arabic literature, and political scientists who worked on Syria. The audience at these events were mainly students who studied Arabic at the cultural centre.'[37]

In an effort to promote Syrian tourism, the centre periodically arranges tourism exhibitions. Exhibits promote Syrian tourist destinations and tours as well as Syrian industrial products; the event in the summer of 2008 was opened by Syria's Deputy Minister of Tourism and attended by a number of tourism companies and officials of the two countries.[38] The head of the Iranian Organisation of Tourism and Culture, Muhammad Sharif Malekzadeh, applauded the Syrian endeavours to widen Syria's appeal as a tourist destination for Iranians, as up to then Iranian tourism to Syria had been confined to religious tourism and the visit of holy shrines. In a separate meeting at the Iranian Hajj and Ziyarat Organisation – a public sector organisation under the supervision of the Ministry of Culture and Islamic Guidance that deals with all matters related to pilgrimages – the two sides discussed further cooperation in the field of religious tourism and ways to improve the existing infrastructure for Iranian tourists in Syria.[39] Up to the present, Iranian tourism to Syria's non-religious tourist sights is almost non-existent.

The Syrian centre does not put on cultural weeks in Iranian provinces in the same organised manner as its Iranian counterpart in Damascus; it does, however, have occasional activities outside the capital. In November 2005, for instance, the centre organised an exhibition of Syrian pictures, traditional costume and books in the city of Mashhad in north-east Iran. This exhibition, which included film screenings and a lecture on Syrian-Iranian cultural and economic relations, was organised in cooperation with the Iran branch of the Syrian student union.[40] The following month, the two institutions organised a similar event in Qazvin.[41] In 2012, a Syrian heritage and tourism pavilion was opened at Isfahan University.[42] Events in cities other than Tehran are generally arranged through the Syrian student union as the Syrian cultural centre lacks the infrastructure and means to run them on its own. The Syrian student union in Iran is attached to the Syrian embassy; its five-member council takes care of issues concerning the Syrian student body in Iran. The members of this council are Syrian students studying in Iran, selected by the embassy to represent their peers.[43]

The cultural centre maintains links with other Iranian cultural centres and institutions, in particular universities. Meshkin Fam, head of the Arabic department at Tehran's al-Zahra University, stresses the role of the Syrian cultural centre. She asserts that it connects Syrian and Iranian cultural institutions, universities, professors, writers and critics.[44] The centre is an important link between Iranian students and Syrian universities; it facilitates trips to Syria for Iranian students for instance, and arranges for them to stay at Syrian university dormitories.[45] The centre also cooperates with Iranian cultural institutions such as the Farhangserai Melal, a religious cultural centre in Tehran that strives to bring together different cultures and teach the Quran and religious principles to children.[46]

Language classes form an integral part of the Syrian cultural centre's calendar. They focus on improving the students' skills in pronunciation, conversation and dictation, and use various teaching tools including newspapers, magazines and films.[47] The language classes are held at the centre and are especially popular with Iranian academics and students.[48] One student remembers:

'The students who took part in the language classes I participated in often majored either in Arabic literature at university or in Persian literature (as classical Persian was quite influenced by Arabic). There were also students who did religious studies and wanted to be more fluent in colloquial Arabic in order to make visits to Arabic speaking countries. I should also note that there were many students who did not need to learn Arabic for their studies or career but merely wanted to learn Arabic and enjoy the music and the culture! Most students I met with were happy with the class and found it useful in terms of conversation specifically [...] The centre had also arranged scholarships for students who had earned the highest grades at the end of the semester to study a semester in Syria. I personally attended the

Syrian cultural centre to learn Arabic and improve my conversation skills as my major is Middle Eastern studies and it is quite
necessary for my academic and career goals. I heard about the
Syrian cultural centre from a friend. I found the centre useful to
start with, but I think after a while it would be better to spend
time in an Arabic speaking country which would speed up the
learning process.[49]

The language classes and their reach, as well as the role of the centre
in advancing the level of Arabic in Iran, will be discussed in detail in
Chapter 6. Suffice it to say here that activities in the field of language
teaching form the backbones of the centre's operations in Tehran.

Events at the centre are mostly advertised by sending out official
invitations to people the centre would like to participate, such as officials from ICRO,[50] representatives of Hezbollah and Hamas, or the
Iranian tourism industry. Alternatively, the centre advertises language
classes and its activities in one of Iran's main newspapers, *Hamshahri*,
which has a large advertising section, or distributes leaflets in public
places to inform Iranians about the Syrian cultural centre.[51] The centre
generally attracts an audience that knows about the events and language classes either through their university or institution or by word
of mouth. Its existence is not well known among the larger Iranian
public. The Iranian cultural centre in Damascus is located in the heart
of the city and close to many of the hotels catering to Iranian religious
tourists, thus contributing to an Iranian character of part of Damascus.
The Syrians by contrast are barely visible in Tehran. This leads us to
the limits of the centre's reach.

Limits of the Centre's Reach

Syria does not have a strong presence in Iran. Most Iranians will never
have heard of the existence of a Syrian cultural centre in Tehran, unless
they are involved in the Arabic language faculties at Iranian universities, or if they work at an institution that has contacts with the centre,
such as ICRO or the Iran Language Institute.[52] Although the centre
advertises its activities, it caters more for an audience that actively

seeks it out rather than attracting a wider more general crowd. Unlike the Iranian cultural centre in Syria, which has extensively documented its activities in its journal, in printed booklets or on its website, the Syrian cultural centre lacks information about its programmes. It has neither a website nor a regular programme published periodically.

One major constraint on the Syrian centre's work is its lack of a budget. Unlike the Iranian centre in Damascus, which does not seem to suffer from a shortage of money for any of its projects, the Syrian centre does not have a large budget to organise events. As one Iranian student in Syria, who knows the Syrian cultural centre in Tehran, put it:

'One big difference between the Syrian centre in Tehran and the Iranian centre in Damascus is that the Syrians do not have money to spend on cultural activities in Iran. Iran on the other hand has a lot of money for this kind of activity.'[53]

The limited financial means are one of the reasons why the Syrians do not often invite artists to come from Syria to exhibit their works, but instead invite artists resident in Iran. Alternatively, they exhibit paintings and photographs from the Syrian Ministry of Culture's collection hosted by the centre – the centre stores around 600 paintings and posters from Syria.[54] The lack of budget can be explained by the lack of ambition on the Syrian part to promote its culture to a wider audience, reflecting the low priority given to cultural diplomacy. It feeds into the argument that the Syrian cultural centre's purpose is as much symbolic as actually serving as a medium for Syrian cultural diplomacy.

While the centre is easily accessible for Iranians once they have located it, there is a language barrier for Iranians not comfortable in Arabic. Whereas the Iranian staff at the Syrian centre in Tehran is bilingual, the director and librarian speak no Persian, and lectures are generally held in Arabic, which limits the audience to those proficient in Arabic. This stands in contrast to the Iranian centre in Damascus where the vast majority of activities are held in Arabic and thus easy to understand for a general Syrian public. It has to be added, however, that the case of the Iranians in Syria is the exception, not the case of the Syrians in Iran – it is common for foreign cultural centres to undertake activities in their own language rather than the host country's language.

Conclusion

The existence of the Syrian cultural centre in Tehran has to be understood as a political statement. It was opened at a time of heightened diplomatic interaction, when both Syria and Iran felt targeted by the international community. This is reflected in the content of the cultural activities Syria undertakes in Iran, which largely focus on themes connected to the resistance against Israel as well as anti-imperialism. Its activities are largely confined to the Iranian capital, with a few events taking place in other cities, organised in cooperation with the Syrian student union. While the centre's ideological activities do not seem to leave any impact on Iranian students and visitors to the centre, the latter is appreciated largely as a place to study Arabic.

Syria's cultural diplomacy is limited in Iran. In contrast to other countries' cultural work in Tehran, which is limited by constraints imposed on the countries by the Iranian authorities, Syria's work is limited mainly by its own lack of motivation and financial resources. The Iranian side supports the Syrian centre, and officials participate in its activities. It seems the centre reaches out to a small crowd of Iranians who know about the Syrian centre's events mainly through their universities or the institutions they work at; generally Syria does not have a visible presence in Iran. The Arabic language programme is genuinely popular, however, and the Syrians play a particular role in furthering Arabic language teaching in Iran, as will be explained in the next chapter.

CHAPTER 6

STUDENTS: FOSTERING THE BONDS OF THE FUTURE

The role of students in fostering bilateral relations between Syria and Iran will be examined in this chapter, as a case study of the extent to which cultural diplomacy reaches down to the people. Students are an attractive group to take as an example of how Syrian-Iranian relations play out at the popular level. While contact between students and the culture of the other country was facilitated by the two governments, students constitute non-governmental actors whose education might lead them to become involved in keeping the bonds tied in the future, a key goal of cultural diplomacy. An analysis of the make-up and motivation of the student body and the support it received from the governments will throw light on the effectiveness of building bridges through education in the Syrian-Iranian case. It will be argued that language teaching and academic exchanges had potential to build bridges between the Syrian and Iranian peoples. While the number of people involved was small, it was growing until 2011 as more people with no prior connection to the other country were becoming interested in the other side. This held true particularly for Syria, where Iran was actively seeking to expand its sphere of influence. Especially the newly established Persian language departments in Syrian universities and the academic exchanges contributed to an increased interaction between the two peoples.

In this chapter, I will introduce the importance of language learning and academic exchanges in cultural diplomacy before turning to the role of language students. Persian language teaching in Syria will be analysed by looking at Persian language institutions and Persian language departments in Syrian universities as well as at the profile of Syrians studying Persian. In the case of Arabic language teaching in Iran, the special place of Arabic in Iran – Arabic being the language of Islam – and the role of the Syrian cultural centre will be examined. The focus will then shift to academic exchanges between Syria and Iran and the role of exchange students, namely the case of Iranian students studying in Syria and Syrian students studying in Iran. Lastly, the joint project of setting up a Syrian-Iranian postgraduate university on the Syrian coast will be looked at.

The Importance of Language Learning and Academic Exchanges in Cultural Diplomacy

'Currently, the closest competitor to the United States in soft power resources is Europe. [...] Taken individually, many European states have a strong cultural attractiveness: half of the ten most widely spoken languages in the world are European.'[1]

'Many observers agree that American high culture produces significant soft power for the United States. For example, [former] Secretary of State Colin Powell has said, "I can think of no more valuable asset to our country than the friendship of future world leaders who have been educated here." International students usually return home with a greater appreciation of American values and institutions, and, as expressed in a report by an international education group, "the millions of people who have studied in the United States over the years constitute a remarkable reservoir of goodwill for our country".'[2]

Language learning and academic exchanges play an important role in fostering relations between states. Language is a central element of cultural diplomacy, as it is strongly linked to cultural identity.

Nye in the first quote above equates European cultural attractiveness with the fact that its languages are shared with a lot of people worldwide; language is a soft power resource. In an article in the *Islamic Culture* journal it is suggested that the 'language of any people is the only gate through which others can grasp the culture and heritage of this people'.[3] Language teaching has always been one of the core components of cultural diplomacy work, and one of the main tasks of foreign cultural centres across the world.

Academic student exchanges between two countries are an effective way of introducing one's culture to the new generation of the other country, and of building lasting ties between the intellectual elites. As Nye points out in the second quote cited above, international students who have studied in the United States constitute an invaluable bridge between the students' home countries and the United States. Government-sponsored scholarship programmes enabling students to study in foreign countries play into this potential of building bridges, and have become integral to cultural diplomacy. While international students do not always bring home a positive picture of the country in which they studied, they nevertheless return to their country knowing the language and ways of life of the place they studied in. Former US Senator William Fulbright has been quoted as saying: 'Education is in reality one of the basic factors in international relations – quite as important as diplomacy and military power in its implications for war and peace.'[4]

In their cultural agreements of 1975 and 1984, Syria and Iran acknowledge the importance of education – and within that of language learning and academic exchanges – in strengthening their bilateral relationship. The first section of the 1984 agreement is dedicated to education; Article 3 calls for both sides to 'encourage granting scholarships to students of the other country and work towards providing space in the fields of study, teaching and research' (Article 4 in the 1975 agreement), Article 5 calls for 'creating Persian language chairs in Syrian universities and Arabic language chairs in Iranian universities, and to support the existing ones' (Article 7 in the 1975 agreement).[5]

Specific stipulations on how to apply this exchange were not put down until the first implementation programme for the 1984 cultural agreement was drafted a decade later. In the programme for the years 1995–1997, Article 9 called for the exchange of ten university scholarships in different subjects. Article 19 again called for efforts on both sides to set up a chair for Persian in Syrian universities and a chair for Arabic in Iran's universities. Other articles called for exchange of university professors to give lectures and take part in conferences in the other country, for agreements to be concluded directly between universities in both countries, and for an exchange of journals and publications.[6] More details on cooperation in the field of higher education were set down in subsequent implementation programmes, and the number of scholarships to be exchanged was increased.[7] To what extent cooperation in the field of education was implemented will be examined in the following.

The Role of Language Students: Persian Language Teaching in Syria

Persian Language Institutions and Persian Departments in Universities

'In Syria, the Persian language has spread; through its cultural representatives the Islamic Republic of Iran is providing all things necessary for learning and teaching the Persian language and literature on university level and in the cultural centre.'[8]

Thus writes an Iranian lecturer teaching Persian at Damascus University in 1996. Persian language teaching had started at Damascus and Aleppo University in the 1970s, as a module in the departments of history and Arabic language and literature. Tishrin University (Latakia) started Persian language teaching in 1995, and Ba'th University (Homs) in 1996. The study of one of Aramaic, Hebrew, Latin or Persian – subject to availability – was mandatory for students reading history or Arabic Literature.[9] However, things were not as straightforward as they sound.

In 1994, only two years before the Iranian lecturer praised the progress of Persian language teaching in Syria, the director of the Iranian cultural centre in Damascus, Muhammad Shariati, reports back to the

Persian language desk of the cultural department for the Arab world and Africa at the Iranian Ministry of Culture and Islamic Guidance about the not quite perfect situation of Persian language teaching at Damascus University. Shariati forwards a letter of his colleague responsible for public relations at the cultural centre, in which the latter stresses the need for Iran to cooperate with Syria in teaching Persian. He explains that Persian is an optional language for students at the faculty of literature and humanities at Damascus and Aleppo University, and that many students would like to choose Persian in view of the cultural commonalities and the presence of numerous Iranian visitors to Syria, but are prevented from doing so by the lack of teachers. He is amazed how second year students at Damascus University were nearly forced to abandon the study of Persian and take Hebrew instead, because there was no one to teach the language to them; only cooperation with the Iranian cultural centre – which in the end managed to send a teacher to the university – prevented this. He underlines how important it was for Iran to post trained Persian language teachers to Syria, as the only permanent Persian language teacher in the country – the Syrian Muhammad al-Tounji – was based in Aleppo and overloaded with teaching between Aleppo and Damascus, which consequently affected the quality of the students' education. Moreover, teaching material was required and students should have access to literary sources, which should be sent to the library of Damascus University.[10]

One can discern from this account that spreading the teaching of the Persian language in Syria – although called for rhetorically – had not been taken too seriously by Iranian cultural officials until the mid-1990s. The situation then gradually started to change, following the drafting of the first cultural implementation programme. The change coincided not only with the formation of ICRO in Tehran, but also with a renewed interest on both the Syrian and Iranian side for greater cooperation in view of regional developments such as the Turkish-Israeli rapprochement. By 1996, Persian was offered at a basic level in the four major Syrian state universities, in Damascus, Aleppo, Latakia and Homs, facilitated by the Iranian cultural centre. According to Iranian sources, a large number of students had chosen Persian over the other languages due to the close relationship between Syria and

Iran, and commonalities between the two languages. Around 4,500 students had taken Persian courses in the universities up to 2005.[11] The Iranian cultural centre provided some of the teachers, the others being Syrian professors who held post-graduate degrees from Iran. One has to bear in mind, however, that the level of these classes was very basic and most students who took the classes were probably only very superficially interested in learning the language – the classes were much more a course requirement to be fulfilled. Persian as a subsidiary language in the Arabic literature faculties was thus only marginally effective as a cultural diplomacy tool.

The main location for learning Persian remained the Iranian cultural centre itself. With language teaching being a promising medium of creating links between two peoples, one of the first steps the centre undertook after its establishment was to set up Persian language courses. Initially, these were offered only on the centre's own premises in Damascus, but in 1995, the Iranian cultural centre also started providing Persian language classes in the Sayida Zaynab area, a Damascene suburb and the main destination of Iranian pilgrims to Syria.[12] The recently established outlet of the Iranian cultural centre in Latakia also offers Persian language courses at beginner, intermediate and advanced levels.

Improving the state of Persian language teaching at Syrian universities was next on the agenda of the Iranian cultural centre. In 2000, the centre for teaching foreign languages attached to Aleppo University started offering Persian courses, in 2001 the centre attached to Damascus University followed suit.[13] However, although the situation of Persian language teaching was gradually improving in Syria, the Iranian side heavily criticised the fact that none of the Syrian universities hosted a department for Persian language and literature as such – especially in view of there being several departments for Arabic literature at Iranian universities.[14] This changed in 2005, when departments of Persian language and literature opened at Damascus and Ba'th University. The department of Persian language and literature at Damascus University officially opened in May 2005, in the presence of the Syrian and Iranian Ministers of Higher Education, the Supreme Leader's representative in Syria, the Iranian ambassador,

Persian teaching facilities in Syria, with year of establishment.[15]

Persian teaching facility	Location	Year of establishment
Departments of History and Arabic Literature, Damascus University	Damascus	1975
Departments of History and Arabic Literature, Aleppo University	Aleppo	1975
Iranian Cultural Centre	Damascus	1984
Iranian Cultural Centre	Sayida Zaynab	1995
Departments of History and Arabic Literature, Tishrin University	Latakia	1995
Departments of History and Arabic Literature, Ba'th University	Homs	1996
Centre for teaching foreign languages, Aleppo University	Aleppo	2000
Centre for teaching foreign languages, Damascus University	Damascus	2001
Iranian Cultural Centre, Muhsiniya School (language classes for Iranians resident in Syria)	Damascus (al-Amin quarter)	2003
Iranian Cultural Centre, al-Mehdi Complex (language classes for Iranians resident in Syria)	Damascus (Zayn al-Abdin quarter)	2004
Department of Persian language and literature, Damascus University	Damascus	2005
Department of Persian language and literature, Ba'th University	Homs	2005
Iranian Cultural Centre	Latakia	2006
Department of Persian language and literature, Aleppo University	Aleppo	2007
Department of Persian language and literature, Tishrin University	Latakia	Planned

and the president of Damascus University. The opening speeches focused on the importance of language teaching in fostering bilateral relations, as a means of increasing the understanding between nations and peoples, and the exemplary role of Syrian-Iranian relations in furthering Arab-Iranian dialogue.[16] Both Syrian and Iranian officials underlined the role of languages as a means to bring about appreciation and unity between different nations, realising the importance of language teaching in promoting bilateral cultural relations. In the academic year 2007–2008, Aleppo University opened a department, coinciding with the 50-year anniversary of the university; Tishrin University is set to open one in the future. Persian language teaching also started at the Universities of Tartous and Hama, but only as an optional part of the curriculum for students of Arabic literature. As with the establishment of the Syrian cultural centre in Tehran in 2005, the strengthening of the Syrian-Iranian relationship during the last decade also clearly showed itself on the level of educational cooperation.

Each department of Persian language and literature takes in between 30 to 60 students each year; places are limited to this comparatively small number as the universities lack the capacity for more, due to a shortfall in qualified Persian teachers. There are currently a handful of Syrian students completing their PhDs in Persian language and literature in Iran under the umbrella of the student exchange programme; upon their return to Syria, they will be assigned teaching positions in one of the Persian departments, which are currently understaffed. Where no experienced professor of Persian literature is available, the head of the department is chosen from another department – the heads of the Persian departments at Damascus and Baʻth University for instance are professors of Arabic literature.

While teachers can decide what texts to teach within each subject, the general curriculum is set by the Council for Persian Language Teaching. The council, which meets every two weeks at the Iranian cultural centre, had been set up by the Iranian side to coordinate and unify Persian teaching in Syria. Members include the director of the Iranian cultural centre, the Iranian cultural attaché from the embassy, and all Persian language teachers. One Persian teacher at Damascus

University underlined the usefulness of this fortnightly meeting, as it provided teachers with a forum to exchange their teaching experiences.[17] In 2012 the Iranian cultural centre formed a committee to evaluate the work of the departments of Persian language and literature at Syrian universities.[18]

Students are not given much choice in the courses they study, as all courses are compulsory; they include language, literature, history and Islamic philosophy. The departments are integrated into the faculties of literature of each university, but work in close cooperation with the Iranian cultural centre in Damascus. According to the head of the Persian department at Ba'th University, the Iranian cultural centre acts like the 'godfather' of the department as it ultimately supervises the department's work.[19] While other language departments exist in Syrian state universities – Damascus University for instance hosts eight language departments, namely Arabic, German, Spanish, English, French, Persian, Japanese and Russian[20] – in general the governments of the languages under instruction are not involved in setting the curriculum or providing the teaching material.

The Iranian cultural centre is directly or indirectly involved in all the Persian teaching facilities in Syria mentioned above. It also serves as the mediator between the Syrian and Iranian ministries of higher education, being thus informed about every development in the field. In addition to providing Persian language teachers – Iran usually sends four Iranian university professors to Syria – the centre supplies relevant university departments with books and teaching material, coordinates exchanges between Syrian and Iranian students and academics, and the exchange of academic journals between universities; it organizes book fairs and scientific weeks in Syrian universities, and sends Syrian scholars to annual cultural festivals in Iran such as the international book fair.[21]

Persian faculty members questioned about the state of cooperation between their departments and the Iranian cultural centre mostly replied that cooperation was good, and that the centre was helpful in sending books and teaching materials, and organising seminars on historical and contemporary (revolutionary) literary figures,[22] but that the departments still had shortcomings in teaching tools and qualified teachers.[23] One former Syrian professor of Persian language and literature in Aleppo was less positive about the role of the Iranian side in the university departments – he said the universities were simply a tool for the Iranians to spread their propaganda in Syria, and had nothing to do with academia.[24] He resented the fact that Persian language and literature teaching at Syrian universities had become strongly associated with the politics of the Islamic Republic. The statement of an Iranian official in fact confirmed that Iran was not only aiming to teach language and literature. When President Ahmadinejad's former Minister of Culture and Islamic Guidance, Husyan Saffar-Harandi, came to Damascus in 2008, he joined one of the meetings of the Persian teaching council at the Iranian cultural centre, telling the teachers: 'Our goal is not to teach Persian, but to teach the values of the Islamic Republic.'[25]

One Syrian professor of Persian language also complained that the Iranians made them work too many hours, and that they wanted to be involved in everything but did not provide enough facilities:

'When the Iranian cultural centre said they wanted to set up the department of Persian language and literature at Damascus University, the university did not dare to say no, to tell them "we don't have the facilities, we don't have the personnel, we can't do it", because of the good relationship between the two states. The cultural centre said they would build everything and bring everything, but they did not do anything, or certainly not enough. The director of the cultural centre just wanted to say to his superiors in Iran: "Look, we have set up a language department in Syria, we have done this and that", in order to get promoted. They do it for their personal benefit.'[26]

Another Persian teacher disagreed, stressing that the Iranian cultural centre was very helpful, and that if it did not exist, it would make their work much more difficult. The centre helped the faculties obtain teaching materials, and the students from Damascus University also made use of the centre's library – seeing that Damascus University did not have its own specialised library for Persian literature, unlike Ba'th

University (which was supplied by the Iranian cultural centre). Of course they could always do with more books and teaching material, he agreed, but the centre was already very helpful.[27] There were thus different views on to what extent the Iranian cultural centre should be involved in Persian teaching at Syrian universities.

Syrians Studying Persian

So who are the people the Iranians are reaching out to through their language programmes? Who are the students taking up the opportunity to study Persian in Syria? How do they come to study Persian? What are their motivations? How do they aim to make use of the language in the future? In the following, the background and motivations of students at Syrian universities and at the Iranian cultural centre in Damascus will be examined, to discern the reach and effect of Iran's language programme.

The Syrian university system provides for a varied background of students in the departments of Persian language and literature. Students choose their subjects according to their grades of the state exam taken at the end of secondary school. Subjects like medicine and engineering are reserved for students with higher grades; arts and humanities subjects like languages and history rank much lower.[28] On this account, students in Syria do not necessarily choose to study Persian, but happen to study it, as this is the department their grades puts them in. The student body is mixed – a minority chooses to study Persian out of interest, the majority have a limited choice due to their grades, and just want to obtain a university degree, no matter in what subject.[29] One result is that the student profile in the Persian department cuts across all confessions present in Syria; religion plays no role in the choice of Persian as a subject. On average, more girls than boys are studying Persian, reflecting the overall gender proportion of students at the faculty of letters. According to one Persian literature teacher, who had extensive experience teaching Persian to foreigners in Iran, the Syrian students in the Persian department were average, neither brilliant nor bad.[30]

None of the students had been to Iran prior to their studies, but were interested in going there to learn more about the place they were studying.[31] The Iranian cultural centre organises an annual trip in the summer for 40 of the most promising students of the Persian departments, heavily subsidised by the two ministries of higher education.[32] Syrian students who visit Iran are in general pleasantly surprised by the country – before they go, they believe Iran is a backward country, and are surprised to see how developed it is once they are there. Iran exceeds their expectations. To encourage more students to visit the other country, the head of Tehran University concluded an agreement with Damascus University in 2010 that stipulated for a group of Iranian students of Arabic literature to spend the summer in Damascus studying Arabic at the Language Centre of the university, and for a group of Syrian students of Persian literature to spend the summer in Tehran.[33]

Work opportunities for the students of Persian language and literature have not yet clearly emerged, seeing that the departments are still new. However, teachers see possibilities for their students in working for Iranian companies in Syria, or working for the vast religious tourist industry of Iranian pilgrims in Syria. The head of the Persian department at Aleppo University explained: 'It is not yet clear what students will do after graduation, but there are opportunities for them as there are good economic and cultural relations between Syria and Iran; they could also work in the field of tourism.'[34] A small number of students might continue their education in Iran, obtaining post-graduate degrees within the cultural exchange programme, and return to teach in the Persian departments.[35] The first round of students graduated in the summer of 2009. In Damascus University, 17 students graduated – down from 30 when they started their degree in 2005. Every year a couple of students dropped out, as was normal in the faculty of letters, so the number had decreased. Of the students who graduated, several started to work with Iranian companies in Syria, and some in the hotel business. A few obtained scholarships to continue their studies in Iran.[36]

It can be argued that the main motivation of students at the Persian departments is to graduate from university, which has little to do with Iranian efforts as such. However, by providing students with the opportunity to study Persian, regardless of whether students take it up by choice or not, the Iranians are playing a crucial role in generating interest in Iran amongst Syrians with no prior connection to the country. Upon graduation, the majority of students are trying to find work where they can take advantage of their Persian language skills. Through the Persian departments at universities, Iran is fostering relationships with key individuals, a future generation of Persian speaking Syrians, one of the main purposes of cultural diplomacy.

Students learning Persian at the Iranian cultural centre have a different background and motivation in learning the language. While students at the universities' Persian departments come from a mixed confessional background, many of the students at the centre are Syrian Shi'a. They want to learn Persian because they consider it the second language of Islam, and/or because their work is in some ways related to Iran, either through business or the tourist industry. It is also a forum to meet like-minded people, and language students form friendships that continue beyond the classroom. However, having observed two sets of Persian language classes at the Iranian cultural centre, one in the first half of 2008 and one in the first half of 2009, different student profiles have been encountered. While most students in the courses observed in 2008 met the above-mentioned profile, the students in the 2009 class I attended had a different background. In my 2008 classes, students were between the age of 20 and 45, religious, all of the women veiled, and predominantly Shi'a.[37] In my 2009 class, while some language students met the same profile, the majority were university students in their early 20s – possibly attesting to a greater visibility of the Persian language in Damascus University since the establishment of a Persian department there. They were students of various disciplines, including journalism, international relations, pharmacology, engineering, Arabic and French literature, all studying at Damascus University. The journalism and international relations students learned Persian as they saw work opportunities in their fields provided by the two governments' strong relationship, the pharmacology and engineering students wanted to continue their education in Iran, the Arabic literature student attended Persian classes at the centre as he considered the basic classes provided at university for Arabic literature students too basic, and the French literature student learned Persian out of interest in literature, and because he felt he was enhancing his marketability.[38]

Classes at the Iranian cultural centre thus do provide an environment where the goal of strengthening cultural relations between the two countries could be addressed, albeit for two different audiences. On the one hand there is the audience that already has an interest in Iran and the form of Islam it represents, which has been the main audience for years. On the other hand more recently there is also the younger audience that seized the opportunities offered by their country's existing excellent relationship with Iran. However, even in the latter case language students at the centre were mostly not from a Sunni background. It was one thing to study Persian at the university, which was a neutral ground. It was another thing to learn Persian at the Iranian cultural centre, which was an agency of the Islamic Republic. It seems, however, that the existence of the Persian departments at Syrian universities is slowly changing this hesitancy to take part in activities at the centre itself. While they may not be participating in the language classes offered at the centre, seeing that they learn it at university, Syrian students of all backgrounds had started to make use of the cultural centre. They take part in seminars organised especially for them in the Arab-Iranian Cultural Studies Centre, and use the library for their studies. There is also a third audience, namely foreign students like myself, who come from a number of countries and learn Persian for various reasons, which we are not concerned with here; they are a clear minority.

It can be argued that the establishment of Persian departments at Syrian universities is a promising medium to foster relations on the popular level. As the majority of students in these departments have no prior interest in Iran, they provide an effective way of introducing young Syrians to Iran's language and culture, and building potential bridges for the future. The Iranian cultural centre had a different profile as students actively sought it out to study Persian – students at the centre had a genuine interest in learning the language. The centre traditionally attracted language students that were pious and wanted to learn Persian as the second language of Islam; only more recently has it attracted a considerable group of young Syrians seeing opportunities for their own future in learning Persian. In both cases has the centre been successful in maintaining and furthering people's interests – although it is generally the first group that participates in the centre's regular activities.

The Role of Language Students: Arabic Language Teaching in Iran

Constitution of the Islamic Republic of Iran, Article 16: 'Since the language of the Quran and Islamic texts and teachings is Arabic, and since Persian literature is thoroughly permeated by this language, it must be taught after elementary level, in all classes of secondary school and in all areas of study.'[39]

The case of Arabic language teaching in Iran differs notably from that of Persian language teaching in Syria. Firstly, Arabic has a special status in the Islamic Republic of Iran, being the language of the Quran. The teaching of Arabic is mandatory in secondary school education, provided for by Article 16 of the Iranian constitution. Secondly, the Arabic language is not mainly identifiable with Syria as a country; it is the language of the Arab world as a whole. While Persian is spoken not only in Iran, it can nevertheless be directly identified with Iran as a country, in particular the way it is propagated in Syria. Therefore Arabic in Iran is not connected to Syria as such, whereas Persian in Syria is connected to Iran. Third, unlike Iran in Syria, the latter is not directly involved in Arabic departments at Iranian universities. However, especially since the establishment of the Syrian-Arab cultural centre in Tehran in 2005, Syria has started to play a role in the field of Arabic language teaching in Iran – not least due to the fact that it is Iran's closest Arab partner. After introducing the state of Arabic language teaching in Iran, the role of Syria and the Syrian cultural centre will be discussed.

Arabic language teaching in Iran has profited greatly from the Islamic revolution. Up to the Islamic revolution, only three universities had departments of Arabic, namely Tehran, Isfahan and Mashhad University, which were set up in the 1970s.[40] Before that, Tehran

University had a department called *al-manqul* (the transmitted) and *al-m'aqul* (the logical), where Arabic was taught as part of religious and philosophical studies. The 'bourgeois Iranian environment', however, was not conducive to studying Arabic, according to one prominent professor of Arabic in Tehran.[41] Very few students read Arabic at university. This changed with the revolution, which elevated Arabic to Iran's second language after Persian and firmly embedded it into its constitution. Now there are around 24 departments of Arabic language and literature at Iranian state universities at least at the undergraduate level, many up to Masters level, and a few up to PhD level, and private universities also have Arabic departments.[42] The fact that many Iranian universities have Arabic departments was one of the reasons Iranian cultural officials were complaining about the lack of Persian departments at Syrian universities.

Although Arabic has a special status in Iran, and is being taught throughout secondary school education, the standard of Arabic amongst Iranians is surprisingly low. Even at university level, most teachers teach Arabic language and literature in Persian. Students' Arabic proficiency is weak. To date, only Alameh Tabataba'i University ensures that all Masters and doctoral theses are written in Arabic – as a university specialising exclusively in the humanities, it has a strong Arabic department.[43] There are teachers actively trying to change this situation, but have not succeeded yet – one of the problems being that even some of the teachers are not fluent in speaking Arabic.[44]

This is where Syria and the Syrian cultural centre come in. Due to the close relationship between Syria and Iran, the stipulations in the bilateral cultural agreement and subsequent cultural implementation programmes, and geographic proximity, many Arabic language professors have travelled to Syria through official channels, be it for visits of the country or for an extended stay to deepen their language skills or make use of Arabic literary sources.[45] The Syrian cultural centre often facilitates these trips. What is more, the centre in Tehran provides a forum for Arabic language teachers to meet, and an opportunity to practise and further their language skills with native speakers.

Since May 2005, the Syrian cultural centre offers language classes in four different courses: conversation, translation from Arabic to Persian, translation from Persian to Arabic, and dictation. There are no beginner classes; students are put in a class according to their level following a placement test – there are between 120 and 150 students across the courses. Courses last for three months.[46] The vast majority of students frequenting the centre are current students or graduates from Arabic language departments of different Iranian universities, or Arabic language teachers at the latter and at schools. As they cannot practise Arabic conversation at university and have no regular access to native speakers, they come to the Syrian cultural centre that fills these gaps. Courses at the centre are held in classical Arabic, but students can ask questions about Arabic dialect in class. Teachers are generally Syrians studying post-graduate degrees in Iran.[47] Although Syria is not directly involved in Arabic language teaching at Iranian universities and institutions, it is thus indirectly involved by assisting in the formation of teachers. Arabic language classes at the centre are popular as the standard of teaching is higher than in most Iranian institutions. One of the functions of the Syrian cultural centre, besides offering language classes, is to raise the level of Arabic teaching in Iran, for which it sets up special seminars and workshops.[48]

One such activity was the conference on Arabic language teaching, which the Iran Language Institute – a state-run language institute founded in 1979[49] – organised in cooperation with the Syrian cultural centre, the Arabic departments of Tehran and Tarbiyat Modarres University,[50] and the Iranian Association of Arabic Language and Literature.[51] The three-day conference, which took place in Tehran in June 2009, provided a fascinating insight into the state of Arabic language teaching in Iran, and showed how Syria contributed to the discussion. The director and staff of the Syrian cultural centre attended the conference; being one of the hosts, the former gave an opening speech in which he declared his pride in the strong relationship between Syria and Iran, and explained how the Syrian cultural centre was working towards deepening these ties further, and spreading the Arabic language through its language courses. Two Arab ambassadors attended the opening of the conference: the Syrian and the Palestinian ambassadors, the latter being the dean of the diplomatic corps. Participants were teachers of Arabic language and literature in Iranian and Arab universities and institutes.

The largest Arab delegation taking part in the conference was Syrian; there were other Arab academics mainly from Iraq, Algeria and Tunisia. The Syrians were Arabic language teachers from the Centre for teaching foreign languages at Damascus University, which had concluded an agreement of cooperation with the Iran Language Institute the previous year – another sign of the growing academic interaction between the two sides. Iranian participants came from across Iran.

Throughout the conference, one point was made repeatedly: the special position of the Arabic language in Iran. Arabic was considered the second language of Iran; it was not really a foreign language; Iran was the only country in which teaching Arabic in school was a law; Persian speakers could not understand their own language's literature without knowing Arabic; Arabic was important in Iran for cultural, religious and historical reasons; Arabic was the language of Islam. One Arabic teacher from Yazd raised the point that one of the problems in Iran was that many students did not consider Arabic a language that could be used in day-to-day life; they did not consider Arabic a live language.[52] This problem is connected to the often poor standard of Arabic teaching in Iranian schools, where pupils mainly learn Arabic grammar and how to read religious texts – but certainly not how to have a conversation in Arabic.

This is where the Syrian cultural centre seemed to be helpful. In conversations with Iranian conference participants, it emerged that they valued the Syrian centre as a meeting place, to further their Arabic skills with native speakers, and not least as a medium for travelling to an Arab country.[53] The conference brought together all those interested in developing Arabic language teaching in Iran, and it was clear that Syria was a firm partner in this initiative. It has emerged that although Arabic will never be primarily identified with Syria as such, Iranian professionals in the field of Arabic language and literature are happy to turn to Syria for assistance in improving their language skills, and Syria is happy to extend its hand to its partner. Syria is also the Arabic country most accessible to Iranians, as they no longer need a visa to visit it and both sides encourage travels of academics to the other country. Many other Arab countries impose restrictions on Iranian entries to their countries.

The Role of Exchange Students

Background: Academic Exchanges

'Familiarity breeds the ground to be critical. [...] The benefits from study abroad should be sought not so much in minds won over as in the strengthening of academic disciplines and of links between institutions, the increase of enlightenment, the diffusion of skill and expertise, and the promotion of understanding.'[54]

Syrian-Iranian cooperation in the field of Higher Education started in earnest following the drafting of the first cultural implementation programme for the years 1995–1997. This programme called for partnerships and exchanges between Syrian and Iranian universities in different fields, including student and teacher exchanges.[55] The goal was to strengthen academic disciplines and links between institutions, to diffuse skills and promote understanding between Syrian and Iranian students and academics. Syria in particular needed Iranian Persian language teachers for its universities, while it sent its own students to complete post-graduate degrees in Persian language and literature in Iran in order to be able to teach Persian in Syrian universities upon return. Iran wanted to send its students to pursue post-graduate studies especially in Arabic language and literature, to raise the level of Arabic amongst its own academics. Fostering relations with key individuals and building lasting relationships are crucial components of cultural diplomacy. Students who studied in another country are likely to keep ties to that country, speaking the language and being familiar with how the country works – they are ideal candidates to keep up and strengthen bilateral relations between their country of study and their own country. This is not to say that all international students' experiences are positive, which in fact they are not; however, it is likely that students will keep up a bond with their country of study.[56]

In their cultural implementation programmes, Syria and Iran provide for a number of scholarships to be exchanged between the two sides. The academic exchange got fully started after the signing of the 2003–2005 implementation programme in 2002, parallel to an intensification of diplomatic cooperation.[57] Aside from students who study

Number of scholarships according to implementation programmes.[58]

Implementation programme	Iranian scholarships to Syrian students	Syrian scholarships to Iranian students	Further stipulations
1995–1997	10 scholarships each year between the two countries		N/A
2003–2005	35 for BA students 5 for MA students 5 for PhD students	10 for BA students 20 for MA students 5 for PhD students	N/A
2006–2008	20 for BA students 15 for MA students 5 for PhD students	20 for BA students 5 for MA students 5 for PhD students	2 of the Iranian scholarships for Syrian PhD students for the study of Persian language and literature

in the other country through the scholarship exchange programme, a larger number of students study abroad on their own initiative. Article 21 of the 2003–2005 implementation programme provides that the two sides will consider requests from the other side about study places positively, facilitating students to study in the other country independently.[59] In addition to the general implementation programme, there are separate agreements between several Iranian and Syrian universities that equally call for and encourage student exchanges between their institutions.[60]

Iranian Students in Syria

According to the cultural attaché at the Iranian Embassy in Damascus, there are around 150 to 200 Iranian students in Syria at any one time, undergraduates as well as postgraduates, who study in Syria through the cultural exchange programme. The total number of Iranian students is around 400, but apparently a number of those are *Iraniyan muqim*, Syrians of Iranian origin whose families have been in Syria for generations but still hold Iranian nationality.[61] Students who come on a scholarship are chosen through the Iranian Ministry of Education, and are placed under the supervision of the embassy in Damascus. The Iranian cultural centre is in contact with the students for day-to-day matters, if they need assistance finding their way around life in Syria at the beginning of their stay for instance.[62] Most of the students who come to Syria as part of the student exchange programme study either medicine or dentistry, or subjects in the humanities, in particular Arabic language and literature, and history, focusing within the latter on subjects such as Islamic history and Islamic architecture. The majority studies at Damascus University. At Aleppo University, there are no Iranian students in the humanities, but a number in the faculties of medicine and dentistry.[63]

Apparently a considerable number of Iranians come to Syria to study medicine or complete their medical specialisation. These are students who are forced to study outside of Iran as they did not manage to obtain one of the competitive places in medicine in an Iranian university. Syria is a popular choice for those who cannot afford to go far; it is comparatively cheap to live and study in, and it is easy for Iranian students to obtain a residence permit and place at university.[64] Conservative students also appreciate cultural commonalities between Iran and Syria, according to an Iranian language teacher at Aleppo University.[65] However, this is not to say that these medicine students are necessarily happy to study in Syria – if they had the choice, they would have stayed in Iran. According to one student who was just finishing her five-year dentistry degree, the level of study in Syria was much lower than in Iran. Upon her return to Iran, she will have to spend one year completing a conversion course in order for her degree to be recognised there and for her to be able to practise dentistry.[66]

A student of Islamic architecture also maintained that in her subject the level of study was lower than in Iran. 'What students write for their PhD theses here, students in Iran write for their Masters' theses', she claimed. She did not complain about being in Syria, however, as it was very useful for her in terms of finding sources and obtaining material. Her supervisor was also extremely helpful, not only in terms of her academic work but also assisting her in dealing with the Syrian bureaucracy. Syrians were generally helping her with her research, and it was easier for her to obtain material here than in Isfahan, where people were not as friendly and forthcoming. Her spoken Arabic was still very weak, however, and she did not spend much time socializing with Syrians. When she was not studying, she spent most of her time with other Iranian students at the university dormitories – also due to the language barrier.[67]

At the public PhD examination of one of the Iranian doctoral students at Damascus University, some of the ideological differences between Iran and Syria came to the fore. The student was defending his thesis in the Arabic literature department on a comparative study between an Iranian and an Arab writer. All four examiners criticized the language mistakes the student made, while acknowledging that it could not have been easy to write a thesis in a foreign language. One of the professors attacked him for mentioning the 'Persian Gulf', telling him that in Syria it was called 'Arab Gulf' and that he could not write 'Persian Gulf' in a thesis submitted at Damascus University – 'Syrian students in Iran cannot say Arab Gulf either, they have to say Persian Gulf, otherwise they might be expelled from the university,' he added. The same professor also criticized the student for apparently attacking Russia and the Soviet Union in his work. 'Why do you attack them?' he asked. 'Russia is a friend of Syria and has helped her a lot.'[68] While the professors' comments to the student were quite critical and some not particularly friendly, the student obtained a good grade for his thesis in the end.

The students' experience in Syria is mixed. Initially some struggle with the language barrier, not being able to communicate in Syrian dialect. Others integrate quickly, and profit from the Iranian cultural centre to meet Syrians interested in Iran who can teach them dialect and about life in Syria in general. Iranian students in Syria – whether in the country on their own initiative or on state scholarships – are not completely independent, but are closely watched by their own community and Iranian intelligence. Iranian students have to follow Islamic dress code for instance while in Syria, and the embassy keeps track of them.[69] One student claimed that the atmosphere amongst the Iranian student body in Syria had changed in the second half of Ahmadinejad's term, with most new students coming to Syria being the children of government officials or Revolutionary Guards in Iran, such as the son

of Ali Akbar Velayati, the Supreme Leader's senior advisor on international affairs and former Foreign Minister. They spied on each other
and often only stayed in Syria for a short period of time until they
managed to obtain a place at a good Iranian university through their
connections.[70] To what extent this holds true could not be verified.

Whereas minds might not always be won over, understanding is
certainly promoted. As one student put it:

> 'Arabic has a bad image in Iran as it is only associated with religion.
> But most people have never visited an Arab country. Only once one
> knows a country like Syria does one understand that people here
> have similar concerns and problems, we are not so different.'[71]

One of the main contributions of academic exchanges to the Syrian-
Iranian relationship is to increase familiarity with the other side, one of
the core purposes of cultural diplomacy – which is clearly taking place.
The dentistry student said that one of the most difficult things for her
at the beginning was to have a proper conversation with Syrians:

> 'People here are very helpful and friendly, but I have found it difficult
> for us to talk to each other on the same level – people here gener
> ally do not understand what I am thinking. We have mostly had
> quite superficial conversations. But in the end I learnt how to speak
> to people here, and I have made some very good friends.' Asked
> whether she would keep up a link with Syria after her return, she
> promptly replied: 'Of course! I have spent five years studying here,
> I know Damascus better than Tehran by now, I speak the lan
> guage, I have made friends, of course I will come back.'

Before coming to Damascus to study, she did not know any Arabic,
and had never been to Syria.[72]

Syrian Students in Iran

In Iran, the number of Syrian students varies between 300 and 500 at
any one time, according to the Syrian embassy. The Syrian Ministry

of Higher Education chooses students for the scholarship programmes
depending on their grades. Students are not necessarily involved in the
decision making process to determine which country they are being
sent to; they take part in a general competition to study abroad. Most
Syrian students who are in Iran through the scholarship programme
are postgraduates. The majority of students come to Iran independently, financing their studies themselves. They go to all major Iranian
cities with good universities, but predominantly to Tehran. Studying
at Iranian state universities, in particular in large cities such as Tehran,
is attractive since the universities provide good education and maintain high standards: they have a rigorous entrance examination that
foreign students do not have to take. Students generally have no prior
knowledge of Persian, but study at the language institute in Qazvin
before starting their course of study. The choice of subjects is varied,
but science subjects like engineering are particularly popular amongst
the students. The Syrian embassy in Tehran is responsible for all
students, and there is a Syrian student union in Iran that provides
a link between Syrian students and Iranian student organisations, as
well as a link with the embassy.[73] According to the Syrian embassy,
students constitute the largest number of Syrians in Iran. As such, they
form an important link between Syria and Iran. However, the fact that
the comparatively small number of Syrian students constitutes the largest number of Syrians in Iran also demonstrates how little exchange
there in fact is.

Like their Iranian counterparts in Syria, Syrian students in Iran
have a mixed experience. Many do not particularly enjoy their experience, especially as they are often not too well received in Iran, being
Arab. Comments such as 'you know what it's like, they don't really
like us, they don't like Arabs and they think we are all the same' are
frequently made by Syrian students in Tehran when asked about their
experiences.[74] Tehran apparently has the strongest prejudices against
Arabs, not least because many Tehranis have visited Dubai and believe
that Gulf Arabs are representative of the wider Arab world, according
to one Iranian student in Syria.[75] As a result Syrian students often
stick together with other Syrian or foreign students and do not mingle.
Others – in particular Persian language and literature students – are

fascinated by Iran and have integrated well, speaking Persian fluently and conversing comfortably about Iranian poetry and literature. One such student stated that everyone who has spent some time in Iran must miss it after his departure. Another student, studying archaeology at Isfahan University for her undergraduate degree, had fallen in love with Iran. Missing Isfahan upon her return to Syria after over five years in Iran, she started assisting with the Persian teaching at the Iranian cultural centre in Latakia.

As students in most cases do not choose Iran as a destination for their studies but are either sent there as in the case of scholarship recipients, or are recommended to go there as the cultural agreement facilitates acceptance at Iranian state universities with a high standard of teaching, it is understandable that students have different experiences studying in Iran. Experiences are also not always black or white; as one student affirmed, living and studying in Iran was 'at times difficult, and at times good'. She never experienced any prejudices against her because she was Arab, however. 'I mostly stayed in an academic environment where people did not care where I was from, I never had a bad experience because I was Syrian,' she underlined. This student, who had finished her doctoral studies in Iran several years ago, still frequently goes back to Iran, mostly for conferences or seminars.[76]

Joint Project: al-Farabi University

Syria and Iran's academic cooperation was further strengthened with their decision in late 2007 to set up a joint Syrian-Iranian university on the Syrian coast, in the Latakia region. The two sides signed an agreement to establish the joint university – to be called al-Farabi university – with the aim of strengthening scientific research and to offer teaching at postgraduate level to Syrian students. The agreement was concluded between the Syrian Minister of Higher Education and the Tarbiyat Modarres University in Iran. The university, which will be a branch of the Tarbiyat Modarres University, is to be specialised in around ten subjects, mostly engineering and humanities.[77] The language of instruction will be English, while the scientific framework will be set by Iran. Teachers will be sent from the Tarbiyat Modarres University.

Students will be Syrians chosen though a competition, or *concours*, in accordance with the Iranian higher education system.[78]

The process of setting up the university is ongoing; according to an official at the Iranian Ministry of Science, Research and Technology, officials had hoped students could apply for admission to the university starting in 2010.[79] It turned out, however, that the building work had not even commenced by the summer of 2010 – the opening date of the university has therefore not yet been confirmed, but the building work will likely take several years to complete.[80] Committees have been formed between the two sides to supervise the development. While Tarbiyat Modarres University has scientific cooperation with a number of foreign countries and universities, the project in Syria – setting up a joint university – is the first of its kind.[81] According to Press TV, however, Syria is not the only country Iran is establishing branches of its universities in; apparently there are currently projects underway to open branches of Iranian universities in Lebanon, Afghanistan, Pakistan, Dubai and Comoros.[82] In terms of cultural relations between Syria and Iran, the project of al-Farabi University provides a further step to build lasting ties between the two sides as it reinforces institutional cooperation on a long-term basis – provided the project sees the light of day.

Profile: Muhammad al-Tounji

As an example of someone who has been involved in Syrian-Iranian academic exchange and pioneer of Persian language teaching in Syria, we will consider the profile of Muhammad al-Tounji: Muhammad al-Tounji was the first Syrian to teach Persian in Syrian universities, after studying in Tehran in the 1960s. Passionate about literature, he came to be interested in the Persian language and literature through the encouragement of his mentor at university. Born in Aleppo in 1933, Muhammad al-Tounji studied Arabic language and literature at Damascus University, from which he graduated in 1960. After completing a Master's degree in education, he expected to be awarded a scholarship from Syria to be sent to Europe to study Hebrew. He already had a basic knowledge of Hebrew, as it was a compulsory requirement for students in the humanities at the time. The head of the literature department and his advisor, Said Afghani, had other plans for him – he suggested that Tounji should go to Iran instead. When Tounji objected that there was no Hebrew teaching in Iran and he did not know Persian, the former told him that he should learn Persian in order to teach the language in Syria upon his return.

So Tounji went to Lebanon to speak to Muhammad Muhammadi, Persian professor and chair of the Centre for Persian Language and Literature at the Lebanese University, to ask him how to obtain a scholarship to study in Iran.[83] Muhammadi advised him to go back to Syria for two months and study Persian by himself – at that time there was no Persian teaching in Syria – and then return to him in order that he could assess whether Tounji had a talent for the language. After Tounji arrived home, he sought out two old gentlemen who had studied Persian at Ottoman government schools in the late Ottoman period, borrowed their Persian schoolbooks, and taught himself. After two months he revisited Muhammadi in Beirut, took a Persian exam and succeeded in it, upon which Muhammadi proposed to the Iranian embassy in Damascus to assist Tounji. They offered him a plane ticket to Tehran as well as a doctoral scholarship, and he set off to Iran.

As an indication of how little interest there existed in an exchange between students at the time, in return for offering al-Tounji a scholarship to study at Tehran University as well as a return flight, Damascus University offered the same to an Iranian student. However, a year after the offer was made – and Tounji had started his studies in Iran – Tehran University had still not found a student to take it up.[84] What is more, when offering Tounji the scholarship to study in Iran, the Iranian side had offered scholarships for two students. Whereas Tounji arrived in Tehran on 30 July 1962, the second scholarship was never taken up.[85]

Tounji was the first Syrian to study in Iran on a scholarship, and the only one for years to come. In Iran, he was part of a group of foreign students for whom a special course in Persian literature had been organised, under the patronage of the Shah's wife, Farah Diba. He obtained his PhD in comparative literature from Tehran University in 1966. Later on, he obtained a second doctorate in Abbasid literature from St. Joseph University in Beirut, upon the urging of his Iranian supervisor who maintained that if he wanted to be able to compare Arabic and Persian literature, he needed to know both literary traditions equally well. Upon Tounji's return to Syria, Afghani had become dean of the faculty of letters and employed him immediately to teach Persian at Damascus University. Afghani himself had visited Tehran at the time Tounji was studying there, together with several of his colleagues from Damascus University.[86]

Tounji taught at the Arabic literature faculties of Damascus and Aleppo University until his retirement in the late 1990s, for the largest part being the only permanent Persian language teacher at both institutions. Throughout his academic career, he has written and translated many books to further the Persian language and literature in the Arab world, including a Persian-Arabic dictionary – of which more than 22 editions have been printed to date – as well as an Arabic-Persian one; he wrote the first Persian language textbook for Syrian university students in 1967, a guide to the Persian language and a compilation of Persian texts.

Tounji had mixed feelings about the Islamic Republic's cultural activities. Before the revolution, cultural relations between Syria and Iran were not good, he explained, as Iran had no ambition to help people like Shi'ism or Persian literature in Syria. At the beginning of the revolution, cultural cooperation started off well. In his view it soon emerged, however, that the Islamic Republic wanted to teach Persian not to those who liked literature, but to those who had an inclination to Shi'ism – the promotion of the language was at the same time also a tool for the promotion of the Shi'i school of thought, he believed. According to Tounji, the Iranians mostly did not teach real Persian literature anymore: it was all propaganda for the Islamic revolution. Tounji himself taught Persian, but not Iranian propaganda – he had also taught Hebrew for instance, but had no connection whatsoever to Israel: the one was unconnected to the other. He neither liked the Shah – especially 'because the latter's secret service was everywhere and also because he was a friend of Israel' – nor did he like the Islamic Republic.

Tounji has nevertheless been cooperating with the Iranian cultural centre and its officials. The *Islamic Culture* journal of the centre, for instance, used to be a journal of very good standard according to Tounji, and he translated a number of texts from Persian to Arabic for them. Respected scholars used to write for it, such as the Syrian scholar Abd al-Karim al-Yafi. For some reason the standard then dropped and the journal was stopped. Tounji's experience with the Iranian cultural centre has not always been positive. When the Iranians set up the Persian department at Damascus University several years ago, he recounts, they invited him to speak for 20 minutes at the opening ceremony about his long experience teaching Persian language and literature in Syria. The night before the opening they called him and told him his speaking time had been cut down to ten minutes. Once he arrived at the ceremony, they told him that the Iranian ambassador had taken his speaking slot and he should just go up to the podium, greet the audience and leave again. This infuriated Tounji, he recalled, shouting that he had taught Persian in Syria for nearly 50 years and now was not even allowed to speak for ten minutes! He left and went back to Aleppo. Tounji generally kept his contact with the Iranian cultural centre to a minimum, but did participate in regular meetings such as the Persian language council while he still taught at university.[87]

Muhammad al-Tounji was a pioneer of Persian language teaching in Syria, but had been keen on working in the field of comparative literature and language teaching due to his enthusiasm for literature, not for the Islamic Republic. He had a genuine interest in Persian language, literature and culture, but not the discourse of the Iranian cultural centre, which he dismissed as revolutionary propaganda. Having been employed by Syrian state universities, he did take part in the cultural centre's activities, however, when he was invited to do so, and regularly travelled to Iran to participate in academic conferences. Tounji taught Persian out of interest, but cooperated with the Islamic Republic's cultural centre when necessary due to his position at university.

Conclusion

The importance of education in Syrian-Iranian cultural cooperation had been put down on paper with their cultural agreement of 1984, but had only been realised in practice starting in the mid-1990s and in particular in the early 2000s – in line with the further strengthening of bilateral relations taking place during this period. The Iranian cultural centre in Damascus is heavily involved in the teaching design not only at its own centres but also at Syrian universities' Persian departments, which it helped create. Persian language students in Syria come from two groups, one that has chosen to learn the language often for religious reasons, and one that has not necessarily chosen the language out of interest but hopes to profit from the good bilateral relationship between the two countries to offer work opportunities. Arabic language teaching in Iran has a different basis, Arabic being a compulsory school language according to the Iranian constitution. Arabic language students at the Syrian cultural centre in Tehran mostly come from within the universities' Arabic departments and are often Arabic language teachers, using the cultural centre as a meeting and training place. In particular in the case of Syria, language teaching has proven a useful way to increase awareness of the partner country and start building up a group of Syrians who have an interest in maintaining bilateral bonds in the future.

Likewise, the student exchanges taking place between Syria and Iran are a good start to build up relationships between the two countries on the popular level. Even if the students' experiences are not only positive, students nevertheless become familiar with the other country and are likely to keep up a working relationship. While it is difficult to measure the success rate of academic exchanges as there are no records of what returning students go on to do or to what extent they do in fact keep up ties with their country of study, it is clear that student exchanges increase contact and understanding between the two peoples – albeit on a small scale. The language and exchange students are largely products of the cultural diplomacy efforts between the two states, as the existing bilateral agreements facilitate their exchange. In the case of students, cultural exchange thus does reach down to the popular level and fosters the bonds of the future. Whether they have taken up the language of the other country or studied in the other country by choice or by chance, students are important actors in keeping a Syrian-Iranian exchange alive on the non-state level. Unlike the case of religious tourists, which will be examined in the following chapter, numbers involved in the educational exchange are still small, however.

CHAPTER 7

RELIGIOUS TOURISM: THE BLESSEDNESS OF CULTURAL TIES

This chapter focuses on the case of Iranian religious tourism to Syria, and what role tourism plays in bilateral relations. While the Iran-Iraq war prevented Shi'i Iranians from going on pilgrimage to Karbala and Najaf, the emerging alliance between Tehran and Damascus allowed for a growing tourist industry of Iranian pilgrims to Syria. The main destinations for these pilgrims were sites in and around Damascus, most prominently the shrines of Sayida Zaynab and Sayida Ruqayya, the sister and daughter of Imam Husayn respectively. Both shrines showed a strong Iranian influence, and had been renovated and partly built by Iranian donations. In Raqqa, two shrines were built in the 1990s and added to the pilgrimage route. A complete infrastructure had been set up to provide for the Iranian visitors, with trade taking place around the sites and a hotel industry in specific areas catering exclusively to Iranians. Although a significant number of Iranian pilgrims visited shrines in Syria every year, contact between pilgrims and Syrians was restricted. Whilst Iranian religious tourism drew directly on the shared cultural religious heritage the two sides wanted to promote, it also showed the limits of interaction between the peoples.

At first, the connection between tourism and cultural policies will be introduced, looking at tourism in terms of cultural diplomacy, the formal institutions involved in running the tourism exchange in both countries, and the state of Syrian tourism to Iran and Iranian tourism to Syria. Religious tourism will be defined, and its importance for the Shi'i community explained. The role of heritage and geopolitics in tourism will be analysed, by introducing Shi'i places of interest in Syria that drew on a shared Islamic history, and explaining the emergence of Iranian religious tourism to Syria. We will then turn to Iranian involvement in Syrian religious sites, both before and after the Islamic revolution in Iran. Finally, interaction and trade between Iranian pilgrims and Syrians will be discussed, to assess to what extent Iranian religious tourism fostered relations on the popular level.

Tourism and Cultural Policies

Tourism and Cultural Diplomacy

'Culture and heritage are primary drivers of international tourism. [. . .] Tourism is important not just for its economic impact, but for the significance that it has in creating impressions about a country. The experience of a visit – how visitors are treated, what they see, hear and learn – will remain with them for years and be communicated to family and friends. [. . .] It is particularly vital that visitors see their own cultures being cared for and respected.'[1]

Tourism enables people to visit other countries and observe other cultures. It gives them the opportunity to experience another country, and form an opinion about it, which they then convey to those around them upon their return home. Tourism is therefore closely connected to issues of reputation and perception.[2] As such, it forms part of cultural diplomacy. Heritage plays a crucial role in attracting visitors, which is evident in the case of tourism between Syria and Iran. The vast majority of tourists going back and forth between the two countries were Iranian pilgrims to Syria's religious sites, in particular the tombs of the ahl al-bayt, the family of the Prophet. The pilgrims in fact visited sites that formed part of what they perceived as their own heritage.

Their travel took place in a specific sphere, which was pre-determined by the purpose of their visit and the nature of the Syrian-Iranian relationship. Hence, while there is a theory that tourism matters in intercultural exchange 'because it provides both a lens onto and an energy for relationships with everyday life',[3] the everyday life that Iranians were subjected to in Syria was not the everyday life other tourists to Syria experienced. Iranian pilgrims in Syria moved largely in spheres sketched out for them by a combination of their own itin-erary – visiting holy shrines and shopping – political circumstances and the infrastructure that had developed to accommodate them.

Tourism has an important economic dimension to it. Not only in terms of the money tourists spend in a country while travelling, but also in terms of longer term commerce tourism brings about. Iranian religious tourism to Syria certainly encouraged trade between the two countries, as pilgrims used their trips to engage in commerce. Trade in fact was one of the main forums of interaction between the pilgrims and the local population in Syria.

There are thus three main points to make about tourism and cul-tural diplomacy. First of all, tourism enables visitors to experience another country and interact with the local population, and to gain insights into local values and beliefs. Secondly, it draws on heritage and geopolitics to attract visitors. Thirdly, it encourages trade. To what extent this holds true in the Syrian-Iranian case will be discussed in this chapter.

Institutions

In Iran, the link between culture and tourism was institutionalised during the first decade of the Islamic Republic, by uniting the minis-tries of tourism and culture in the 1980s, culminating in the formation of the Ministry of Culture and Islamic Guidance in 1987.[4] Both the Iran and International Tourism Organisation (sazeman-e irangerdi va jihangerdi), and the Hajj and Pilgrimage Organisation (sazeman-e hajj va ziyarat) were affiliated to this ministry, whose basic responsibilities included finalising tourism agreements, and establishing, expanding, improving and operating facilities and infrastructures for domestic and international tourism.[5] The Hajj and Pilgrimage Organisation, for instance, appointed agents in charge of dispatching pilgrims to Syria and monitoring the pilgrimage, as well as organising pilgrimage affairs by way of coordinating between the concerned governmental and non-governmental institutions in Iran and Syria.[6]

In Damascus, the Ministry of Tourism managed Syria's tourist affairs, in cooperation with the General Directorate of Antiquities and the Ministry of Awqaf. In the case of Iranian tourism to Syria, the latter was relatively involved in the exchange, as the vast majority of Iranian tourists came to Syria for religious tourism. The Ministry of Awqaf – in place since 1961 – was generally responsible for religious administrative matters, including the administration of mosques, donations and Islamic religious education.[7] In theory the Ministry of Awqaf and the Syrian cabinet supervised Shi'i religious sites. In practice, Iran was also involved in the expansion and running of some of these places, in particular in terms of giving financial support.[8]

In the 1984 cultural agreement between Syria and Iran, tourism was included in Article 13, which called for working towards mutual understanding between the two peoples by way of encouraging and facilitating cultural and tourist travels, including the visits of holy sites in both countries.[9] Tourism came up frequently in bilateral meetings between high-ranking representatives of both states.[10]

Syrian Tourism to Iran, Iranian Tourism to Syria

In cultural diplomacy, tourism is a place where internal and external cultural policies meet. Countries use their representations and cultural centres abroad to promote tourism in their own country. Tourists are drawn to a country not only by its heritage but also by the cultural scene and living arts.[11] Exhibiting art and organising performances by artists of one's country abroad are staples of cultural diplomacy practice. They introduce a country's culture and might attract spectators to visit the country. Due to the specific nature of activities at both the Iranian cultural centre in Damascus and the Syrian cultural centre in Tehran, which were ideologically inspired, they did not encourage cultural tourism between the two sides. While the religious tourist industry from Iran to Syria was booming, conventional tourism between the two countries was in need of promotion.

In theory, both sides agreed to advertise tourism in each other's country, and called on each other to promote Iranian cultural tourism to Syria and Syrian tourism to Iran.[12] However, other than verbal agreements little promotion was made other than a number of Iranian tourism weeks in Syria,[13] Syrian tourism exhibitions in Iran and the participation at various fairs.[14]

To show the limits of these weeks, we will look at the 2008 Iran tourism week in Damascus, which took place in an exhibition room at the Meridien Hotel. The exhibitors offered Persian food samples, showed Iranian handicrafts, held a calligraphy workshop, promoted Iran tours, had a small exhibition of copies of Iranian antiquities, and put photos of Iranian tourist sites on display. Dolls dressed in traditional clothes were decorating the centre of the exhibition space, there was a well-stocked bookshop with books about Iran in Arabic, Persian and English, and a musical group was performing a traditional dance. The exhibitors had come from Iran for the occasion, except for the ones offering food samples who were running a restaurant in the Sayida Zaynab area, and were either independent or worked in one of the national museums or agencies, like Iran Air.[15] The fact that it was held at one of the large upmarket hotels of Damascus, an entirely secular venue that was accessible to all, suggests that Iran wanted to reach out to cultural tourists. Most of the attendees were those already familiar with Iran, however, including those involved with the Iranian cultural centre such as language students at the centre.

Syria occasionally made use of its cultural centre in Tehran to promote non-religious tourism to Syria. This translated largely to hanging posters of Syrian tourist sites at the centre, however, so was not far-reaching. In July 2008, the centre organised a Syrian Tourism Exhibition held at its premises, in which they showed pictures of Syrian handicrafts, tourist destinations and tourist activities. The aim was to expand Iranian tourism to Syria to include cultural tourism, not only religious tourism and the visit of holy shrines.[16] It is questionable what reach these activities had, as they barely connected with those that were not already interested in the other country. Neither country tried to promote itself on a large scale in the other country, by putting up an advertising campaign through posters, television adverts and the like. Thus tourism between Iran and Syria remained largely confined to a one-way religious tourism from Iran to Syria.

Religious Tourism

The purpose of religious tourism is a pilgrimage; the journey revolves around travelling to holy places for religious reasons. Due to the existence of numerous saints' tombs and holy places in the Middle East, the birthplace of monotheistic religions, pilgrimage has a strong presence in the region, and is a phenomenon shared by the different religions and confessions.[17] Islam has placed pilgrimage at the heart of its dogma, by making the hajj – the pilgrimage to Mecca – a religious duty.[18] For the Shi'i community, pilgrimage holds a special place and is central to their ritual practice. The visitation of the shrine cities of the Imams, located in Iraq, Iran and Saudi Arabia, is recommended to Shi'i believers.[19] The Twelver Shi'a doctrine is based on the belief that religious authority is passed on to the direct descendants of the Prophet Muhammad's daughter Fatima with Ali, the Prophet's cousin and son-in-law, who was the fourth caliph of Islam and first Shi'i Imam. The line continued until the twelfth imam, Imam al-Mahdi, went into occultation.

Buchta explains that the Shi'a believe that all imams – with the exception of the last one – died as martyrs. As such, they took part of human sin upon themselves, which in turn protects humankind from God's retribution; the martyrs act as mediators between God and humankind. As a sign of gratitude to the imams for taking the suffering upon themselves, believers can wail at their tombs or express readiness to die as martyrs themselves, at least symbolically.[20] This is one of the reasons why the visit of the tombs of the imams has been important to the Shi'a since early days. Shi'i rituals that have evolved over the centuries, such as the visitation of the shrines, were also intended to boost the position of the imams and their descendants as the focus of devotion for Shi'i believers. Among the shrines, those of Ali and his son Husayn – located in Najaf and Karbala respectively – are the most important.[21] Apart from the tombs of the imams, the shrines of the ahl al-bayt are also places of worship. Members of the family of the Prophet are considered examples of moral values and virtues.[22]

While the objective of a pilgrimage is religious in nature, it also has an economic and political dimension to it. Like in conventional tourism, pilgrimages have always been an occasion for trade fairs and commerce, and there is often a whole cluster of industry – including transportation, hotels and trade – involved in religious tourism. Politically, as pilgrimages are usually mass gatherings, they can be seen as places for political mobilisation and propaganda.[23] The gatherings can be used to spread messages and rally people. In the case of Syria and Iran, the political message was more connected to the scale and organisation of the pilgrimage rather than actual messages spread amongst the visitors. The mass pilgrimage of Iranian Shi'a to Syria did, however, influence the religious rituals of the Shi'i communities in Syria, and incorporated the latter in the religious framework of transnational Shi'ism.[24]

Heritage and Geopolitics

Heritage: Shared Islamic History and Shi'i Places of Interest in Syria

Heritage plays an important role in tourism in attracting visitors. A number of places of interest for the Shi'a are located in Syria. The presence in Syria of shrines of companions of the Prophet and members of the ahl al-bayt, the Prophet's family, is largely due to two events that play a crucial role in Shi'i history: the battle of Siffin and, more significantly, the battle of Karbala.

During Ali's caliphate (656–661), the first civil strife broke out between fractions of the divided Muslim community. Ali had been elected as fourth caliph in 656, an election that was contested amongst others by members of the Bani Umayya under the leadership of Mu'awiya, the cousin of the third caliph 'Uthman and powerful governor of the province of Syria. Ali was accused of not prosecuting 'Uthman's murderers and thus implicated in his murder. Mu'awiya's and Ali's armies met in the battle of Siffin, which took place in the summer of 657 near present-day Raqqa in north-east Syria. Ali subsequently lost much of his influence to Mu'awiya and was killed in 661 by one of his own former followers.[25]

Upon Ali's death, Mu'awiya took power and founded the Umayyad Dynasty. Hassan – Ali's eldest son – had concluded a contract with Mu'awiya recognising the latter's succession to the caliphate. His brother Husayn adhered to this contract until Hassan's death, after which he felt free to challenge the Umayyads. After Mu'awiya died in 680, Husayn – on the urging of his followers – seized the opportunity to confront Yazid, Mu'awiya's son and designated successor. However, he was overwhelmed by Umayyad forces at the plains of Karbala, and killed after ten days of siege that culminated in a bloody battle, in which Husayn's followers were by far outnumbered by Yazid's troops. The martyrdom of Husayn in Karbala in the year 680 was a seminal event for Shi'i Islam, and symbolically marked the split between Sunnis and the Shi'a. Husayn's head was brought as a trophy to Damascus, and some of his entourage who survived the massacre, such as his sister Zaynab and infant daughter Ruqayya, were taken along to Syria as prisoners.[26]

The mausoleum of Husayn's sister Zaynab, referred to as Sayida Zaynab, is the most important Shi'i shrine in Syria, and the focus of Shi'i pilgrimage to the country. It is located several kilometres southwest of Damascus, in what used to be a village called Rawiya. It is now a suburb of Damascus. After Karbala, Zaynab became a symbol of courage; she stood by her brother during the battle, and it was she who protected Husayn's son, Ali Zayn al-Abidin. There are different hypotheses where Zaynab was buried in the end. The shrine for Imam Husayn at the Umayyad Mosque in Damascus, which is believed to house his head that was brought to Damascus after the battle, is another main destination for Iranian pilgrims. As with Sayida Zaynab, similar confusion arises as to where Husayn's head was finally buried.[27] An Iranian guidebook for pilgrims to Syria notes that Husayn's head was hanged for three days in front of Yazid's palace on the latter's instruction, before being put in a corner in the Umayyad Mosque, where it stayed for several days.[28] What is important is that both places are recognised places of worship, dedicated to the two saints, regardless of whether they in fact contain their human remains or not.

Near the Umayyad Mosque is the shrine of Sayida Ruqayya, Husayn's daughter who died there as an infant. The story goes that the prisoners' caravan coming from Karbala came to rest in Damascus, next to Bab al-Faradis. Ruqayya, who was then only three or four years old, saw her father in a dream in the middle of the night and woke up; she cried and persistently asked for her father. Hearing her weeping, the rest of the group also started crying. From the sound of weeping, Yazid woke up and ordered the head of Imam Husayn to be placed close to her so that she would keep quiet. When Ruqayya saw her father's bloody head, she died after a couple of days of great sorrow and grief, and was buried in the same place where they had rested.[29]

Just outside of the Damascene city gate of Bab al-Saghir in the south-west of the old city lies the cemetery of the same name. A large number of companions of the Prophet, martyrs of Karbala, ahl al-bayt and other historical figures are buried in this graveyard. Amongst them are Husayn's sister Umm Kulthum, and his daughter Sukayna, two of the Prophet's wives (Umm Salama and Umm Habiba) and some of their children, as well as a mausoleum dedicated to the martyrs of Karbala, containing their heads.[30]

In Daraya, ten kilometres south-west of Damascus, is the shrine of Sukayna, the daughter of Imam Ali. This shrine was only rediscovered in the late 1980s, and has been added to the Iranian pilgrimage route. Thirty kilometres north of Damascus, in the town of 'Adhra, are the headless bodies of Hujr bin 'Adi and six of his friends. Hujr was a companion of the Prophet; he later fought with Ali in the battles of the Camel, Siffin and Nahravan and was in charge of parts of Ali's army. Hujr and his six companions were captured in Kufa by Mu'awiya's governor Ziad bin Abih, who sent them to Damascus where they were killed in Adhra, and their heads brought to Mu'awiya.[31]

Going north, Homs hosts the mausoleum of Abu Dharr al-Ghifari, one of the first converts to Islam and a companion of the Prophet.[32] In Hama, there is a mausoleum for Husayn's son Ali Zayn al-'Abidin; the shrine is not his tomb but was built to celebrate his passing.[33] Neither shrine is mentioned in the Iranian guidebook for pilgrims

Main Shi'i shrines in Syria.

Name of shrine	Location
Sayida Zaynab (sister of Imam Husayn)	Rawiya (Damascus suburb)
Imam Husayn (Umayyad Mosque)	Damascus
Sayida Ruqayya (daughter of Imam Husayn)	Damascus
Bab al-Saghir cementary: Umm Kulthum (sister of Imam Husayn) Sukayna (daughter of Imam Husayn) Umm Salama (wife of Prophet) Umm Habiba (wife of Prophet) Mausoleum dedicated to martyrs of Karbala	Damascus
Sukayna (daughter of Imam Husayn)	Daraya (Damascus suburb)
Hujr bin 'Adi (companion of the Prophet) and six of his friends	'Adhra (30km north of Damascus)
Abu Dharr al-Ghifari (companion of the Prophet)	Homs
Ali Zayn al-'Abidin	Hama
Al-nuqta/Mashhad al-Husyan	Aleppo
Al-saqt/Muhsin bin al-Husayn	Aleppo
Shahab al-Din Suhrawardi	Aleppo
Ammar bin Yasir (companion of the Prophet)	Raqqa
'Uways al-Qarani (companion of the Prophet)	Raqqa

to Syria, which suggests that they only carry minor importance for Iranian pilgrims.

There are two main pilgrimage sites for Shi'a in Aleppo, *al-nuqta* (the drop) and *al-saqt* (the fall). *Al-nuqta*, which is also called *mashhad al-husayn*, is a mausoleum built around a stone on which Husayn's head was placed on the way from Karbala to Damascus; several drops of blood fell on the stone. *Al-saqt* is a mausoleum dedicated to al-Muhsin bin al-Husayn. His mother had lost him during pregnancy, and called him Muhsin. Sayf al-Dawla al-Hamdani ordered the building of the mausoleum.[34] The story goes that one night in his dream, Sayf al-Dawla saw that light was rising into the air from one point of the city. Since dawn was imminent, he hurried to the said place.

After some digging, a stone emerged on which was written: 'This is the tomb of Muhsin bin al-Husayn bin Ali.' He then ordered a shrine to be built around it.[35] Another tomb of interest to Iranians, but maybe less on the traditional pilgrimage route, is the shrine of the philosopher Shahab al-Din Suhrawardi, who was born in Zanjan in 1155 and died in Aleppo in 1191.[36]

In Raqqa in the north-east of Syria are the mausoleums of Ammar bin Yasir and 'Uways al-Qarani, companions of the Prophet and loyal supporters of Ali. Both died in the battle of Siffin in 657, where they fought alongside Ali. The battle took place around 40 kilometres west of Raqqa; the numerous tombs scattered between Siffin and

Map of Syria with main locations of Shi'i shrines marked.[37]

Raqqa have been Shi'i pilgrimage destinations for centuries, but Raqqa never became home to a Shi'i community, and has only been added to the Iranian pilgrimage route after the Islamic Republic rebuilt the tombs of 'Ammar and 'Uways.[38]

Syria thus hosts a number of shrines of importance to the Shi'a. Ironically this is largely due to the fact that Syria was home to Mu'awiya and Yazid, the adversaries of Ali and Husayn. Most of the shrines house heroes of the battles of Siffin or Karbala, who either died in battle or were brought to Damascus as captives. These shrines have become the main destinations for Iranian religious tourism to Syria. Their presence in Syria is a result of the heritage and shared Islamic history between the Shi'i community and the lands of the Umayyads, even if both were positioned on opposing ends. The fact that the shrines are thus located in the land of Mu'awiya and Yazid does not deter Shi'i pilgrims from visiting these sites. However, as one Iranian friend in Syria remarked:

'Iranians are only friends with dead Arabs, they come here to visit dead Arabs: if it wasn't for the tombs, they would never come to Syria. Quite on the contrary, they would not like to come because of the Umayyads.'[39]

While he was joking when he said this, he was also half-serious about his statement, pointing to the underlying cultural divide between the two peoples. What brought about the large number of Iranian pilgrims visiting the shrines in Syria was more due to geopolitical reasons, which we will discuss in the following.

Geopolitics: Emergence of Iranian Religious Tourism to Syria

While Iranian pilgrims had come to Syria before the Islamic revolution in Iran, it was not until after the revolution and the outbreak of the Iran-Iraq War that the number of Iranian visitors increased drastically. The example of the Iranian Shi'i pilgrimage movement shows to what extent pilgrimage can be dependent on geopolitics. In theory, Iraq was the top destination for Shi'i pilgrims, as it hosted the two most important Shi'i tombs, the shrines of Imam Ali in Najaf and Imam

Husayn in Karbala. Other key destinations in Iraq were Kazimayn, where the seventh imam – Musa al-Kazim – was buried, and Samarra, which houses the tombs of the tenth and eleventh imams as well as a shrine indicating where the twelfth imam allegedly disappeared.[40]

Before the First World War, around 90 per cent of all foreign pilgrims to Iraq were Iranians, amounting to an annual average of 100,000.[41] The nature of Iranian pilgrimage to the shrine cities changed in the mid-1920s, and numbers were reduced following strained Iraqi-Iranian relations. Pilgrimage became dependent on the government policies of both Iran and Iraq. During most of the 1930s, 1940s and 1950s the Iranian government restricted pilgrimage to the shrine cities, a process that had begun under Reza Shah in the 1920s. After Saddam Hussein had come to power in Iraq, Iranian pilgrims were not allowed to visit the shrine cities during much of the 1970s and the Iran-Iraq War in the 1980s.[42] Even after the end of the war in 1988, Iraq remained mainly off-limits for Iranian pilgrims; Saddam, who suppressed his own Shi'i population and had banned large religious gatherings like the commemoration of Husayn's martyrdom, certainly did not welcome his Iranian neighbours.[43]

Syria largely came into the picture as a religious tourist destination after the Islamic revolution in Iran. While there had been a constant traffic of Iranian pilgrims to the shrines of Sayida Zaynab and Ruqayya since at least the 1950s, often en route to Mecca, they did not amount to great numbers until the early 1980s. As Syria and Iran formed a close partnership following the revolution, this was soon reflected in religious tourism as Iranian pilgrims were diverted to Syria. As Pinto notes, the Shi'i shrines in Syria 'became the target of a joint political, economic, and symbolic investment of the Syrian and Iranian regimes, which, despite having very different approaches to religious identities and practices, had an interest in promoting pilgrimage as a religious dimension of their strategic alliance.[44] The construction of the shrine complexes in Raqqa is a good example of this geopolitical collaboration – it affirms Syria's ties to Iran by allowing the Islamic Republic to extend its religious territory across Syria.[45]

Chiffoleau and Madeouf suggest that Shi'i pilgrimage is so dependent on geopolitical factors that whereas Syria may have been favoured as a destination after Iraq was made inaccessible to Iranian pilgrims during much of Saddam Hussein's rule, this could turn around once Iraq's holy cities were reopened.[46] To this effect, Vali Nasr observes how Iranian pilgrims poured into Karbala after the fall of Saddam:

> 'As soon as Saddam Hussein's regime was crushed in the spring of 2003, tens of thousand of Iranians, many poor and elderly women with nothing more than a black cloth covering their heads and small bundles of food in their hands, walked across the Iran-Iraq border, traversed minefields, and made their way through the desolate landscape of southern Iraq to visit the shrine of Imam Husayn in Karbala, which Saddam had for years barred to Iranian pilgrims.'[47]

However, while Iranian pilgrimage to the shrine cities in Iraq certainly picked up, this did not seem to have affected the number of pilgrims visiting Syria after 2003.[48] Travelling to Syria was attractive to a certain type of Iranian tourists as it was cheap and could be combined with trade.

Iranian Involvement in Syrian Religious Sites

Pre-Revolutionary Involvement

Even before the Islamic revolution and the redirection of Iranian pilgrims to Syria for geopolitical reasons, Iranians had been coming to Syria to visit the shrines of the ahl al-bayt in and around Damascus, often en route to perform the hajj, the pilgrimage to Mecca. In particular starting in the 1950s, as road infrastructure improved and transport was facilitated, the number of Iranian pilgrims visiting the shrines of Sayida Zaynab and Ruqayya increased.

In a letter from the Iranian embassy in Damascus to the Shah's private office, written in 1954, the Minister Plenipotentiary explained the situation. Sayida Zaynab, he wrote, was until recently a very small and neglected village around ten kilometres outside Damascus. However, after the efforts of some Syrian Shi'a who were influential in government circles, as well as actions taken by the Iranian representation, the Syrian state had put asphalt on the road leading to the village of al-Sitt (the Lady) – as Sayida Zaynab was referred to. Since then, every day the numbers of Syrian as well as Iranian visitors increased, and more attention was paid to the shrine.[49] The renovation of the shrine of Sayida Zaynab had in fact begun in 1952, under the supervision of the Murtada family.[50] The Murtada family has held the responsibility for Sayida Zaynab's mausoleum and lands since the fourteenth century.[51]

Whereas the shrine complex's renovation was in Syrian hands, Iranians gave generously, largely through mediation by an Iraqi called Hajj Behbahani. They donated mostly on an individual basis, but included the Shah and his wife.[52] In a letter to the Iranian embassy dated February 1955, Behbahani informs the embassy that with the help of Iranian Shi'a and under the special auspices of the servants of His Imperial Majesty and the voluntary donation of Queen Soraya Pahlavi, the expenses of the lighting of the courtyard and the mausoleum had been guaranteed.[53] There was a steady exchange of letters between Hajj Behbahani, the Iranian embassy in Damascus, individual donors and the Shah's Office in Tehran.[54] This shows that while the Iranian state as such made no donation to Zaynab's shrine, the Iranian embassy coordinated the efforts and worked closely with Behbahani. Even the Shah's wife had given money to improve the mausoleum; it is possible that she liked the idea of donating to a female saint. It has also been suggested that the money for the shrine's renovation was sent from Qom directly to Muhsin al-Amin, the *marja* of the Syrian Shi'a.[55] This implies a channel of communication parallel to the official route through the Iranian embassy.

Iranians were donating not only money, but also goods. The amount of objects was such that the Syrian awqaf administration requested the Iranian embassy to demand of Iranians who wanted to donate goods to the shrines of Sayida Zaynab and Ruqayya to register these with the Ministry of Awqaf, to prevent embezzlement.[56] Iranians offered carpets in particular,[57] but also other objects. The embellishment of the dome of Sayida Zaynab in 1965 for instance was a gift of a Hajj Qasem Hamdani.[58] In 1960, an Iranian businessman offered a golden door, which was put on the Western entrance to the sanctuary.[59]

The inlaid box for the tomb of Sayida Zaynab was donated by the Iranian people and built by an Iranian artist, Sani'a Khatem, who also built the tombs for the shrines of the Imams in Iraq.[60] Iranians also gave a golden chest for the shrine of Sayida Ruqayya.[61] These donations contributed to the shrines gradually acquiring a more Iranian-style architectural character.[62] While these donations came mostly from the Iranian people and not the state as such, much of the correspondence went through the Iranian embassy in Damascus.

However, things were not all rosy. In 1957, the Iranian ambassador to Syria lodged complaints to the Syrian Prime Minister's office about the shrine of Sayida Ruqayya. Many Iranians came to Syria to visit the tombs of the ahl al-bayt such as the tomb of Sayida Ruqayya, he wrote, but most of those visitors complained to the embassy about the treatment they received by the caretakers of the tomb. Moreover, visiting times and thus the performance of religious rituals were restricted, and the courtyard of the mausoleum should be widened to facilitate access to the shrine. He had already written to the general awqaf administration, but to no avail. He requested the Syrian state to give directions to the awqaf administration to appoint new caretakers to the shrine, and open daily from 5 a.m. until 10 p.m., so that visitors could easily complete their prayer duties; the tomb should not just be opened for prayer times but also throughout the day to perform other religious rituals. The neighbouring house, which the general awqaf administration had already pulled down, should quickly be added as a courtyard to widen the complex. Lastly, electricity to the shrine should be provided from evening until morning.[63] They also wanted a hall to be built for Ruqayya's new tomb that Iranians were donating.[64] The Syrians were cooperative. The Prime Minister's office forwarded the requests to the awqaf administration, which accommodated most of their wishes; in return, they requested some money to help towards enlarging the courtyard although they had at first agreed to pay for it themselves.[65]

The repeated complaints show that Iranian pilgrims coming to Syria did not always feel well treated by the host country, but were not shy to speak up for themselves to demand more services. We mentioned above that it is important that visitors see their own cultures being cared for and respected. Here, Iranian pilgrims felt restricted in carrying out their religious rituals at a tomb that they considered also part of their own heritage. The Syrian side did take the complaints seriously and acted upon them. Two decades later, after Hafiz al-Asad assumed the presidency in Syria, Syria had another motivation to support the shrine's restoration. In 1974, Syrian president Hafiz al-Asad signed a document purchasing 23 properties around Sayida Ruqayya to expand the shrine – it has been suggested that this took place within the framework of an Alawi-Shi'i rapprochement starting in the 1970s.[66]

We have seen that Iranian involvement in Syrian religious sites pre-1979 emanated largely from Iranian individuals, who often acted through the mediation of Iranian institutions such as the embassy, but of their own initiative. As relations warmed up in the early 1970s, the state got more involved. An agreement was concluded in 1973 between the authorities of both countries to renovate the shrine of Sayida Zaynab, for which Iran would give 10 million tuman in view of its 'special relationship with the ahl al-bayt'.[67] It is likely that this agreement was only implemented in 1979, coinciding with the

The shrine of Sayida Zaynab. Syria, 23 December 2005.

revolution and renewed restoration plans.[68] The degree of Iranian involvement largely reflected the state of bilateral relations between Syria and Iran – before the revolution relations were stronger on an individual level than on a state-to-state level. What has become clear is that Iranians were pushing for an enlargement and improvement of pilgrimage facilities long before the revolution and the rapid increase in numbers of visitors. Following the 1979 revolution, the Iranian state itself became more involved.

Post-Revolutionary Involvement

In 1979, the shrine complex of Sayida Zaynab was further expanded. A committee headed by the Murtadas bought several neighbouring lands, under recommendation from the Ministry of Awqaf, and allocated the budget to start the expansion project.[69] Pinto maintains that the building of the mosque-mausoleum complex was largely sponsored by the Iranian government.[70] There is no mention of Iran on the official Syrian Ministry of Tourism website with respect to Sayida Zaynab's restoration, however – the Syrians do not like to advertise Iran's involvement, as the majority of Syrians remain wary of Iran's interests.

While Iran contributed to the renovation of Sayida Zaynab, it was responsible for the restoration and enlargement of the mausolem of Sayida Ruqayya, albeit in cooperation with the Syrian Ministry of Awqaf.[71] To do so, an old quarter had been erased, which met with the disapproval of the inhabitants of the old town. Mervin points out that the Iranian appropriation of Sayida Ruqayya was the result of an agreement between the Syrian and Iranian states, in fact depriving the Syrian Shi'a of the shrine.[72] Since its latest renovations, Sayida Ruqayya's mausoleum has acquired an Iranian character with its ornamental dome and architectural layout. Tabbaa suggests that as late as 1970 the shrine of Sayida Ruqayya was little known.[73] The correspondence between the Iranian embassy and Syrian authorities cited above, however, demonstrates that at least since the 1950s the shrine was clearly a pilgrimage destination, and that Iranians were donating objects to the mausoleum and pushing for its enlargement. This shows that while it is true that Iran became involved in Syrian religious sites on a much larger scale following the 1979 revolution, and numbers of Iranian pilgrims to Syria increased manifold, the choice of Syria as a destination for Iranian religious tourism is based on an existent devotion to the shrines present on Syrian soil, which has been exploited by the Iranian and Syrian governments for political reasons post-1979.

The case of Raqqa shows how religious tourism can play an important symbolic role. Whereas the shrines of Sayida Zaynab and Ruqayya had been Iranian pilgrimage sites before the revolution, the mausoleums of Raqqa only emerged as a destination for Iranian pilgrims in the 1990s. They have become part of an organised Iranian pilgrimage route. The work on the mausoleums of the Prophet's companions 'Uways al-Qarani and 'Ammar bin Yasir, as well as a smaller one dedicated to the Prophet's secretary, had started in 1988. The construction was at least partly financed by Iran.[74] Work was interrupted between 1994 and 2001 – apparently due to Iranian financial problems – and only completed in 2005.[75] The architectural style is typically Iranian and stands out from its surroundings. Since their completion, the shrines cater to Iranian pilgrims who are being brought there by bus from Aleppo for half-day trips. Ababsa explains that the new mausoleums are largely ignored by the local authorities and population who had previously used them for local rituals and practices.[76] Instead, they have become a symbol of Syrian-Iranian cooperation: for Syria, they serve as a political symbol of their close ties to Iran; for Iran, they represent a manifestation of Shi'i presence in Syria.[77]

In the same vein, a new project was officially announced in 2004: the *mawqib al-sabaya* (procession of captives), in which all places on which Husayn's head had rested or lost a drop of blood on the way from Karbala to Damascus in 680 were to be marked, and a pilgrimage route established alongside it. Some shrines already existed on that itinerary, most notably the *mashhad al-husayn* in Aleppo, but Iran wanted to mark the whole route to extend its reach into Syria.[78]

Interaction and Trade

Having discussed how Iranian religious tourism to Syria emerged, and what sites were of interest to the pilgrims, we will turn to the actors

Tourist Entries to Syria (2000–2010).

	2000	2001	2002	2003	2004	2005	2006	2007	2008	2009	2010
Iranians	221,380	216,542	310,839	213,913	196,699	247,662	250,076	304,956	333,789	430,588	792,258
Non-Arab tourists	578,679	562,722	663,700	541,786	683,933	858,992	892,397	965,397	1,160,433	1,436,679	2,378,260
% of non-Arab tourists	38	38	47	39	29	29	28	32	29	30	33

Source: Syrian Ministry of Tourism, www.syriatourism.org

and infrastructure. Who were the actors in Iranian religious tourism to Syria? What were the services provided to religious tourists, and who provided them? To what extent did tourism create a space for interaction between Iranians and Syrians? How did Iranians experience the country they visited? How did Syrians perceive their Iranian visitors?

Actors and Infrastructure for Iranian Religious Tourists in Syria

The actors were first of all the tourists themselves. Iranians came to Syria in their hundreds of thousands every year, the largest number of non-Arab visitors Syria received. The vast majority came for religious tourism, which they often combined with trade or personal shopping. Of over 360,000 Iranians coming to Syria in 2008, more than 333,000 were tourists, according to official statistics.[79] The main point of entry for Iranians into Syria was the Salama border crossing (north of Aleppo) from Turkey, followed by Damascus Airport, and the Jdeideh border crossing from Lebanon.[80] The number of Iranian tourists entering Syria has steadily risen over the last ten years, constituting an average of 34 per cent of non-Arab tourist entries to Syria between 2001 and 2010.[81] Unofficial numbers place the number of Iranian tourists even higher than the official numbers.[82] Overall non-Arab tourist entries to Syria quadrupled between 2000 and 2010 – the largest increase could be seen in Turkish tourists, from just over 9,000 in the year 2000 to nearly 865,000 in 2010, following the drastic improvement of bilateral relations between Turkey and Syria during the 2000s.[83] Numbers for 2011 and 2012 are not yet available, but a huge drop can be expected. However, Iranians have been some of the few nationalities that continued to come to Syria following the beginning of the crisis.

The main destination for these Iranian tourists was the shrine of Sayida Zaynab, followed by that of Sayida Ruqayya and Imam Husayn's head in the Umayyad Mosque. Raqqa was integrated into the pilgrims' route, but was not a prime destination. To visit Raqqa, religious tourists came either on a three day tour from Sayida Zaynab, going to Homs, Aleppo, and from there to Raqqa before returning to Damascus,[84] or they visited the shrines in Raqqa from Aleppo, en route on their way from Turkey to Sayida Zaynab by bus.

In the early 1980s, to boost Iranian religious tourism to Syria as bilateral relations were expanding, both states supported the pilgrimage from Iran to Syria by facilitating visa requirements and subsidising journeys.[85] Even in cases where pilgrims had to pay for their trips themselves, Syria was still a cheaper and easier option than travelling to places such as Mecca in Saudi Arabia. As Mervin has termed it, visiting the shrine of Sayida Zaynab in the outskirts of Damascus was a 'pilgrimage of the poor' (hajj al-fuqara').[86] In the 1980s, many of the Iranian pilgrims to Syria were mothers or widows of those who had fallen in the Iran-Iraq war, who received a sponsored journey to Damascus from Iran's Martyr's Foundation.[87] Up until 2011, women continued to make up a large number of the Iranian pilgrims coming to Syria. They visited the shrines of Sayida Zaynab and Ruqayya, seeking 'the intercession of these female saints for various familial problems, including marriage, conception and cure.'[88] The pilgrimage to Syria was often the first time these women travelled outside Iran; the journey allowed them to experience a new place and engage in commerce, while being reassured by the presence of their fellow travellers and the infrastructure set out for them.[89]

So what did this infrastructure consist of and who provided it? Iranian pilgrims usually travelled in groups to Syria; the whole trip was organised for the group, including not only transportation and accommodation but also all meals. They stayed in hotels that catered for pilgrims, where employees often spoke Persian, and were being taken care of by tour operators, travel agents or private mediators. The hotels were concentrated in specific areas, such as the area around Martyr's Square in central Damascus, or generally the Sayida Zaynab region. The majority came by bus through Turkey, others flew by plane directly to Damascus. Apart from the two national carriers, Iran Air and Syria Air, which had two to three weekly flights each between Tehran and Damascus, there were a number of Iranian charter planes catering for religious tourists; they used the pilgrimage terminal in Damascus and only exceptionally took on non-pilgrims as passengers.[90] In 2001, rail service between Iran and Syria was resumed after it had been suspended in 1982 during the Iran-Iraq war. The service, which ran once a week from Damascus to Tehran via Turkey, was restarted in order to further encourage religious tourism between the two countries at a time of increased interaction.[91] The train was a cheaper option than flying and faster than taking the bus. The rail service was again interrupted in April 2011 following the general suspension of rail travel in Syria.

There were a large number of bus companies catering for Iranian pilgrims, both Syrian and Iranian. One only needed to walk along Malik Faysal Road in central Damascus to get an idea about some of the bus agencies. One bus after the other was lined up on that road, the closest point of access by bus to the shrine of Sayida Ruqayya. Until the mid-1990s, there was only one tour operator that was allowed to take pilgrims to the site of Sayida Zaynab: Transtour, the tourist agency of Saeb Nahas.[92] Nahas, a Shi'a and one of Syria's most prolific businessmen, maintained close ties to Iran and was founder and head of a 'Commission of economic coordination between Syria and Iran'. This commission was created in 1988 with the aim of building a large hotel complex close to Sayida Zaynab. Nahas was in fact behind much of the hotel and commercial development of the Sayida Zaynab area.[93] The Nahas Group and Transtour ran the hotel Safir al-Sayida Zaynab, for instance, provided services to pilgrims and generally took care of matters concerning the welfare of the shrine's visitors – services that were largely lacking in an organised manner.[94]

Until the onset of the crisis in 2011, around 30,000 visitors came to the mausoleum of Sayida Zaynab every day, which called for the provision of adequate services in order to avoid chaos – which apparently had been prevalent in the shrine areas. In 2005 negotiations had taken place to further widen and renew the mausoleum complex, and offer more services to the pilgrims; for this purpose, the president had issued a decision to appropriate the area neighbouring the shrine.[95] In 2009, the situation did not seem to have improved a lot, however. Travel agents in the Sayida Zaynab region complained about electricity cuts, lack of water and dirtiness, buses waiting around and blocking the roads here and there, and the popular markets that ruined the view. In particular as religious tourism represents more than one-fifth of tourism to Syria, religious areas should be invested in and more services provided, travel agents maintained. According to one tourist agency close to Zaynab's shrine, many of the hotel owners in the area were 'peasants who lacked all kind of experience in dealing with tourists'; many of the hotels were licensed as buildings and not as hotels, and thus avoided having to meet certain standards.[96] Tourist agencies furthermore complained that transport agencies were taking their customers, by providing accommodation and food in addition to transport. Even worse in their view was that ordinary people without any agency behind them were organising tourist groups from Iran and Iraq; they only needed to have friends in these two countries and then rent buses and hotels without taking official permission or paying taxes.[97] Cooks, who took care of pilgrims' meals, were sometimes brought from Iran with the groups; otherwise members of the group took care of cooking.[98]

Hajj Khanum fell into the category of individuals taking the initiative to organise groups from Iran. The Iranian anthropologist Fariba Adelkhah, who joined a bus tour to Damascus from Tehran, described her case. The wife of a grocer, Hajj Khanum recruited people for the pilgrimage to Damascus (and other trips) during religious meetings she organised at her house, or by word-of-mouth. She worked together with a travel agency through which she obtained Syrian visas for her group; she either organised the trip herself, renting a bus and taking care of her group, or brought people to the travel agency and got free seats in return. Adelkhah's trip, which met the second profile, was Hajj Khanum's seventeenth journey to Damascus. During the trip, she engaged in commerce, buying all kinds of products that she sold in Iran upon her return.[99] She was not alone in this trade – the majority of Iranian religious tourists divided their time between visiting the shrines, selling goods they brought from Iran, and going shopping. The latter was facilitated by the merchants in the markets surrounding the shrines.

Trade

'In Damascus old town, it is common to hear vendors using Farsi as they welcome Iranian customers and bargain over Syrian-made

Iranians shopping close to the shrine of Sayida Ruqayya. Damascus, August 2010.

clothes and lingerie. Some shops have Farsi on their signs and sellers usually accept the Iranian rial.'[100]

Walking around the small alleys surrounding the shrine of Sayida Ruqayya in the old town of Damascus, one felt as if one were in an Iranian bazaar. 'Come here, come here, two tuman, two tuman', vendors shouted out in Persian to the Iranian crowds passing, trying to attract their attention. They offered clothes, scarves, tablecloths, sweets, dolls, toys, shoes and other goods, haggled with the pilgrims in Persian and accepted the Iranian currency.

Around the corner, in Souq al-Hamidiya, the Damascus main market thoroughfare, the same scene was unfolding. Merchants were quick to spot their customers, and swift in approaching them in a language familiar to them. They called out in Persian to the Chador-clad ladies and Iranian-style veiled girls, while saying 'welcome, welcome, look here' to Europeans passing. Many businesses in the market relied on Iranian tourists. While the Iranian pilgrims bought mostly cheap products, and knew how to drive the prices down, their sheer numbers and willingness to buy made them attractive and consistent consumers.[101] Some acted as traders, buying goods in Syria that they then sold with a profit back in Iran, often financing their pilgrimage in this way. Others simply bought souvenirs to bring back to their family and friends.

Pilgrims, who both sold goods they brought from their home countries and bought goods they sold upon their return, dominated the market around the shrine of Sayida Zaynab. The merchants of Damascus came to the shrine area to buy Iranian carpets and pistachios from the pilgrims.[102] The pilgrims-cum-traders occupied a particular place in the Syrian-Iranian economic exchange: according to a Syrian importer who worked with Iran, it was difficult to trade in certain commodities as the pilgrims controlled part of the market through their informal exchanges.[103] The Syrian Shi'i shrine areas also attracted a large number of vendors selling religious commodities, such as religious texts, key-chains in the shape of the sword of Ali and mosque-shaped alarm clocks.[104]

Iranian tourist groups in Souq al-Hamidiya. Damascus, August 2010.

Interaction and Perceptions

When Iranian pilgrims first started to arrive in Syria in large groups in the early 1980s, interaction between Iranians and Syrians was very limited. There was little love lost between Syrians and the religious tourists, often revolutionary activists remunerated for their services, or mothers and widows of victims of the Iran-Iraq war. Several clashes occurred over differences in ideology. According to some accounts, for instance, Iranian tourists attempted to put up posters of Ayatollah Khomeini and religious slogans at Damascus airport upon their arrival; the Syrian police had to stop them by force.[105] The efforts of some to propagate Iran's revolutionary ideology was a headache for the Syrian authorities, who tried to keep the tourists separate – which did not help in bringing the two peoples together.[106] The Iranians protested against their accommodation in Damascus, complaining that the hotel bars should be shut down and requesting that female staff wore chadors.[107] To avoid further conflict, Iranian tourists soon stayed at hotels designated entirely for them.

Ali Montazeri, Iranian cultural attaché to Syria in the early 2000s, explains that at the beginning, there was very little interaction between Syrians and Iranians. With time, however, Syrians got used to the presence of the Iranians, and to their language. In the end, the language and traditions became familiar. And Syria is very familiar to Iranians from certain circles: there are many Iranians who have never travelled anywhere, have never been to Europe or even Mecca, but they have often been to Damascus.[108] Adelkhah describes how the traffic of pilgrims between Tehran and Damascus was so high that pilgrims remained in an environment familiar to them, as on the one hand many Iranians had settled along the main stops of the route, to engage in commerce, and on the other hand the local people (Turks and Syrians) had learned sufficient Persian to communicate with the pilgrims. Often pilgrims ate Iranian food throughout, and saw pictures of Iran's former and current revolutionary leader on hotel walls.[109]

Iranian pilgrims felt at ease in Syria. The following two accounts illustrate this feeling of comfort:

'The busy historic market of Damascus is a familiar sight for Siya Shahidi. The Iranian housewife and mother of three has

Persian and Arabic language sign for women's entry and exit to Sayida Ruqayya's shrine, and pilgrims in front of the entrance to the shrine. Damascus, December 2005.

been coming here from Tehran at least twice a year for years
with her family to shop and visit holy sites. "When I walk in
this market, it feels like walking in Tehran," said Shahidi [. . .].
Shahidi, who considers Damascus "the cheapest and closest city"
to Tehran, is one of hundred of thousands of Iranians who visit
Syria every year for religious tourism, recreation or business.'[110]
'The first thing you notice about the Iranian women waddling
around Damascus markets in black-clad two- or three-somes is
how happy they are, and how in their own element. There is none
of the anxieties of a new traveller in a foreign country, none of
the self-consciousness of invading a place to which one does not
belong, no unease about the absence of a common language.'[111]

Pilgrims moved in an Iranian sphere, communicating in their own language and relying on a network of services catering for them. Signposts
at the mosques and shrines frequented by Iranians were written in
Persian in addition to Arabic. The pilgrims seemed to take for granted
that everyone around them spoke their language. Watching the crowds
in front of the Umayyad Mosque in Damascus, an Iranian pilgrim
standing next to me turned and asked me something in Persian.
When I replied to her in Persian she showed no reaction to the fact
that I had understood her; it was normal for her.[112] Adelkhah notes
that a number of pilgrims had no concept of 'Syria' or 'Damascus', but
knew that they were travelling to 'the shrine of Sayida Zaynab'.[113] For
some, geography was defined by religion, which traversed national
borders.

Iranian pilgrims were easily recognisable; they generally stayed in
groups or families. Women were mostly dressed in black or flowery
chadors; some – especially younger girls – dressed in *manteau* (knee-
length coat) and *rusari* (headscarf). There were few all-male groups,
so the women usually gave them away as Iranians. In and around
Damascus the Iranians dominated some market areas through their
sheer numbers. Ababsa maintains that in Raqqa they were discreet –
though still easily recognisable. They came mainly to the shrine of
'Ammar bin Yasir, where they prayed and attached green straps of fabric
on the silver fence surrounding the tomb while making a wish.[114]

Iranian tourists walking in the old town of Damascus. Damascus, December 2005.

While Iranian tourists felt at ease in Syria, their presence did not improve interaction between the two peoples or perceptions the two had of each other. Whereas the two sides did not clash anymore as they did at times during the 1980s, at a time when Iran was still trying to export its revolution, Syrians without professional interest in Iran or in the pilgrims stayed clear. And as Iranians barely left the sphere mapped out for them, interaction between the two sides remained very limited. The main interaction took place between the pilgrims and those working in the tourist industry, as well as the shopkeepers in the markets. While Iranians constituted a consistent customer base, one worth learning Persian for, this did not translate into any particular affinity. Some of the shopkeepers in old Damascus mocked the pilgrims, calling them 'black bag' (*kis aswad*) – referring to the women's dress.[115] Syrians moreover got the impression that all Iranians were just like the pilgrims who came to their country, while the latter represented a conservative and traditional segment of society that was not characteristic of Iran as a whole. Tourists mostly came from rural Iran, and often from conservative provinces such as Isfahan.

Iranian tourists were thus rather counterproductive in terms of advertising for their own country in terms of cultural diplomacy. Their own experience of Syria was largely positive, however, and judging by the yearly numbers of Iranian tourists coming to Damascus, they spread the word about their travels upon return – a good sign for cultural diplomacy. The only drawback there is that it is not clear to what extent they associated their trip with Syria as such. Some of the evidence we have discussed implies that they were in fact oblivious of the country they were in. While they enjoyed their journey, prayed at the shrines and profited from the markets, they remained in their own world.

Non-pious Iranian visitors, who at times ended up staying in the same hotels as pilgrims, could have mixed experiences in Syria, obtaining a very different impression of the country than non-Iranian tourists. The story of one Iranian-Italian student who came to Damascus on a university trip illustrates this point:

'Several years ago I spent one semester at Tehran University, studying archaeology. The university organised a trip to Syria for all the students of my class. We went to Damascus by bus through Turkey, sleeping either in the bus or in parks along the way. In Damascus, we stayed in a very basic hotel near Sayida Zaynab. Most of the students were disappointed and got a bad impression of Syria. They thought they were going on a trip outside Iran, they wanted to go out dancing and enjoy themselves for a bit, but here they were having to visit holy shrines. In our free time we were encouraged to go shopping.'[116]

Iranians visiting Syria and staying at hotels frequented by their compatriots were not entirely independent but watched by the Iranian community and expected to behave as though they were in Iran. One Iranian girl visiting Damascus in order to apply to the Canadian Embassy for immigration – the Canadian embassies in Syria and Turkey were the two main contacts for dealing with Iranian immigration issues until all immigration affairs were moved to Turkey in 2011 – was told to wear her headscarf in the hotel, for instance, after she had removed it believing she was out of Iran and thus no longer obliged to adhere to its rules.[117] Even Iranians who came to Syria inde-pendently were thus often not able to leave the sphere created for them by the two governments' strong relationship.

Conclusion

To what extent has tourism contributed to the strengthening of bilateral relations between Syria and Iran? As we have seen, tourism between the two countries was largely confined to Iranian religious tourism to Syria. Efforts on both sides to extend the industry to non-religious tourism going both ways have been weak so far. We will go back to the three main points mentioned above, that is tourism enabling visitors to experience another country and interact with the local population, tourism drawing on heritage and geopolitics to attract visitors, and tourism encouraging trade.

As for the first and most important in terms of fostering relations between the two peoples, we can say that Iranian religious tourism to Syria did not encourage interaction between Iranians and the local population, except for those involved in the tourist industry and trade, as Iranians largely stayed on a route drawn out for and by them. Nevertheless, it did accustom Syrians to Iranians – they subconsciously learned about the other's customs and traditions by observing them in the shared markets. This was not the best advertisement for Iran, however, as the pilgrims were generally from lower classes, traditional and religious, and conveyed the impression that all Iranians were like them – which did not persuade many Syrians to visit Iran.

As for heritage and geopolitics, both played an important part in the Syrian-Iranian exchange. The presence of Shiʻi shrines in Syria was largely the result of shared Islamic history. The fact that the shrines were located in Syria because it was the capital of Muʻawiya and Yazid, the main adversaries of Ali and Husayn, did not deter Shiʻi pilgrims from visiting the sites. As the main shrines in Iraq had for a long time been inaccessible to Iranian pilgrims, and bilateral relations between Syria and Iran grew strong, the pilgrimage was diverted to Syria in the early 1980s, but had existed on a much smaller scale in the preceding decades.

The trip to Syria gave Iranians who otherwise had little opportunity and means the chance to travel. One reason for this was the strong connection between pilgrimage and trade in the Syrian-Iranian case. The vast majority of Iranian pilgrims in Syria combined the visitation of the shrines with shopping; those with a business sense also brought goods from Iran that they sold upon their arrival in Syria. Trade with the Iranians encouraged Syrian merchants in the shrine areas to learn Persian, and provided one of the main forums of interaction between the two peoples – albeit an interaction limited to the buying and selling of goods. While tourism in the Syrian-Iranian case thus offered only a limited opportunity to foster relations on the popular level, it provided the most visible manifestation of Iran in Syria. As such, following the start of the Syria crisis it exposed a number of Iranian pilgrims to kidnappings by Syrian opposition forces who wanted to put pressure on the Iranian state.[118]

CONCLUSION

CULTURAL DIPLOMACY, SOFT POWER AND THE SYRIA-IRAN AXIS

It has emerged that cultural relations between Syria and Iran largely took place on the official level, promoted by the two governments, and had limited reach on the popular level. Having established a historical narrative of cultural diplomacy between Syria and Iran, both continuity and change could be observed. Cultural diplomacy between the two countries in its current form, having gradually developed starting in the early 1980s, did not emerge out of a void. The 1984 cultural agreement, the basis for subsequent bilateral cultural exchange, closely resembled the pre-revolutionary agreement of 1975. This earlier agreement had largely been neglected due to lack of motivation and resources on both sides. Cultural diplomacy between Syria and Imperial Iran was dependent on enthused individuals who were constrained in their work by lack of institutional support. Except for sporadic visits to Iran by Syrian academics, it played out in Syria, where the Iranian cultural attaché based at the Iranian embassy organised a number of film screenings and exhibitions, and got involved in Persian language teaching at the Arabic faculties of Damascus and Aleppo University. It did not seem to have had an impact on the Syrian cultural scene, and Iran had problems attracting Syrian students to take up graduate studies in Iran.

Following the Iranian revolution, Iran continued to be the driver in pushing for greater cooperation on the cultural level, with the difference that – unlike Imperial Iran – the Islamic Republic did not spare efforts and resources for its cultural endeavours in Syria. The cultural centre set up by the Ministry of Culture and Islamic Guidance in 1983 had all the financial support and human resources it needed. Syria continued to remain largely passive in its own cultural diplomacy work, mainly cooperating with the Islamic Republic in the latter's activities but not taking an initiative of its own. This only changed as late as 2005, when it set up its own cultural centre in Tehran. However, the centre suffered from the same constraints as Imperial Iran's cultural efforts, in that it lacked resources and motivation, showing the low priority given to cultural diplomacy by the Syrian side.

Continuity was also visible in Iran's involvement in Syrian Shi'i shrines. While the number of Iranian pilgrims visiting shrines in Syria had increased dramatically since the early 1980s, Syria had existed as an Iranian pilgrimage destination before the revolution, in particular from the 1950s onwards when road infrastructure and transport facilities to the Syrian shrines improved. Throughout the 1950s, 1960s and 1970s Iranians donated generously to the shrines of Sayida Zaynab and Sayida Ruqayya. While the number of pre-revolutionary Iranian tourists to Syria cannot be compared with the hundreds of thousands of annual visitors in the years before the Syrian uprising, it was substantial enough for the Iranian embassy in Damascus to lodge complaints about the lack of adequate facilities provided to its nationals. Iranian religious tourism to Syria thus did not develop out of nothing in the early 1980s when the Iran-Iraq war prevented Iranian Shi'a from going on pilgrimage to Iraq, but was based on a genuine interest in the Shi'i shrines on Syrian soil.

Looking at Syrian-Iranian cultural diplomacy through formal representative structures has demonstrated that both sides were engaged in building bridges between the two peoples, although Syria only half-heartedly and both within the official framework of their relationship. The Iranian cultural centre in Damascus has been trying to promote its culture and Islamic values to the Syrian people since its inception in the 1980s. While its publications, cultural weeks, seminars and conferences did find an audience in Syria, its reach was mainly confined to those that already had an interest in Iran and the religious culture promoted by the Islamic Republic. It was largely the Syrian Shi'i community that frequented the Iranian cultural centre, and others who saw opportunities to work in the bilateral field or were simply interested. The majority of cultural players and intellectuals generally stayed clear of the centre and its activities, unless people were involved with an institution that cooperated with the Iranian side out of professional interests against the background of the political relationship between Syria and Iran.

The Syrians opened their cultural centre in Tehran more for symbolic reasons than out of a true desire to build bridges between the Syrian and Iranian peoples. The ideological content promoted by Syria in Iran, mainly focusing on resistance against Israel and anti-imperialism, went largely unnoticed. Having a low profile in Iran and mostly known to those with a connection to Arabic language departments at Iranian universities or institutions the Syrian centre cooperated with in Iran, the Syrian cultural centre was appreciated for its Arabic language teaching. Although the Syrian centre had the potential to be a bridge between Iran and the Arab world, as it offered a product one segment of the Iranian population was genuinely interested in – the Arabic language – it made little out of this opportunity.

One group the cultural exchange did reach were students. It is nothing new that language teaching and academic exchanges can foster relations between countries, and the case of Syria and Iran was no exception. The Iranian cultural centre in Damascus was involved in all the Persian teaching facilities in Syria, and played a significant role in the setting up and running of Persian language and literature departments at Syrian universities – albeit to the dismay of some Syrian academics. Language teaching had proven a useful way to increase awareness of Iran in Syria and to start building up a group of Syrians interested in maintaining ties between the two countries in the future. While language students at the Iranian cultural centre generally learned Persian out of interest or for religious reasons, many of the students at the university did not choose to study Persian but had become interested in Iran through their studies. Arabic language students at the Syrian cultural centre in Tehran were often students or teachers of Arabic at Iranian universities or schools, and appreciated the centre as a forum in which to improve their language skills.

Overall, contact between Syrians and Iranians on the popular level remained slight. The example of Iranian pilgrims going to Syria emphasizes the limits of interaction. Communication between pilgrims and Syrians was largely confined to those that were involved in the tourist industry or trade. While Iranian religious tourism did introduce Syrians to Iranians and their traditions due to the sheer number of Iranian tourists visiting Damascus and other Syrian cities, it did not contribute to bridging the cultural divide between the two peoples. Quite on the contrary, it created an impression amongst Syrians that all Iranians were like the pilgrims visiting their country, namely religious, of modest background and conservative, which did not persuade many Syrians to visit Iran. The main interaction between the two sides took place in the markets, where many shopkeepers had learned some Persian to sell their goods to Iranian visitors, who were reliable customers. Non-religious tourism between the two countries remained as good as non-existent.

The Islamic Republic's efforts to promote its ideas and values in Syria thus largely reached an audience of those already interested in Iran, mainly for religious reasons, and of opportunists who had a stake in the political system and needed to follow the official line with regards to Syria's foreign relations and friends. While Iran understood the importance of soft power in foreign policy, it could only wield it in a limited sphere in Syria as its cultural diplomacy was so intertwined with the two countries' political relationship, and the official culture it propagated only attractive to selected groups. Nevertheless, Iran considered its cultural diplomacy work in Syria as exemplary, which can be explained by the fact that precisely due to the strong relationship between the two governments the activities of the Iranians were supported in Syria, and events always well attended. What is more, since culture constitutes a nation's identity, Iran considers its cultural diplomacy work successful since it emphasised precisely the identity the Islamic Republic wanted to construct, regardless of it being one of many cultural identities actually present in Iran. Syria had never pretended to want to wield soft power as such in Iran, opening the doors of its cultural centre as a visible sign of their strong official relationship on the cultural as well as political level. Its message of anti-imperialism and resistance formed part of the bilateral cultural dialogue but found resonance mainly amongst Iranian official circles and was largely ignored by the students frequenting the centre.

In terms of soft power, while Syrians might have been wary of the Islamic Republic's cultural activities in their country, Iran's president Mahmud Ahmadinejad did enjoy some popularity amongst the Syrian population. He was seen to stand up to the United States and Israel, one of the triumvirate of the 'Axis of Resistance' – posters of which adorned many shop windows. One Iranian student in Syria put it like this:

'Syrians often tell me they like my president, Ahmadinejad, because he stands up to America. It is funny, because in that respect he enjoys greater popularity here than he does in Iran, where people don't dislike America the way they do here.' Then she added, laughing: 'Maybe they also have to say that they like our president, as he is good friends with the president here.'[1]

Quo vadis? Ahmadinejad, Asad and Nasrallah on the back of a minibus. Damascus, June 2012.

The fact that the 2009 presidential elections in Iran were disputed did not make any difference to Iran's cultural policies in Syria or to the two countries' bilateral relationship. Asad recognised Ahmadinejad immediately after the latter was sworn in for his second term. According to Iran's state-owned Press TV, most Iranians voting in Damascus chose Ahmadinejad.[2] Some Syrian university professors were saying it was a shame that Iranian demonstrators threatened their country's security by setting objects on fire, referring to pictures shown on international news.[3] The official sector clearly stood by the Iranian president.

On the other side of the coin, young Syrians sympathised with their Iranian counterparts who were asking for greater freedom and recognition of their voice in the presidential election. Many young Syrians with access to the Internet sympathised with the Green Movement and demonstrated this by turning their Facebook profiles green – the symbolism followers of the Green Movement used inside and outside Iran. Likewise, young Iranians feel the Syrian people are currently going through a similar process as they did during the period following the 2009 presidential elections, when many voicing their opposition to the process were imprisoned and tortured. In solidarity with the people of Homs, an Iranian rapper composed a song in 2012, 'The Battle of Homs', in which he supports the Syrian protesters and warns Asad that he will pay for his crimes.[4] The song by Emad Ghavidel featuring Hamed Fard was widely shared on social media platforms. One line states that 'in Damascus few special people are laughing but people of Homs are crying', and the refrain goes:

'I swear to laments of grieving mothers, I swear to tears of grieving mothers, you will pay for it Bashar al-Asad, even if I am drowned in my blood, I would not shut up; you better know that Iranians cannot keep quiet while you kill; your name is lion but you are a lion with no mane; what I am saying, you are not a lion, you are not even a hyena; you do not even deserve to be treated with anger.'[5]

United by rejection of violence and authoritarianism, young people show their solidarity independently in the information age.

Since the on-going crisis in Syria has turned into a regional and international power struggle, with Iran as the Syrian government's principal regional ally playing a key role, bilateral relations are viewed even more within the context of support or opposition for one's own regime. Iranians and Iranian institutions in Syria are considered targets for the Syrian opposition to harm their regime and its allies – as evident in the kidnapping of Iranians in Syria or throwing sound explosions in front of the Iranian cultural centre in Damascus as in April 2012.[6] In terms of soft power, supporting the resistance in Lebanon is no longer enough for Iran to win the hearts and minds of the Syrian people.[7]

Since Syrian-Iranian cultural relations have taken place in an official sphere, cultural diplomacy in its current constellation would crumble were either of the two regimes to change. However, there exists a real potential to develop broader cultural ties between the two peoples if cultural exchange loses its strong official character and more people travel to the other country for reasons other than religious tourism. Maybe we are starting to see a trend in this direction by the virtual support young Syrians and Iranians give each other.

NOTES

Introduction

1. Billows, William and Körber, Sebastian (eds), *EUNIC Culture Report, Europe's Foreign Cultural Relations* (Stuttgart, 2011), p.24.
2. Hirschfeld, Yair, 'The odd couple: Ba'athist Syria and Khomeini's Iran' in M. Ma'oz and A. Yaniv (eds), *Syria under Assad: domestic constraints and regional risks* (London, 1986).
3. Ehteshami, Anoushiravan and Hinnebusch, Raymond, *Syria and Iran: Middle Powers in a penetrated regional system* (New York, 1997), p. 2.
4. McMurry, Ruth Emily and Lee, Muna, *The Cultural Approach: Another Way in International Relations* (Chapel Hill, 1947), pp. 2–3.
5. Maaß, Kurt-Jürgen, *Kultur und Außenpolitik* (Baden-Baden, 2009), p. 25. [translation from German author's own].
6. Bound, K., Briggs, R., Holden, J. and Jones, S., *Cultural Diplomacy* (London, 2007), pp. 11–20.
7. Haigh, Anthony, *Cultural Diplomacy in Europe* (Strasbourg, 1974), p. 28.
8. Mitchell, John M., *International cultural relations* (London, 1986), pp. 2–7.
9. Melissen, Jan, 'Between Theory and Practice' in J. Melissen (ed), *The New Public Diplomacy* (London, 2005), p. 8.
10. Ibid, p. 22.
11. Nye, Joseph, *Soft Power: The means to success in world politics* (New York, 2004), pp. 107–110 [Emphasis author's own].
12. Wang, Jian, 'Localising public diplomacy: the role of sub-national actors in nation branding' *Place Branding* 2, no 1 (2006), p. 37.
13. Leonard, Mark, *Public Diplomacy* (London, 2002), pp. 8–10.
14. Ibid.
15. Nye, Joseph, *The paradox of American power: Why the world's only superpower can't go it alone* (Oxford, 2002), pp. 8–9.
16. Interview with Joseph Nye, Oxford, 17 May 2010.

17. Nye, *Soft Power*, pp. 14–5.
18. Wang, Introduction.
19. Leonard, p. 8.
20. Melissen, 'Between Theory and Practice', p. 16.
21. Ibid, p. 18, quoting from Henderson, E.H., 'Toward a Definition of Propaganda' *Journal of Social Psychology*, vol.18 (1943), p. 83.
22. Haigh, p. 32.
23. Interview with Joseph Nye; Nye, Joseph, 'Public Diplomacy and Soft Power' *The ANNALS of the American Academy of Political and Social Science*, vol.616 (March 2008), p. 95.
24. Nye: 'Public Diplomacy', p. 95.
25. McMurry and Lee, pp. 4–5.
26. Bates, Gill and Huang, Yanzhong, 'Sources and Limits of Chinese 'Soft Power'' *Survival*, vol.48 no.2 (2006), pp. 19–20.
27. Chaubet, Francois and Martin, Laurent, *Histoire des relations culturelles dans le monde contemporain* (Paris, 2011), p. 86; Haigh, p. 29; McMurry and Lee, p. 40.
28. *The Times*, 20 March 1935, as quoted in McMurry and Lee, pp. 139–40.
29. Hartig, Falk, 'Mit Konfuzius ins 21. Jahrhundert – Chinas Auswärtige Kulturpolitik' in K.J. Maaß (ed), *Kultur- und Außenpolitik* (Baden-Baden, 2009), p. 404.
30. Chaubet and Martin, p. 257.
31. Hartig, p. 405; Bates and Huang, p. 18.
32. Hartig, pp. 405–8; http://english.hanban.edu.cn/hbsm.php.
33. European Cultural Foundation, *Cultural Policies in Algeria, Egypt, Jordan, Lebanon, Morocco, Palestine, Syria and Tunisia. An Introduction.* (Amsterdam, 2011). For the Cultural Influence Algeria Agency, see its official website: www.aarcalgerie.org/index.php [last accessed 17/05/2012].
34. Chaubet and Martin, p. 261.
35. Lafi Youmans, William, 'Humor Against Hegemony: Al Hurra, Jokes, and the Limits of American Soft Power' *Middle East Journal of Culture and Communication* 2 (2009), pp.76–99.
36. Interview with Joseph Nye.

Chapter 1. Historical Backdrop

1. Olmert, Yosef, 'Iranian-Syrian Relations: Between Islam and Realpolitik', in D. Menashri (ed), *The Iranian Revolution and the Muslim World* (Boulder CO., 1990), p. 171; Parsi, Trita, *Treacherous Alliance. The Secret Dealings of Israel, Iran, and the U.S.* (New Haven and London, 2007), pp. 20f.

2. Hunter, Shireen, 'Iran and Syria: From Hostility to Limited Alliance' in H. Amirahmadi and N. Entessar (eds), *Iran and the Arab World* (New York, 1993), p. 207; Seale, Patrick, *Asad: The Struggle for the Middle East* (Berkeley and Los Angeles, 1989), p. 353. For Egyptian-Iranian relations in the 1970s see Sabbagh, Said, *Al-alaqat al-masriya al-iraniya bayna al-wasal wa al-qati'a, 1970–1981* (Cairo, 2007).

3. Seale: Asad, p. 352 and Hunter: 'Iran and Syria', p. 207.

4. Emami, Muhammad A., *Siyaset va Hukumet dar Suriyeh* (Tehran, 1997), p. 234. [Author's own translation].

5. Goodarzi, Jubin, *Syria and Iran: Diplomatic Alliance and Power Politics in the Middle East* (London, 2006), p. 15.

6. On the friendship treaty, see Chapter 3.

7. Saikal, Amin, 'Iranian Foreign Policy, 1921–1979' in P. Avery, Hambly and C. Melville (eds), *The Cambridge History of Iran, Vol.7: From Nadir Shah to the Islamic Republic* (Cambridge, 1991), p. 442.

8. For a discussion of the Syria's attitude towards the Baghdad Pact, see Seale, Patrick, *The Struggle for Syria: A Study of Post-War Arab Politics 1945–1958* (London, 1965), Chapters 16–17.

9. Ramazani, Rouhollah, *Iran's Foreign Policy 1941–73* (Charlottesville, 1975), p. 398.

10. Archives of the Iranian Foreign Ministry, file: Iranian Embassy Damascus, *Dameshgh 52, number 63.* (hereafter referred to as IFM). Year: 1336–1340, K:8, D: 140–1 (files about Bahrain).

11. Chubin, Shahram and Zabih, Sepehr, *The Foreign Relations of Iran: A Developing State in a Zone of Great-Power Conflict* (Berkeley, 1974), p. 146, Goodarzi, p. 15, Emami, p. 233.

12. Goodarzi, p. 15. The Iranian Red Lion and Sun Society was established in 1922 and recognised by the international committee of the red cross in 1923; following the Islamic revolution its name was changed to the Red Crescent Society of the Islamic Republic of Iran. Website of the Iranian Red Crescent Society: www.rcs.ir.

13. Iranian Foreign Ministry, *Suriyeh {be sefaresh} daftar mutala'at siyasi va bein el-melli.* (Tehran, 2008), p. 223.

14. Ibid, p. 222.

15. Agha, Hussein and Khalidi, Ahmad, *Syria and Iran: Rivalry and Cooperation* (London, 1995), p. 2.

16. Ibid and Saikal, p. 451.

17. Agha and Khalidi, p. 2.

18. Iranian Foreign Ministry: *Suriyeh*, p. 223; Hunter: 'Iran and Syria', p. 206, Goodarzi, p. 16, Agha and Khalidi, p. 2, Kienle, Eberhard, *Ba'th v Ba'th: The*

Conflict between Syria and Iraq 1968–1989 (London, 1990), p. 62. According to Goodarzi, Iran agreed in 1974 to provide a $150 million loan and a $50 million grant to Syria to finance a number of industrial and agricultural projects; in 1975 it gave an additional $300 million in loans to Syria. Goodarzi, p. 16. Hunter states that Iran agreed to set up joint ventures and provide technical assistance, whilst in exchange Iran wanted to increase its exports to Syria. Hunter: 'Iran and Syria', p. 206.

19. Iranian Foreign Ministry: *Suriyeh*, p. 223.

20. Shafi'ai, Husayn, 'al-mustashariya al-thaqafiya al-iraniya bi-dimashq khilala rub'a qarn' in *al-thaqafa al-islamiya* no.100 (2006), p. 100. The 1975 cultural agreement will be examined in detail in Chapter 3.

21. Marschall, Christin, *Syria, Iran and the Changing Middle East Order*, unpublished MPhil thesis (Oxford, 1991), p. 6, Hunter: 'Iran and Syria', p. 206; Amirahmadi, Hooshang and Entessar, Nader. 'Iranian-Arab Relations in Transition' in H. Amirahmadi and N. Entessar (eds), *Iran and the Arab World* (New York, 1993), p. 2.

22. Hunter: 'Iran and Syria', p. 206.

23. Goodarzi, p. 16, Seale: *Asad*, p. 353.

24. Ramazani, Rouhollah, *Revolutionary Iran: Challenge and response in the Middle East* (Baltimore, 1986), p. 176 and Hunter: 'Iran and Syria', p. 207.

25. Iranian Foreign Ministry: *Suriyeh* p.224.

26. Seale: *Asad*, p. 353, Hunter: 'Iran and Syria', p. 207; Drysdale, Alasdair and Hinnebusch, Raymond, *Syria and the Middle East Peace Process* (New York, 1991), p. 94.

27. Goodarzi, pp. 16–17.

28. Agha and Khalidi, pp. 2–3.

29. Stanley, Bruce, 'Drawing from the well: Syria in the Persian Gulf' *Journal of South Asian and Middle Eastern Studies* vol.XIV, no.2 (1990), p. 52 and Seale: *Asad*, p. 354.

30. This action followed the inability of the two sides to reach an agreement over transfer fees for exporting Iraqi oil via the trans-Syrian pipeline. Goodarzi, p. 17.

31. Goodarzi, p. 17, Stanley, p. 52, Seale: *Asad*, p. 354, Kienle, p. 147. For a detailed account of Syrian-Iraqi relations, see Kienle: *Ba'th v Ba'th*.

32. Marschall: *Syria, Iran and the Changing Middle East Order*, pp. 9–10, quoting *al-Ba'th newspaper*, 6 October 1979.

33. Seale: *Asad*, p. 352.

34. Agha and Khalidi, p. 3.

35. Olmert, p. 172, Seale: *Asad*, p. 352, Agha and Khalidi, p. 3, Emami, p. 236. Kramer, Martin, 'Syria's Alawis and Shi'ism' in M. Kramer (ed), *Shi'ism, Resistance, and Revolution* (Boulder Co., 1987), p. 247. Kramer points out

that the Sunni mufti of Palestine, Hajj Amin al-Husayni, had issued a
fatwa in 1936 in which he found the Alawis 'to be Muslims and called
on all Muslims to work with them for mutual good, in a spirit of Islamic
brotherhood'. However, the Alawis had probably only turned to him as they
were not able to extract a similar recognition from Sunni religious authorities within Syria. After the Alawis came to power in Syria, they needed an
external recognition from a recognised Shi'i authority. Kramer, pp. 241–7.

36. Olmert, p. 172, Agha and Khalidi, p. 4, Seale: *Asad*, p. 352.
37. Calabrese, John, 'Iran II: The Damascus Connection' *The World Today* vol.46
    (1990), p. 188. Chehabi suggests that relations between Musa al-Sadr and
    Khomeini had been rather ambiguous. Chehabi, H.E., *Distant Relations: Iran
    and Lebanon in the last 500 years* (London, 2006), p. 159. Also see Alpher,
    Joseph, 'The Khomeini International' *The Washington Quarterly*, vol.3, no.4
    (1980), pp. 54–74.
38. Marschall: *Syria, Iran and the Changing Middle East Order*, p. 8.
39. Agha and Khalidi, p. 5, Marschall: *Syria, Iran and the Changing Middle East
    Order*, p. 8, Hunter: 'Iran and Syria', p. 207.
40. Alpher, p. 61.
41. Agha and Khalidi, p. 6; Calabrese, p. 188.
42. Seale: *Asad*, p. 352 and Hunter: 'Iran and Syria', p. 207. Ghotbzadeh was
    later appointed as head of the national radio and television network. In 1982
    he was executed following an attempted coup against Khomeini. Chehabi,
    pp. 204–208.
43. Alpher, p. 62.
44. Stanley, pp. 50–51, Chehabi, p. 204.
45. Marschall: *Syria, Iran and the Changing Middle East Order*, pp. 9–10, Chehabi,
    p. 204. Ghotbzadeh, Yazdi, Chamran and Tabataba'i were all leading
    members of the *Nehzat-e Azadi*, or Liberation Movement, an Islamic oppos-
    ition group founded in 1961 that was the first political group to send
    members to Lebanon after it ceased all open activity in Iran in the wake of
    the June 1963 events. Chehabi, p. 182f. Also see Alpher.
46. Chehabi, pp. 190/209/223.
47. Ibid, p. 191.
48. Interview with ICRO official, Tehran, 22 April 2006.
49. Jan Zadeh, Ali, *Doktor Ali Shariati* (Tehran, 1969), p. 53; Abassi, Muhammad,
    al-Doktor Ali Shariati (Syria, year unknown), p. 15; Rahnema, Ali, *An
    Islamic Utopian, A Political Biography of Ali Shari'ati* (London, 1998), p. 368;
    Abrahamian, Ervand, *The Iranian Mojahedin* (London, 1989), p. 110.
50. Adelkhah, Fariba, 'Économie morale du pèlerinage et société civile en Iran:
    les voyages religieux, commerciaux et touristiques à Damas' *Politix* vol.20,

no.77 (2007), p. 40; Kramer: 'Syria's Alawis and Shi'ism', p. 250. According to Chehabi, it was Shariati's friends who decided to bury his corpse at the shrine of Zaynab; 'the Iranian government tried to have Shariati's body flown to Iran for an officially sponsored burial and even sent an aeroplane to Damascus, but Musa Sadr used his cordial relations with the Syrian government to sabotage that plan.' Chehabi, pp. 158–9.

51. Adelkhah, p. 40. Al-e Ahmad writes on Zaynab's character: 'Zainab: sister of Imam Husayn. Witnessed his martyrdom at Karbala and was said to have been the first to mourn his death.' Al-e Ahmad, Jalal, *Lost in the Crowd* (Washington D.C., 1985), p. 7.

52. Rahnema, p. 110.

53. Ehteshami and Hinnebusch: *Syria and Iran*, p. 207.

54. In 1979, following the revolution, Iran cut its relations with Israel, closed the Israeli embassy in Tehran and transformed it into a Palestinian one. See Musa al-Gharir, 'B'ad al-malamih al-asasiyya lil-'alaqat al-suriya al-iraniya', unpublished lecture given at several universities in Iran in the academic year 2005–06. Tehran, 2005.

55. Drysdale and Hinnebusch, p. 95.

56. Such as Hirschfeld in 'The odd couple', p. 105.

57. Seale: *Asad*, p. 353.

58. Goodarzi, p. 220.

59. Ibid, p. 18

60. Seale: *Asad*, p. 353.

61. Goodarzi, p. 25. The Iranian Diplomatic Corps Handbook of 1984 states that Younes was appointed Syrian ambassador to Iran on 18 November 1979.

62. Information drawn from Goodarzi, Hinnebusch and Ehteshami: *Syria and Iran*, Agha and Khalidi, BBC/SWB 1979–1989.

63. Olmert, p. 175. The religious tourism from Iran to Syria in connection to cultural diplomacy will be discussed in detail in Chapter 7.

64. Seale: *Asad*, p. 357.

65. Goodarzi, p. 33.

66. Seale: *Asad*, Chapter 21; Goodarzi, p. 35; Kienle, p. 162.

67. Goodarzi, p. 73–4; Ehteshami and Hinnebusch: *Syria and Iran*, p. 208; Kienle, p. 96.

68. Hirschfeld, p. 107; Goodarzi, p. 45.

69. Seale: *Asad*, p. 359; Ehteshami and Hinnebusch: *Syria and Iran*, p. 208; Kienle, p. 163.

70. Hirschfeld, p. 107.

71. Ehteshami and Hinnebusch: *Syria and Iran*, p. 208.

72. Goodarzi, p. 110; Ehteshami and Hinnebusch: *Syria and Iran*, p. 95f.

73. Goodarzi, p. 118 and p. 128.

74. Ibid, p. 135.

75. Goodarzi, p. 281.

76. Asad in press conference on the eve of the Arab League meeting in Tunis, 19 September 1987. Goodarzi, p. 230.

77. Ibid, p. 280.

78. Goodarzi, Chapter 3. Goodarzi, Agha and Khalidi, Ehteshami and Hinnebusch give a detailed account of Syrian-Iranian policy in Lebanon in the 1980s.

79. Ehteshami and Hinnebusch: *Syria and Iran*, p. 211.

80. Goodarzi, p. 245.

81. Agha and Khalidi, p. 26; Hunter, Shireen, *Iran and the World, Continuity in a Revolutionary Decade* (Indiana, 1990), p. 122.

82. Syrian Vice-President Khaddam, 27 May 1988, as quoted in Goodarzi, p. 274.

83. Olmert, p. 179.

84. Hirschfeld, p. 110.

85. Olmert, p. 179.

86. Goodarzi, p. 63.

87. The number of revolutionary guards is unclear, figures range between 800 and 1,500 (Agha and Khalidi, p. 15). Goodarzi puts the figure at 1,500 (Goodarzi, p. 88). Chehabi suggests that Syria and Iran being allies, Syria could hardly refuse the Iranian offer to send in military help; however, according to Chehabi the Syrians refused to give the Revolutionary Guards a role and wanted to keep them for propaganda purposes only, so that most returned to Iran, after which 'a few hundred, assisted by clerics from the Pasdaran's "Cultural Unit" (a total of about 1500), were sent to the Bekaa Valley to train Lebanese', under the supervision of Mohtashemipur. Chehabi, pp. 212–16.

88. Ranstorp, Magnus, *Hizb'allah in Lebanon, The Politics of the Western Hostage Crisis* (London, 1997), p. 110. See Ranstorp, Chapter 4: 'The Influence of the Iranian-Syrian Relationship On the Hizb'allah' for an account of cooperation over the hostage issue.

89. In May 1983, the US brokered a Lebanese-Israeli accord, which soon became irrelevant. Agha and Khalidi, p. 17 and p. 20.

90. Hirschfeld, p. 111, Goodarzi, p. 94, Agha and Khalidi, p. 20.

91. Olmert, p. 181.

92. Hunter: 'Iran and Syria' and Goodarzi, Chapter 2.

93. Jaber, Hala, *Hezbollah: Born With a Vengeance* (London, 1997), p. 20; Ehteshami and Hinnebusch: *Syria and Iran*, p. 123.

94. The creation and evolution of Hezbollah has been covered by a number of authors, see for instance Palmer Harik, Judith, *Hezbollah, The Changing Face of Terrorism* (London, 2004), Jaber, and Norton, Augustus Richard, *Hezbollah: A Short History* (Princeton, 2007).

95. Ma'oz, Moshe, *Syria and Israel, From War to Peace-making* (Oxford, 1995), p. 188.

96. Agha and Khalidi, p. 21.

97. For a detailed discussion of this period, see Goodarzi, Chapter 3.

98. Agha and Khalidi, p. 15; Chehabi, p. 223.

99. Goodarzi, p. 88; Chehabi, p. 209; Ehteshami and Hinnebusch: *Syria and Iran*, p. 123; Jaber, p. 82.

100. Hunter: 'Iran and Syria' and Goodarzi, pp. 263–277.

101. *New York Times*, 11 March 1987.

102. *United Press International*, 13 July 1987.

103. Goodarzi, p. 271; *Christian Science Monitor*, 18 May 1988.

104. BBC/SWB 20 May 1988, ME/0156/A/1.

105. For a detailed account of Iran's stand during the crisis, see Milani, Mohsen, 'Iran's active neutrality during the Kuwaiti crisis: Reasons and ramifications' *New Political Science*, 11, nr. 1 (1992).

106. Goodarzi, p. 289; Hinnebusch and Ehteshami: *Syria and Iran*, p. 213. It has been suggested that Asad did not visit Iran while Khomeini was alive due to ideological differences between the two leaders.

107. Agha and Khalidi, p. 30.

108. Marschall, Christin, *Iran's Persian Gulf Policy: From Khomeini to Khatami* (London, 2003), p. 107.

109. SWB, (ME/0845 i), 18 August 1990.

110. Ehteshami and Hinnebusch: *Syria and Iran*, p. 213; SWB, ME/0881/A/1 'Syrian Radio Commentary stresses continuing unity with Iran', *Syrian Arab Republic Radio*, 28 September 1990.

111. Goodarzi, p. 289.

112. Rafsanjani's delegation included: Foreign Minister Ali Akbar Velayati, Trade Minister Abdulhussein Vahaji, Oil Minister Gholam Reza Aghazadeh, the director of the President's office Muhammad Mir-Muhammadi, the Secretary of the National Security Council Hojjatoleslam Dr. Hassan Rohani, the Member of Parliament Hojjatoleslam Sayyed Mahmud Do'a'i, the Director General of the Foreign Ministry Muhammad Kazem Khonsari, and the Head of the political department at the Foreign Ministry Mahmud Hashemi. See SWB (ME/1060/A/1) 1 May 1991; 'Syrian-Iranian Communiqué stresses self-determination for Iraq and Palestinians', *Syrian Arab Republic Radio*, 29 April 1991.

113. Ibid.
114. Marschall: *Iran's Persian Gulf Policy*, p. 117; Hinnebusch and Ehteshami: *Syria and Iran*, p. 214; Parsi, p. 146.
115. President Bush allegedly stated that 'Iran "as a big country" should not be forever treated as an enemy by the countries in the region', Marschall: *Iran's Persian Gulf Policy*, p. 117.
116. Ibid, p. 117 and p. 163.
117. For a detailed discussion of Syrian-Iranian attitudes towards the peace process, see Ehteshami and Hinnebusch: *Syria and Iran*, Chapter 7: 'Syria, Iran and the Arab-Israeli peace process'.
118. BBC SWB (EE/D2548/ME); 'Syrian vice-president denies differences with Iran on peace process', *Radio Monte Carlo*, 27 February 1996.
119. Ehteshami and Hinnebusch: *Syria and Iran*, pp. 157–9.
120. 'Waiting for Christopher, with Assad poised for the profit-taking', *Mideast Mirror*, 02 August 1993.
121. Agha and Khalidi, p. 60.
122. Ehteshami and Hinnebusch: *Syria and Iran*, p. 215; Agha and Khalidi, p. 62.
123. BBC SWB (ME/1149/A/1), 'Iranian Interior Minister Comments on Talks in Damascus'.
124. Ehteshami and Hinnebusch: *Syria and Iran*, p. 217.
125. 'Iranian Vice President visits Syria', *Xinhua News Agency*, 13 December 1993; Ehteshami and Hinnebusch: *Syria and Iran*, p. 218.
126. 'Countdown to the Geneva summit What Clinton "expects" from Assad', *Mideast Mirror*, 7 January 1994.
127. 'Summit message hazy, but price is clear', *The Jerusalem Post*, 19 January 1994.
128. Goodarzi, p. 290.
129. Ehteshami and Hinnebusch: *Syria and Iran*, p. 221.
130. 'Syrian vice-president denies differences with Iran on peace process', BBC SWB EE/D2548/ME, *Radio Monte Carlo*, 27 February 1996.
131. 'Iran's Habibi in Damascus on eve of Syria's new round of talks with Israel', *Mideast Mirror*, 27 February 1996.
132. Zisser, Eyal, *Asad's Legacy: Syria in Transition* (London, 2001), p. 73; 'Assad in Tehran seen lobbying for new Arab-Iranian alliance', *Mideast Mirror*, 1 August 1997.
133. Goodarzi, pp. 287–288; Ehteshami and Hinnebusch: *Syria and Iran*, p. 135.
134. Ibid, p. 136.
135. Ibid, p. 137.
136. 'Tehran Seeks To Preserve Hizballah, Weaken Peace Chances', *FBIS Trends*, 11 August 1993.

137. Lawson, Fred, 'Syria's Relations with Iran: Managing the Dilemmas of Alliance' *The Middle East Journal* vol.61, nr. 1 (2007), p. 32.
138. Ehteshami and Hinnebusch: *Syria and Iran*, p. 136.
139. *Christian Science Monitor*, 21 August 1990.
140. Ehteshami and Hinnebusch: *Syria and Iran*, p. 214; Agha and Khalidi, p. 72.
141. *Mideast Mirror*, 11 January 1993; 01 March 1996; 01 April 1996.
142. Olson, Robert, 'The Kurdish Question four years on: The policies of Turkey, Syria, Iran and Iraq' *Middle East Policy* vol.3, issue 3 (1994), pp. 137–9.
143. Ehteshami and Hinnebusch: *Syria and Iran*, pp. 221–2.
144. 'Asad and Rafsanjani begin talks in Tehran', *Syrian Arab TV*, 02 August 1997; Goodarzi, p. 290; 'Assad in Tehran', *Mideast Mirror*, 01 August 1997.
145. Ibid.
146. Goodarzi, p. 291.
147. 'Assad in Tehran', *Mideast Mirror*, 1 August 1997..
148. *The Economist*, 13 December 1997.
149. Lawson, p. 34.
150. 'Syria's Asad greeted by Khatami on first day of Iran visit', al-Ba'th newspaper quoted in *AFP*, 24 January 2001.
151. Leverett, Flynt, *Inheriting Syria: Bashar's Trial by Fire* (Washington D.C., 2005), p. 132.
152. Goodarzi, preface to the 2009 paperback edition, p. xii.
153. 'Syrian paper urges joint Iranian-Syrian effort to face "threats"', *al-Thawra*, 17 May 2003.
154. Goodarzi, p. 293.
155. 'Syria, Iran "genuine resistance front" against foreign designs – Tishrin', *BBC SWB*, 22 January 2006.
156. See for instance '"Wedging" Damascus from Tehran', *Forward Magazine*, July 2007; 'Syria's Alliance with Iran', *USIP Briefing*, May 2007; 'Despite U.S. Outreach, Syria Affirms Iran Ties', *Time Magazine*, 07 May 2009; 'Syria Rejects West's Calls for Severing Ties with Iran', *Fars News Agency*, 17 September 2008; 'Mottaki: Iran will keep ties with Syria', *Press TV*, 12 June 2008.
157. SANA, 'Iran/Syria: News agency directors discuss closer ties', *BBC SWB*, 15 October 2002.
158. 'Syrian foreign minister arrives in Iran', *BBC SWB*, 18 January 2003, source: Syrian Arab TV.
159. Syrian Arab Republic Radio, 'Syrian, Iranian presidents discuss Iraq, Mid East', *BBC SWB*, 15 May 2003.
160. Lawson, p. 40.

161. SANA, 'Syrian, Iranian ministers discuss boosting industrial cooperation', *BBC SWB*, 14 October 2003.
162. SANA, 'Syrian, Iranian parliament speakers sign memorandum, hold talks', *BBC SWB*, 20 April 2004.
163. http://mellat.majlis.ir/PARLIAMENTARY%2OFERIENDSHIP%20 GROUPS/SOORIEH.HTM.
164. Lawson, p. 40; Goodarzi, p. 293.
165. Lawson, p. 41.
166. Goodarzi, p. 293; Syrian Arab TV, 'Syrian, Iranian president comment on bilateral talks', *BBC SWB*, 8 August 2005.
167. Tishrin, 'Syrian daily views president's successful Tehran talks, closer cooperation', *BBC SWB*, 12 August 2005.
168. SANA, 'Syrian-Iranian relations are firm and developed; Iranian President', *BBC SWB*, 19 January 2006; Xinhua, 'Iranian President arrives in Damascus on official visit', *BBC SWB*, 19 January 2006.
169. 'Iran, Syria show stronger ties', *The Washington Times*, 20 September 2006; 'A relationship above domestic politics', *Syria Today*, July 2009.
170. *Reuters*, 14 November 2005; 'Iran voices solidarity with Syria; Visiting minister blasts US "manoeuvrings"', *The Daily Star*, 15 November 2005.
171. Lawson, p. 41; 'Syrian daily criticises remarks of Zionist regime's PM', *IRNA*, 18 October 2006; 'Syria's Assad due in Tehran for nuclear talks', *AFP*, 01 August 2008; 'Syria backs Iran nuclear program', *Press TV*, 06 January 2010.
172. Broadcast journalist Charlie Rose Interview with Bashar al-Asad, Damascus, May 2010, www.charlierose.com.
173. See 'Iran and Syria want broader scientific ties', *IRNA*, 21 November 2005; 'Iran, Syria sign agreements on telecommunication, IT', *IRNA*, 3 May 2006; 'Syria, Iran Sign Memo of Understanding on Islamic Affairs', *SANA*, 9 May 2006; Lawson, p. 43; 'Syria's Alliance with Iran', *USIP Briefing*, May 2007; 'Syria and Iran Sign a Memo of Understanding in Maritime Transport', *SANA*, 26 October 2007.
174. Lawson, p. 43.
175. Personal observations, Damascus Winter 2007–2008, Tehran Summer 2006.
176. 'FM: Palestinian problems to be solved through national consensus', *IRNA*, 29 October 2006.
177. I posed the question about Syria's relations with Iran following the indirect talks with Israel to Buthaina Sha'ban during a talk she gave at the Middle East Centre, St. Antony's College Oxford, 17 November 2008.
178. http://www.etemaad.ir/Released/87–06–07/150.htm.

179. 'Mottaki: Iran will keep ties with Syria', *Press TV*, 12 June 2008.
180. 'Iran, Syria Call for Lifting Gaza Blockade', *Fars News Agency*, 10 January 2009.
181. 'Iran, Syria call for unity among Palestinian resistance groups', *Tehran Times*, 28 December 2010; 'Iran, Syria stress support for resistance', *ISNA*, 28 December 2010.
182. 'Iran, Syria plan strategic cooperation', *Press TV*, 26 December 2010.
183. 'Syria's Alliance with Iran', *USIP Briefing*, May 2007; 'Iran, Syria to boost trade ties', *Press TV*, 7 March 2008.
184. 'Iran, Syria Discuss Boosting Mutual Cooperation', *Fars News Agency*, 12 January 2010; 'Iran-Syria-Deals. Iran, Syria keen to follow up bilateral economic deals', *IRNA*, 8 July 2007; 'Iran to build power plant in Syria', *Press TV*, 07 March 2008; 'Iran to export 3bn cu.m. of gas to Syria annually', *Tehran Times*, 6 October 2007; 'Iran increases investment in Syrian construction sector', *Tehran Times*, 20 January 2008.
185. 'Iran, Venezuela and Syria sign MoU on Syrian oil refinery project', *IRNA*, 31 October 2006.
186. 'Mashayee: Iran, Syria Play Most Influential Roles in the Region', *Fars News Agency*, 7 February 2011; 'Islamic Pipeline states to meet in Tehran', *Tehran Times*, 9 February 2011.
187. 'Iran turns Syria into car exporting hub', *Press TV*, 7 May 2009; 'SAIPA opens new car assembly line in Syria', *Tehran Times*, 4 July 2009; '(Iran Khodro) tastadayif jalasat iftitah jama'iyat sadaqa tehran-dimashq', *al-Vefagh*, 8 August 2007.
188. 'Iranian-Syrian free trade agreement', *Syria Today*, January 2012.
189. 'Iran, Syria keen to strengthen ties', *Press TV*, 9 January 2011; .
190. 'Iran, Syria Discuss Boosting Mutual Cooperation', *Fars News Agency*, 12 January 2010; 'Tehran-Damascus sign economic MOU', *Tehran Times*, 12 January 2010.
191. 'Iran, Syria to set uo joint bank', *Press TV*, 25 May 2010; 'Iran, Syria vow to boost economic cooperation', *ISNA*, 3 October 2010.
192. 'Iran, Syria call for further cooperation', *ISNA*, 9 February 2011; 'Iran, Syria free trade agreement takes effect', *Tehran Times*, 28 April 2012.
193. 'Iran insists on need to end Syria violence, renews support for Assad', *Tehran Times*, 9 April 2012.
194. 'Iran will stop U.S. from manipulating Syria crisis', *Tehran Times*, 13 March 2012.
195. 'Iran supports Syria against pressures: ambassador', *IRNA*, 11 December 2011.
196. 'Iran rejects US allegations over Syria', *Press TV*, 18 April 2011; 'Iran denies supporting Syria in dealing with protesters', *Tehran Times*, 19 April 2011;

'Iran dismisses Obama's claim on Syria', *ISNA*, 25 April 2011; 'Iran warns of White House psycho war', *Press TV*, 26 April 2011; 'Iran helping Syrian regime crack down on protesters, say diplomats', *The Guardian*, 9 May 2011.

197. 'Iranian diplomat says Arab countries sending mercenaries to Syria', *Tehran Times*, 10 March 2012.

198. 'Iran lauds Syria's call for referendum on new constitution', *Press TV*, 16 February 2012; 'Iran Renews Support for Syrian Reforms, Voices Opposition to Foreign Interference', *Fars News Agency*, 24 February 2012; 'Salehi says Iran supports Syrians' legitimate demands', *ISNA*, 27 February 2012.

199. 'Annan says Syria promises to respect ceasefire', *Reuters*, 11 April 2012.

200. 'Assad emails: "Suggestions for the president's speech" – translation', *The Guardian*, 14 March 2012.

201. 'Iran will continue supporting Syria: deputy FM', *Tehran Times*, 13 March 2012.

202. 'Syrian youth stage demonstration to support Iran's policy on Syria', *IRNA*, 9 June 2011.

203. 'Kidnapping Iranians in Syria, fear tactic', *Press TV*, 22 December 2011; 'Iranian MP Urges Immediate Freedom of Abducted Nationals in Syria', *Fars News Agency*, 28 January 2012; 'Families of Iranians missing in Syria plead for U.N. probe', *Los Angeles Times*, 11 April 2012.

204. 'Turkish journalists released from Syria with Iran's help', *BBC*, 12 May 2012.

205. 'How strong is their alliance?', *Al-Ahram Weekly*, 7 June 2008.

206. 'Ahmadinejad conveys note to Al-Assad', *Press TV*, 8 March 2011.

Chapter 2. Policy and Values

1. The best attempts to date to explain the power structure of post-revolutionary Iran are Schirazi, Asghar, *The Constitution of Iran: Politics and the State in the Islamic Republic* (London, 1998), and Buchta, Wilfried, *Who Rules Iran? The Structure of Power in the Islamic Republic* (Washington D.C., 2000).

2. Buchta: *Who Rules Iran?*, pp. 2–3.

3. Ramazani, Ruholla, 'Khumayni's Islam in Iran's Foreign Policy' in A. Dawisha (ed), *Islam in Foreign Policy* (Cambridge, 1983), p. 29.

4. Buchta: *Who Rules Iran?*, p. 11.

5. Schirazi, p. 68.

6. Ehteshami and Hinnebusch: *Syria and Iran*, p. 31; Ehteshami, Anoushiravan, 'The Foreign Policy of Iran', in A. Ehteshami and R. Hinnebusch, *The Foreign Policies of Middle East States* (Boulder Co., 2002), p. 291. For a discussion of the different camps within the Iranian leadership, see Buchta: *Who Rules Iran?*.

7. Bakhash, Shaul, 'Iran's Foreign Policy under the Islamic Republic, 1979–2000', in C. Brown (ed), *Diplomacy in the Middle East. The International Relations of Regional and Outside Powers* (London, 2004), p. 248.

8. Schirazi, p. 240.

9. Sick, Gary, 'Iran's Foreign Policy: A Revolution in Transition', in N. Keddie and R. Matthee, *Iran and the Surrounding World* (Seattle and London, 2002), p. 362.

10. Buchta: *Who Rules Iran?*, pp. 22–3.

11. Ehteshami and Hinnebusch: *Syria and Iran*, pp. 32–35.

12. Karim Sadjadpour at the University of Maryland symposium on 'Iran after the 2009 Elections: Domestic, Regional and International Dimensions', 6 November 2009, in a panel entitled 'Iran's Regional Position', available online: http://ms-websvr.ad.eng.umd.edu/DETSMediasite5/Viewer/?peid=3 5639796c7a94e3fbe98a418d04b5662.

13. 'Expansion of ties with Arab states a priority – Dy FM', *IRNA*, 4 October 2007; 'Top Syrian official praises Iran's stand on nuclear right', *IRNA*, 27 September 2005.

14. Chehabi: *Distant Relations*, pp. 190–2, 223. On Mohtashemipur's relationship with Khomeini see his memoirs, Mohtashemipur, Ali Akbar, *Khatirat hojja-toleslam va al-muslimin Sayyid Ali Akbar Mohtashemipur* (Tehran, 1997–9).

15. 'A new ambassador for Iran in Damascus', *arabicnews.com*, 21 July 1998; www.ahl-ul-bait.org/dabirkol/akhtari/index.htm.

16. 'Iran to appoint new Syria envoy', *IRNA*, 8 October 2007.

17. 'Tehran's new ambassadors to Syria, Pakistan, South Africa named', *Tehran Times*, 21 August 2011; 'Iran's new ambassador to Syria arrives in Damascus', *IRNA*, 14 October 2011.

18. Buchta: *Who Rules Iran?*, pp. 47–49.

19. Schirazi, p. 154.

20. Ibid, p. 74.

21. Elements of this section are published in my chapter in Chehabi, H.E., Khosrokhavar, Farhad and Therme, Clement (eds), *Iran and the Challenges of the Twenty-First Century. Essays in Honour of Mohammad-Reza Djalili.* (Costa Mesa, CA, 2013)

22. www.iranculture.org/en/nahad/ertebatat.php (accessed on 09 May 2008).

23. Hunter, Shireen, 'Iran and the Arab World', in M. Rezun (ed), *Iran at the Crossroads, Global Relations in a Turbulent Decade*, (Boulder Co., 1990); Ehteshami and Hinnebusch: *Syria and Iran*, p. 89. Iranian constitution, Article 16.

24. Marschall: *Iran's Persian Gulf Policy*, p. 11.

25. Former Iranian cultural attaché to Damascus. Shafi'ai, p. 98 [translation author's own].

26. Hunter: *Iran and the World*, p. 40.

27. Marschall: *Iran's Persian Gulf Policy*, p. 12.

28. Buchta, Wilfried, 'The Failed Pan-Islamic Program of the Islamic Republic: Views of the Liberal Reformers of the Religious "Semi-Opposition"', in Keddie and Matthee: *Iran and the Surrounding World*, p. 283.

29. Djalili, Mohammad Reza, *Diplomatie Islamique* (Paris, 1989), pp. 63–66.

30. Ramazani: *Revolutionary Iran*, p. 25.

31. Rajaee, Farhang, 'Iranian Ideology and Worldview: The Cultural Export of the Revolution', in J. Esposito (ed), *The Iranian Revolution, Its Global Impact* (Miami, 1990), p. 72.

32. Ibid.

33. www.iranculture.org/en/nahad/tabligh.php.

34. As quoted by Ramazani: 'Khumayni's Islam in Iran's Foreign Policy', p.19.

35. Interview with ICRO official, Tehran, 22 April 2006. For an idea about one aspect of Iran's cultural policies abroad in the first revolutionary decade, see Rajaee: 'Iranian Ideology and Worldview'.

36. www.iranculture.org/en/nahad/ershad.php (accessed on 09 May 2008). For a discussion of the power struggles at the beginning of the revolution, see Keddie, Nikki, *Modern Iran, Roots and Results of Revolution* (New Haven, 2003), Chapter 10.

37. Buchta, Wilfried, *Die iranische Schia und die islamische Einheit 1979–1996* (Hamburg, 1997), p. 246f.

38. These two associations were founded by Khamene'i in October 1990, coming out of the 'World Conference on the ahl al-bayt' held in Tehran in April 1990, with the idea of fostering unity between the Islamic schools of thought. For more on both associations, see Buchta: *Die iranische Schia und die islamische Einheit*, pp. 245ff.

39. Constitution of the ICRO (dated 21 November 1995), Article 10.

40. Constitution of the ICRO, Article 2; www.icro.ir; 'adawa' 'ala rabitat al-thaqafa wa al-'alaqat al-islamiya fi iran' *al-thaqafa al-islamiya* 89, p. 153; Shafia'i, p. 98; Interview with ICRO official, Tehran, 23 September 2008.

41. 'adawa' 'ala rabitat al-thaqafa wa al-'alaqat al-islamiya fi iran', p. 154; Constitution of the ICRO, Article 3c.

42. Constitution of the ICRO, Article 8.

43. In 'adawa' 'ala rabitat al-thaqafa wa al-'alaqat al-islamiya fi iran', the number of countries in which there were Iranian cultural representations was put at over 68 (p. 155); in a discussion with an ICRO official, the latter put the number of cultural centres at around 62, mentioning that the number of countries was lower than this, as Iran had several cultural centres in some countries (such as Pakistan), interview with ICRO official, Tehran 19 April 2006.

44. Interview with Ali Ansarian, Director of the Iranian cultural centre, Damascus, 19 April 2008, and Muhammad Hassan Javid, cultural attaché at the Iranian Embassy, Damascus, 24 June 2008.
45. Interviews with ICRO officials, Damascus April 2008 and Tehran September 2008.
46. Shaffer, Brenda, 'The Islamic Republic of Iran: Is It Really?', in B. Shaffer (ed), *The Limits of Culture: Islam and Foreign Policy* (Cambridge MA, 2006), p. 219.
47. Interview with ICRO officials, Tehran September 2008.
48. See for instance Azarshab, Muhammad Ali, *Al-'alaqat al-thaqafiya al-iraniya al-'arabiya* (Damascus, 2001).
49. See Chapter 4.
50. Ehteshami and Hinnebusch: *Syria and Iran*, pp. 62–3.
51. Seale: *Asad*, p. 433. For an account of the power struggle between the two brothers, see Seale: *Asad*, Chapter 24: 'The Brothers' War'.
52. Ibid, pp. 64–5; Hinnebusch, Raymond, 'The Foreign Policy of Syria', in Ehteshami and Hinnebusch: *The Foreign Policies of Middle East States*, p. 149.
53. Lesch, David, 'The Role of Bashar al-Asad in Syrian Foreign Policy', in R. Hinnebusch (ed), *Syrian Foreign Policy and the United States: From Bush to Obama* (St Andrews, 2010), pp. 44–5.
54. Ibid, p. 45.
55. 'Reshuffling the Cards? (I): Syria's Evolving Strategy' *Crisis Group Middle East Report* nr. 92 (2009), p. 4, drawing on an interview from June 2008.
56. Interview with Hamid Hassan, Syrian ambassador to Iran, Tehran, 13 December 2005.
57. Interview with Samir Altaqi, Director, Orient Centre for International Studies, Damascus, 29 April 2008.
58. Rabinovich, Itamar, *The View from Damascus: State, Political Community and Foreign Relations in Twentieth-Century Syria* (London, 2008), p. 315.
59. Al Khatib, Reem and Yazaji, Rana, 'Syria', in *Cultural Policies in Algeria, Egypt, Jordan, Lebanon, Morocco, Palestine, Syria and Tunisia* (Amsterdam, 2010), p. 181.
60. Interview with Nazih Khoury, Head of the department of foreign affairs of the Syrian Ministry of Culture, Damascus, 8 June 2008.
61. Al Khatib, Reem and Yazaji, Rana, *Compendium. Country Profile Syria* (unpublished manuscript), p. 20f.
62. Dawn, Ernest C., 'The Foreign Policy of Syria', in C. Brown (ed), *Diplomacy in the Middle East. The International Relations of Regional and Outside Powers* (London, 2004), p. 159.

63. Hinnebusch: 'The Foreign Policy of Syria', p. 143.

64. Aflaq, Michel, *Choice of texts from the Ba'th party founder's thought* (Florence, 1977), as quoted in Hopwood, Derek, *Syria 1945–1986. Politics and Society* (London, 1988), p. 132.

65. Al Khatib and Yazaji: *Compendium*, p. 29.

66. Taheri, Abdallah Naseri, 'Limadha?! Kaifa?! Ila ayna?!' *al-thaqafa al-islamiya* no. 4 (1986), pp. 5–6.

67. Hirschfeld: 'The odd couple'; Kabalan, Marwan, 'Understanding Syria-Iran alliance', *Gulf News*, 6 November 2008.

68. Ehteshami and Hinnebusch: *Syria and Iran*, p. 113.

69. Interview with Ali Ansarian.

70. Interview with Bassel Neyazi, Cultural attaché, Syrian Embassy Tehran, Tehran, 17 September 2008.

71. Interview with Ali Ansarian.

72. Murad, Riyad Abdulhamid, *al-tabadul al-thaqafi* (Damascus, 1989), p. 7.

73. Ibid, p. 10.

74. 'Hamdanids' *Encyclopedia of Islam* vol.III (Leiden: Brill, 1971), p. 129; 'Sayf al-Dawla' *Encyclopedia of Islam* vol.IX (Leiden, 1995), p. 103.

75. Interview with Muhammad Ali Azarshab, Former director of the Iranian cultural centre Damascus, Tehran, 5 November 2008.

76. 'Ibn 'Asakir' *Encyclopedia of Islam* vol.III (Leiden, 1971), p. 714; 'al-Sam'ani, Abu Sa'd' *Encyclopedia of Islam* vol.VIII (Leiden, 1995), p. 1024.

77. For short biographies of each, see their entries in the Encyclopedia of Islam.

78. See cultural programmes of the Iranian cultural centre Damascus and list of its publications.

79. Interview with Azarshab, 5 November 2008.

80. Ramazani states seven main principles of Khomeini's Iran's foreign policy: independence of East and West, identification of the USA as main enemy of the Islamic Revolution, fight against the superpowers and Zionism, close relations with all oppressed peoples, especially those in Islamic countries, liberation of Jerusalem and opposition to pro-Israeli states, anti-Imperialism, support of the oppressed/*mustaza'fin* of the world; as quoted in Buchta: *Die iranische Schia und die islamische Einheit*, p. 16.

81. Interview with Palestinian ambassador to Iran, Tehran, 18 September 2008; Ehteshami and Hinnebusch: *Syria and Iran*, p. 89.

82. Interview with Palestinian ambassador to Iran.

83. Pierret, Thomas, 'Sunni Clergy Politics in the Cities of Ba'thi Syria' in F. Lawson (ed), *Demystifying Syria* (London, 2009), p. 77.

84. 'Syrian MP considers World Qods Day as late Imam Khomeini's legacy', *IRNA*, 18 October 2006.

85. See for instance 'suriyeh – bargozari-ye morasem rooz-e jehani-ye qods va 'alam nata'ij mosabeqe (qods az manzur honar va adab)', http://damascus. icro.ir/?c=newsShow&NewsId=570006&t=4, September 2009.

86. Broadcast journalist Charlie Rose Interview with Bashar al-Asad, Damascus, May 2010, www.charlierose.com.

87. Conversation with taxi driver, Tehran, August 2006.

88. Conversation with taxi driver, Tehran, 8 June 2009.

89. Excerpt from report by Syria radio on 15 September 1998, 'Syrian, Iranian Culture Ministers discuss cooperation', *BBC SWB*, 16 September 1998.

90. Buchta: *Die iranische Schia und die islamische Einheit*, p. 251; Kramer, Martin, 'The Global Village of Islam' *Middle East Contemporary Survey* vol.16 (1992), p. 203.

91. Baktiari, Bahman and Bayat, Asef, 'Revolutionary Iran and Egypt: Exporting Inspirations and Anxieties', in Keddie and Matthee: *Iran and the Surrounding World*.

92. For a discussion of the ahl al-bayt Assembly, see Buchta: *Die iranische Schia und die islamische Einheit*, Chapter 8.

93. Ibid, p. 248.

94. Ibid, p. 300.

95. Personal observations of the activities of the Iranian cultural centre in Damascus, 2008 and 2009. For a description of the Abu Nur foundation, see Böttcher, Annabelle, *Syrische Religionspolitik unter Asad* (Freiburg, 1998), p. 154f.; Pierret, p. 76.

96. Pierret, p. 74.

97. As quoted in Böttcher: *Syrische Religionspolitik unter Asad*, p. 207.

98. Ibid, p. 10; Hopwood, p. 99.

99. Böttcher: *Syrische Religionspolitik unter Asad*, p. 207.

100. Böttcher, Annabelle, 'Official Sunni and Shi'i Islam in Syria' *San Domenico, European University Institute working paper* (2002/3), p. 15.

Chapter 3. Pre-1979 Cultural Diplomacy and Foundations for Post-Revolutionary Cultural Exchange

1. Shafi'ai, pp. 96–7.

2. Iranian Foreign Ministry: *Suriyeh*, p. 221.

3. IFM year: 1331–5, K: 4, D: 72, file nr: 203/1, date: 22 January 1952.

4. IFM year: 1331–5, K:4, D: 72, file nr. 158, date: 6 May 1952 and file nr. 384/81, date: 4 June 1952. For an account of Syrian domestic politics in the 1940s and 50s, see Seale: *The Struggle for Syria*.

5. The treaty was signed by Moshfegh Kazemi and the Syrian Minister of Foreign Affairs, Zafer Rifai. IFM year: 1331–5, K: 4, D: 72, file w/out nr, date: 24 May 1953 and file w/out nr, date: 26 June 1955.

6. IFM year: 1331–5, K: 4, D: 72.

7. Ibid.

8. IFM year: 1336–40, K: 8, D: 144, file nr: 261/22, date: 31/02/1336.

9. As a side note on pre-revolutionary cultural diplomacy: the editor of Asadollah Alam's classic account *The Shah and I* added a footnote under the entry of 21 April 1969, when Farah Diba had gone to Paris to open the *Maison d'Iran*, that the latter was intended as a cultural and promotional centre, but ended up doing little more than sell carpets and caviar. Alam, Asadollah, *The Shah and I* (London, 1991), p. 54.

10. IFM year: 1341–45, K:19, D: 302, date: 30 January 1963 (excerpt from book draft about Iranian cultural relations with Syria). 'Musahibe ba ustad Ahmad Aram' *Khabarname farhangistan zaban va adab farsi* 15 and 16 (*esfand* 75 and *farvardin* 76). Beidun, Labib, *Hayat wa dhikriyat fi hay al-amin* (Damascus, 2003), pp. 332–346. Interview with Labib Beidun, Damascus, 29 January 2009.

11. Interview with Labib Beidun.

12. IFM year: 1351–55, K: 156, D: 2255.

13. IFM year: 1341–45, K:19, D: 302, date: 30 January1963.

14. Iranian Foreign Ministry: *Suriyeh*, p. 222, Goodarzi, p. 15.

15. See Chapter 1.

16. Amiri, Kiumarth, *Zaban va adab farisi dar jehan; suriyeh* (Tehran, 2002), p. 132.

17. Iranian Foreign Ministry: *Suriyeh*, p. 223. See Chapter 1.

18. IFM year: 1351–55, K: 157, D: 2260, file nr. 2297, date 21 January 1974. 1975 cultural agreement between Syria and Iran. IFM, file nr. 10476/17, date: 18/08/1353 (9 November 1975) (hereafter referred to as the 1975 cultural agreement).

19. IFM year: 1351–55, K: 157, D: 2260, file nr. 10476/18, date: 18/08/1354. Amiri, p. 134ff. Also see the table below.

20. IFM year: 1351–55, file nr. 175, date: 07/12/1353. File nr. 2050, date 16 March 1975 (also see responses to circulars where he mentions the things not existing in Syria).

21. Shafi'ai, p. 100; Amiri, p. 133; Salmani, Abdulkarim, 'Adawa' 'ala al-lugha al-farisiya' *al-thaqafa al-islamiya* no.100, p. 110. IFM correspondence al-Tounji.

22. IFM year: 1351–55, K: 156, D: 2255.

23. Ibid, various files, and file nr. 185, date: 14/12/1353. The majma' al-lugha al-'arabiya was an institution set up in Damascus in 1918 to revive the Arabic language.

24. IFM various files from the 1970s.
25. IFM file nr. 212, date: 20/07/2536 (1978).
26. IFM file nr. 405, date: 27/12/2536 (1978).
27. Amiri, p. 132.
28. IFM survey of documents.
29. IFM file nr. 1187/24, date: 6 October 1957; see several files of IFM year 1341–1345, K;13, D:215, correspondence between the Iranian embassy Damascus, the Syrian foreign ministry, Damascus University and Tehran University.
30. Pamphlet on Muhammad al-Furati by the ministry of culture printed on the occasion of a special remembrance seminar for al-Furati, Dayr al-Zur, 16 and 17 May 2007.
31. 'Liqa' hiwari m'a al-sayed wazir al-thaqafa al-suri al-doktor mahmud al-sayed' *al-thaqafa al-islamiya* no.100, p. 45. The Syrian Minister of Education in 1984 was Muhammad Najib al-Sayid Ahmad, the Iranian Minister of Culture and Higher Education was Muhammad Ali al-Najafi.
32. Article 12, copy of 1984 cultural agreement between Syria and Iran, obtained from the Syrian ministry of culture, 8 June 2008 (hereafter referred to as 1984 cultural agreement). See also the table above.
33. 1984 cultural agreement.
34. Amiri, p. 150.
35. 1984 cultural agreement, Shafi'ai p. 101, and Amiri, p. 150. Text of cultural implementation programmes between Syria and Iran for the years 2003–2005 and 2006–2008, obtained from the Syrian ministry of culture, 8 June 2009, hereafter referred to as cultural implementation programmes.
36. Cultural implementation programme 2003–2005.

Chapter 4. Iran's Cultural Diplomacy in Syria

* Elements of this chapter have previously been published in my article 'The Case of Iranian Cultural Diplomacy in Syria' *Middle East Journal of Culture and Communication* 2 (2009), 1-18.
1. www.ifporient.org/spip.php?article815.
2. www.ccf-damas.org/rubrique.php3?id_rubrique=4.
3. www.britishcouncil.org/syria-about-us-who-we-are.htm.
4. Goethe-Institut yearbook 2008.
5. The Russian centre was forced to close down in 1973 after its building had been bombed by the Israelis. It re-opened in 1976 in a new (and its current) location. Interview with Head of Administration, Russian cultural centre, Damascus, 31 March 2009.

6. http://damasco.cervantes.es/es/sobre_nosotros_espanol.htm and www.iicdamasco. esteri.it/IIC_Damasco/Menu/Istituto/Chi_siamo/Storia/.
7. IFM, file nr. 179, date: 02/07/2536 (1977).
8. Interview with Turkish embassy official, Damascus, 29 May 2008.
9. Shafi'ai, p. 101.
10. Interview with Muhammad Husayn Hashemi, ICRO, Tehran, April 2006.
11. Goethe Institut yearbook 2008.
12. Interview with Nazih Khoury.
13. ICRO file nr. 136. 'Fa'aliyethaye honari markaz farhangi amrika dar dameshq', 30/08/1374 (1995).
14. ICRO file nr. 5513. 'Gozaresh marakez farhangi khareji dar suriyeh', 30/11/1369 (1991).
15. Markings of cultural centres by author. Map: Syrian Ministry of Tourism, www.syriatourism.org.
16. Interview Muhammad Hassan Javid. Cultural attaché, Iranian Embassy Damascus, Damascus, 24 June 2008; see Chapter 2.
17. http://damascus.icro.ir/, and interviews with Ali Ansarian, and Muhammad Ali Azarshab.
18. ICRO file nr. 3192. 'Ashna'i ba barnameha va fa'aliyethaye farhangi, honari, daneshgahi va pajuheshi raizan farhangi jomhuri eslami iran dar suriyeh'.
19. Table by author. Source: http://damascus.icro.ir/. For a short biography of Dr Aynevand, see www.adabefarsi.ir/Default.aspx?page=5357&section= pfitem&id=37035. While the ICRO website states that he was Cultural Councillor from 1981, the biography states that he was in fact Cultural Councillor from 1983, which makes more sense as that was the year the cultural centre opened. For an idea of the 'Society for the Defence of the Palestinian Nation', see its website www.pngo.ir.
20. http://damascus.icro.ir/.
21. Shafi'ai, p. 101.
22. ICRO file nr. 3192.
23. Table by author. Source: Amrani, pp. 345–412.
24. Amrani, Yaser, 'Fahras mawdua'i 'aam li-'adad al-thaqafa al-islamiya min al-'adad 1–100' al-thaqafa al-islamiya no.100 (2006), p. 387.
25. Taheri, Abdallah Naseri (ed), al-thaqafa al-islamiya no.1 (1406h), p. 148. Quote adapted from the English version of the editorial.
26. Barnamij al-nashatat al-thaqafiya brochure, Iranian Cultural Centre Damascus, Oct/Nov/Dec 2003.
27. Faslnameh Farhangi (Persian). ICRO Syria Website. [http://damascus.icro.ir /?c=newsShow&NewsId=554537&t=4]. For a detailed account of the centre's

activities between 2003 and 2006, see Iranian Cultural Chancellor (ed), *Gahnameh Farhangi* 1–11 (Damascus, 2003–2006).

28. Conversation with member of the editorial board of the *Faslnameh Farhangi*, Damascus, 4 August 2010.

29. There is an automatic count of number of visitors on the ICRO websites. In comparison, the Persian homepage of the Iranian cultural centre in Beirut had received a total of 179,642 hits, the one in London 227,205, and the one in Kuala Lumpur 227,858 hits by 28 May 2012.

30. Survey of this brochure, called *barnamij al-nashatat al-thaqafiya*, nr. 19–23 (winter 2008 – winter 2009).

31. The shrine of Sayida Zaynab, granddaughter of the Prophet Muhammad and sister of Imam Husayn, is one of the main visiting sights for Shi'i pilgrims to Syria, in particular Iranians. Its place in the Syrian-Iranian cultural dialogue will be discussed in detail in Chapter 7.

32. Personal observations at the book exhibition in memory of the 29th year of the Islamic Revolution in Iran, Iranian cultural centre, Damascus February 2008, and at the book exhibition in memory of Imam Khomeini, Sayida Zaynab, June 2008.

33. Personal observations, Damascus International Book Fair, Damascus National Library 2008.

34. ICRO Damascus website, http://damascus.icro.ir/index.aspx?siteid=140&pa geid=11630&newsview=551774 [accessed 9 August 2010].

35. Shafi'ai, p. 106, Interview with ICRO official, Tehran, 22 April 2006.

36. 'adawa' 'ala al-usbu'a al-thaqafi al-irani al-kabir fi al-juhuriya al-'arabiya al-suriya' *al-thaqafa al-islamiya* no.96, p. 242; 'yaftahu al-sayed wa jame'i al-usbu'a al-thaqafi al-irani', *Tishrin Newspaper*, 26 September 2004. For a full account of the Iranian cultural week in Damascus, see 'adawa' 'ala al-usbu'a al-thaqafi al-irani al-kabir fi al-jumhuriya al-'arabiya al-suriya', pp. 235–261.

37. ICRO file nr. 3192.

38. 'Iranian minister, Syrian president discuss improving cultural ties', *IRNA*, 21 September 2004.

39. 'Iranian Cultural Week kicks off in Syria', *IranMania*, 15 August 2005.

40. 'Mas'ul farhangi suri: iraniyan va arab do bal-e umat islami hastand', ICRO Report on cultural week in Safita, http://damascus.icro.ir/?c=newsShow&Ne wsId=548355&t=4. See also statement by Iran's chargé d'affaires in Syria who explained 'the conspiracies of global arrogance and its collaborators against Islamic countries', see 'Iranian cultural week starts in Syrian Qalamoun University', *IRNA*, 28 April 2007.

41. ICRO file nr. 3192.

42. See for instance 'Iranian cultural week in Safita', *al-Thawra*, 3 August 2003; announcement in *al-Ba'th*, 3 August 2003; 'Iranian cultural week in Salmiya', *Tishrin*, 3 September 2003; 'Iranian cultural week in Salmiya', *al-Thawra*, 4 September 2003 and 7 September 2003; 'Iranian cultural week in Latakia', *Tishrin*, 15 December 2003; 'Iranian cultural week in Damascus', *Tishrin, al-Thawra, al-Ba'th*, 20 September 2004, in which the programme of the cultural weeks are laid out.
43. ICRO file nr. 3699. 'Bargozari hafte farhangi jomhuri eslami iran dar lazaqiyeh'.
44. Personal observations, Aleppo 10–11 March 2008.
45. Personal observations at attendance of the opening of the Iranian cinemal festival, Damascus, 23 May 2010.
46. Ibid.
47. Shafi'ai, p. 104.
48. Decision taken on the occasion of the 25th anniversary of the Islamic revolution. See ICRO file nr. 4932. 'Molaqatha ba shakhsiyathaye rasmi suriyeh', 30/10/1382.
49. Mervin, Sabrina, 'Sayyida Zaynab: banlieue de Damas ou nouvelle ville sainte chiite?' *CEMOTI* 22 (1996), p. 154.
50. The academy of Sheikh Ahmad Kaftaru was previously called the *majm'a abu nur*, or Abu Nur foundation.
51. Böttcher: *Syrische Religionspolitik unter Asad*, p. 206.
52. 'al-thawra al-islamiya wa takrim al-nukhub al-thaqafiya', pamphlet, Iranian Cultural Centre Damascus (February 2008).
53. For an account of the profile of attendees at the 2004 ceremony, see ICRO file nr. 5996. 'Hemayesh enqelab eslami va takrim nokhobegan', 27/11/1382 (2004).
54. Various speeches given by the participants of the Fifth Conference on Islamic Unity, Iranian cultural centre and Asad Library, Damascus, May 2008.
55. Böttcher: 'Official Sunni and Shi'i Islam in Syria', p. 5.
56. Pierret, Thomas, 'Les cadres de l'élite religieuse sunnite' *Maghreb-Machrek* nr.198 (2008–2009), p. 14.
57. Böttcher: 'Official Sunni and Shi'i Islam in Syria', p. 11.
58. See *barnamij al-nashatat al-thaqafiya* brochures of the Iranian cultural centre from 2003 onwards.
59. ICRO file nr. 6914. 'Gozaresh safar hay'at bolandpayeh asatid-e daneshgah al-zahra beh jomhori arabi suriyeh', 28/12/1382 (March 2004).
60. ICRO file nr. 433/2/25. Subject not specified in title.
61. Prior to this, the centre had already unofficially been in existence for several years; the library was located on the 4th floor of the cultural centre, a section

for films and seminars in the basement. ICRO file nr. 8043. 'Gozareshi az vazaiyat kitabkhaneh iranshenasi markaz motale'at raizani farhangi jomhuri eslami iran dar suriyeh', 31/02/1380 (2001).

62. Brochure on the Centre for Iranian-Arab Cultural Studies, Iranian cultural centre Damascus (Damascus, 2005).

63. Ibid, and personal observations, Iranian cultural centre, Damascus, February – June 2008.

64. ICRO file nr. 10545. 'Cheshm andazi no beh vazaiyat alaviyan b'ad az riyasat aghaye bashar al-asad', 30/10/1381 (January 2003).

65. Interview with Seyyed Ali Hosseini, Director of the Iranian cultural centre Latakia, Latakia, 10 August 2010.

66. Personal observation at lecture on Arab-Iranian cultural relations, organised by the Iranian cultural centre and held at the Arab cultural centre, Latakia, 12 May 2008.

67. Interview with Hosseini and conversation with several language students, Iranian cultural centre, Latakia, 10 August 2010. 'mudir al-markaz al-thaqafi al-irani fi al-ladhaqiya: al-'alaqat al-suriya al-iraniya watida-tan... wa tabadul lil-'alm wa al-thaqafa wa tawasul hidari 'ariq', *al-Wahda*, 23 November 2009.

68. Personal observations, Iranian cultural centre Latakia, Latakia, 10 August 2010.

69. ICRO file nr. 9286. 'Iraniyan muqim suriyeh va apish nevis asasnameh tashkil komiteh umur iraniyan'.

70. Interview with Muhammad Ali Azarshab.

71. The language classes and their reach are discussed in Chapter 6.

72. ICRO file nr. 3192.

73. Conversation with a Christian girl who took Persian classes at the Iranian cultural centre in the late 1990s, and had to cover up. Her father accompanied her to the classes to support her. Conversation, Damascus, March 2008.

Chapter 5. Syria's Cultural Diplomacy in Iran

1. Dehshiri, Muhammad-Rida, 'Principles and Fundamentals of Islamic Diplomacy From Imam Khomeini's Viewpoint', in M.H. Hafezian (ed), *Imam Khomeini and the International System* (Tehran, 2006).

2. 'Die Strumpfbandaffäre – Iran, Deutschland und die Pressefreiheit', *Süddeutsche Zeitung*, 14 February 2007, available: http://www.sueddeutsche. de/kultur/798/319670/text/.

3. Interview with Alfred Walter, representative of the Goethe-Institut, German Embassy Tehran, 30 October 2008.

4. Interview with German cultural attaché, German Embassy Tehran, 30 October 2008.

5. Interview Alfred Walter.

6. British Council statement on Iran, 4 February 2009. Available: http://news. bbc.co.uk/1/hi/world/middle_east/7870699.stm.

7. UK culture body halts Iran work. BBC, 4 February 2009. Available: news. bbc.co.uk/1/hi/world/middle_east/7870503.stm.

8. www.ambafrance-ir.org/article.php3?id_article=19.

9. Interview German cultural attaché, German Embassy Tehran, 30 October 2008.

10. Ashura is on the 10th of Muharram (Islamic Calendar) and commemorates Imam Husayn's martyrdom in the battle of Karbala; it is a day of national mourning in Iran.

11. Interview Austrian cultural attaché, Austrian Embassy Tehran, 10 June 2009, and website of the Österreichisches Kulturforum Teheran, http:// www.austria-iran.com/.

12. http://english.hanban.org/node_10680.htm (last accessed 28 July 2010).

13. Text of 1984 cultural agreement. This article was highlighted in the Syrian ministry of culture's file.

14. 'Tarhib irani bi-iftitah markaz thaqafi suri fi Tehran', *Tishrin*, 3 November 2004.

15. Interview with Nazih Khoury.

16. The Expediency Council is an advisory body for the Leader of the Islamic Republic; for an explanation of its official functions and how it is embedded in the Iran's power structure, see Buchta: *Who Rules Iran?*, p. 62.

17. 'al-usbu'a al-thaqafi al-suri fi Tehran, 28/02–08/03/2002' *al-thaqafa al-islamiya*, pp. 188–191.

18. Interview with Ibrahim Zarur, Damascus University, Damascus, 9 June 2008.

19. See brochure of the Arab-Syrian cultural centre in Tehran, published by the centre in summer 2007.

20. 'Bahth majalat al-ta'awun al-thaqafi m'a iran', *Tishrin*, 2 February 2005.

21. al-Gharir, 'B'ad al-malamih al-asasiyya lil-'alaqat al-suriyya al-iraniyya'.

22. Interview Musa al-Gharir, Arab-Syrian cultural centre, Tehran, 23 April 2006.

23. Interview Musa al-Gharir, Arab-Syrian cultural centre, Tehran, 4 November 2008.

24. Interview with Syrian professor of Persian language and literature, Aleppo, 1 June 2009.

25. Personal observations, Arab-Syrian cultural centre, Tehran, 2006–2009.

26. Interview Husayn Idriss, Syrian Cultural Centre, Tehran, 15 September 2008.

27. 'Amsiya sh'ariya bil-markaz al-thaqafi al-suri fi Tehran', *Tishrin*, 10 March 2005.

28. 'Nashatat thaqafiya wa faniya fi al-Thaqafi al-suri bi-tehran', *Tishrin*, 12 April 2009; 'Amsiya sh'ariya wa m'arad lil-fann al-tashkili bi-tehran bi-munsabiat "aid al-jala"', *Tishrin*, 24 April 2006.

29. 'al-thaqafi al-arabi al-suri fi Tehran yahtafi bi-dhikra harb tishrin al-tahririya', *Tishrin*, 1 October 2009.

30. 'Amsiya sh'ariya fi al-markaz al-thaqafi al-suri fi Tehran hawil al-muqawama al-lubnaniya wa al-falestiniya', *Tishrin*, 25 September 2006.

31. 'Nadwa hawil intisar al-muqawama al-lubnaniya fi "al-thaqafi al-suri" fi Tehran', *Tishrin*, 28 September 2006.

32. 'Syria urges Iran to make joint film on 33-day war', *IRNA*, 21 December 2008.

33. 'Fa'aliyat thaqafiya fi al-markaz al-thaqafi al-'arabi al-suri bi-Tehran hawla al-mu'amara 'ala suriya wa al-mukhatat al-sahiu-amirki wa adawatihi fi al-mintaqa', *SANA*, 26 April 2012.

34. Conversation with Iranian student of Arabic, Tehran, 20 August 2010.

35. Interview with former student at the Syrian cultural centre in Tehran, by Email, 6 August 2010.

36. 'Ihtifaliya Nizar Qabbani fi Tehran', *Tishrin*, 6 May 2009.

37. Interview with former student at the Syrian cultural centre in Tehran, by Email, 6 August 2010.

38. 'Iftitah al-m'arad al-siyahi al-suri fi Tehran', *Tishrin*, 30 July 2008.

39. Ibid; 'Hadj and Pilgrimage Organization', www.iranculture.org/en/nahad/haj.php.

40. 'al-Ma'alim al-siyahiya al-suriya fi m'arad bi-mashhad al-iraniya', *Tishrin*, 27 November 2005.

41. 'M'arad thaqafi siyahi suri fi Tehran', *Tishrin*, 25 December 2005.

42. 'Iftitah al-jenah al-suri al-turathi wa al-siyahi fi jami'at Isfahan', *SANA*, 21 May 2012.

43. Interview with Husayn Idriss.

44. Brochure of the Arab-Syrian cultural centre in Tehran (2007).

45. Interview with Husayn Idriss.

46. Brochure of the Arab-Syrian cultural centre in Tehran (2007); official website of the *farhangserai melal*: www.fsm.ir.

47. Brochure of the Arab-Syrian cultural centre in Tehran (2007).

48. Interview with Abdelmetin, Syrian Cultural Centre, Tehran, 4 November 2008. See Chapter 6 'The role of language students: Arabic language teaching in Iran' below.

49. Interview with former student at the Syrian cultural centre in Tehran, by Email, 6 August 2010.

50. Interview with Musa al-Gharir, 4 November 2008.
51. Interview with Husayn Idriss.
52. For the Iran Language Institute's involvement with the Syrian centre, see Chapter 6.
53. Conversation with Iranian student in Syria, 30 July 2010.
54. Interview with Husayn Idriss and interview with Musa al-Gharir, 4 November 2008.

Chapter 6. Students

1. Nye: *Soft Power*, p. 75.
2. Ibid, pp. 44–45.
3. Maskarnejad, Jalil, 'Ahmiyat t'alim al-lugha' *al-thaqafa al-islamiya* no.67 (1996), p. 194.
4. Mitchell, p. 9.
5. 1984 cultural agreement and 1975 cultural agreement. See table above.
6. Amiri, pp. 150–52.
7. See texts of cultural implementation programmes 2003–2005 and 2006–2008.
8. Maskarnejad, p. 197.
9. Iranian Cultural Chancellor (ed), *Gahnameh Farhangi 1, Iranian Cultural Centre Damascus* (Damascus, 2003), p. 30. 'Waza'iyat zaban-e farsi dar suriyeh' *pajuheshha-ye mutal'ati nr. 4* (mordad mah 1383/July 2004), pp. 17–20.
10. ICRO file nr. 1877. 'Gozareshi az vazaiyat fa'eli tadris va adabiyat farsi dar daneshkadeh adabiyat dameshq', 30/10/1372 (January 1994).
11. Shafi'ai, p. 106; *Gahnameh farhangi 1*, p. 30.
12. 'Waza'iyat zaban-e farsi dar suriyeh', p. 17ff.
13. Ibid, p. 21.
14. *Gahnameh farhangi 1*, p. 29.
15. Table by author, information drawn from several sources including Amiri and 'Waza'iyat zaban-e farsi dar suriyeh'.
16. 'Waqa'ia hafl iftitah qism al-lugha al-farsiya wa adabiha fi jam'at dimashq' *al-thaqafa al-islamiya* 98, pp. 225–231.
17. ICRO file nr. 444. 'Fa'aliyat raizan farhangi jomhuri eslami iran dar suriyeh dar zamineh gostaresh zaban va adabiyat farsi dar iin keshvar'; Interview with Muhammad Hassanzadeh, Persian literature professor sent from Iran, Damascus University, 2 August 2010.
18. http://damascus.icro.ir/index.aspx?siteid=141&pageid=11631&newsview=583291 [last accessed May 2012].

19. Interviews with members of staff of the Persian departments at the universities of Aleppo, Ba'th, and Damascus, Aleppo, March 2008 and June 2009, Homs, April 2008, Damascus, June 2009.
20. www.damasuniv.shern.net.
21. Shafiʻai, p. 107.
22. For an idea of subjects of literary evenings organised by the Iranian cultural centre for students of the Persian departments, see the *barnamij al-nashatat al-thaqafiya* brochures (Arabic and Persian) of the Iranian cultural centre from 2008 onwards.
23. Interviews with members of staff of the Persian departments at the universities of Aleppo and Damascus, June 2009.
24. Interview with a former Persian language teacher, Aleppo, 1 June 2009.
25. Conversation with Iranian student and former Persian language teacher, Damascus, 2 August 2010.
26. Interview with a Persian teacher, Damascus University, 2 August 2010.
27. Interview with Persian teacher, Damascus University, 2 August2010.
28. Majlis al-taʻlim al-ʻaali, al-qarar raqam 220, al-mada 12, 13 June 2009.
29. Interviews with members of staff of the Persian departments at the universities of Aleppo and Damascus, June 2009.
30. Interview with Muhammad Hassanzadeh, Damascus University, 2 August 2010.
31. Conversations with members of staff and students of the Persian departments at the universities of Aleppo and Ba'th, Aleppo, March 2008 and Homs, April 2008.
32. Conversation with Persian teachers at the Iranian cultural centre, Damascus, 9 April 2008.
33. Interview with Muhammad Hassanzadeh.
34. Interview with Abbas Sabbagh, Director of Persian department at Aleppo University, Aleppo, 1 June 2009.
35. Interviews with Abbas Sabbagh, Muhammad Shabanan, Persian teacher at Aleppo University, 1 June 2009, with Nada Hassoun, Persian teacher at Damascus University, 31 May 2009, and Persian teachers at Ba'th University, 8 April 2008.
36. Interview with Muhammad Hassanzadeh and Nada Hassoun, Damascus University, 2 August 2010.
37. As sectarian issues are a taboo topic in Syria, I did not directly ask my classmates about their confessional background, but it could easily be derived from their place of residence, their names, the way they spoke about Imam Husayn and the family of the Prophet etc.

38. Participant observation of Persian language classes at the Iranian cultural centre, Damascus, February to June 2008, January to March 2009.
39. Constitution of the Islamic Republic of Iran, Article 16.
40. Meshkin Fam, Batul, 'al-lugha al-arabiya fi iran: al-waqi'a wa al-murtaja' *al-dirasat al-adabiya* nr. 48–52 (2005–06), p. 72.
41. al-Azhari, Nada, 'Hewar m'a ra'is qism al-lugha al-'arabiya fi jami'at Tehran... Azartash Azarnoush: ta'thir al-'arabiya fi al-farisiya gharib wa mustamir', *al-Hayat*, 24 June 2008.
42. Ibid; Meshkin Fam, p. 73; Parvini, Khalil, 'al-lugha al-'arabiya fi iran, bayn al-manahij al-jami'aiya wa al-turath al-makhtut' *al-dirasat al-adabiya* nr. 48–52 (2005–06), pp. 89–90.
43. Conversation with former MA student of Arabic literature at Tehran University, Tehran, August 2008.
44. Parvini, pp. 93–4.
45. Conversations with Arabic language teachers at several Iranian universities, Conference for teaching Arabic, Tehran, 16–18 June 2009.
46. 'Bad' dawrat t'alim al-'arabiya fi 'al-thaqafi al-'arabi al-suri' bi-tehran', *Tishrin*, 16 May 2005; Interview with Husayn Idriss; Interview with Abdelmetin.
47. Interview by email with Hajar Kashani, secretary of the Syrian cultural centre Tehran 2005–06, 10 May 2006; conversation with Syrian teacher at the centre, Tehran, 16 June 2009.
48. al-Gharir: 'B'ad al-malamih al-asasiya lil-'alaqat al-suriya al-iraniya'; conversation with Arabic language teachers at several Iranian universities, Conference for teaching Arabic, Tehran, 16–18 June 2009; conversation with Iranian Arabic language student, now a student in Syria, Damascus, 30 July 2010.
49. http://www.kanoonzaban.net/ilicms/Index.aspx.
50. Tarbiyat Modarres University is a post-graduate university located in Tehran.
51. The Iranian Association of Arabic language and literature was established in 2004 on the initiative of Dr Khalil Parvini, the head of the department of Arabic language and literature at Tarbiyat Modarres University, with the aim of improving links between Arabic departments across the country. http://www.iaal.ir/history.htm; Parvini, p. 94.
52. Personal observations at the Conference on Arabic Language Teaching, Tehran, 16–18 June 2009; see also conference programme and handouts, Iran Language Institute; 'al-markaz al-thaqafi al-suri fi Tehran yusharik fi mu'tamar al-lugha al-arabiya', *Tishrin*, 17 March 2009; 'mu'tamar dawli li-t'alim al-lugha al-'arabiya fi Tehran', *Tishrin*, 11 June 2009.
53. Conversations with Iranian Arabic language teachers, participants of the Conference on Arabic Language Teaching, Tehran, 16–18 June 2009.

54. Mitchell, p. 146.
55. Amiri, pp. 150–52.
56. For an elaboration on foreign students' relationship to their host country, see Mitchell, pp. 145–150.
57. Interview with Bassel Neyazi.
58. Table by author. Sources: Cultural Implementation Programme 1995–1997 as quoted by Amiri, p. 151; Article 20, Cultural Implementation Programme 2003–2005; Article 21, Cultural Implementation Programme 2006–2008.
59. Article 21, cultural implementation programme 2003–2005.
60. See for instance report on Iranian delegation from Semnan University visiting Tishrin University, 'al-wafd al-irani al-'almi zar jami'at tishrin', *Tishrin*, 13 June 2005; Agreement between Tishrin and Isfahan University, Syria file ICRO 3269; Damascus University has agreements with a number of Iranian universities, including Tehran, Tarbiat Modarres, Semnan, Imam Sadeq and Isfahan University. Interview with Nada Hassoun, 31 May 2009; Aleppo University has agreements with, amongst others, Tehran and Tabriz University. Interview with Abbas Sabagh, 1 June 2009.
61. Interview with Mousa Tabataba'i, Counsellor, Iranian Embassy Damascus, 12 August 2010.
62. Interview with Muhammad Hassan Javid.
63. Interview with Abbas Sabagh; Interview with Mohammad Shabanan.
64. Conversation with Iranian student, Damascus, University 1 October 2009.
65. Interview with Mohammad Shabanan.
66. Conversation with Iranian dentistry student, Damascus University, 4 August 2010.
67. Conversation with Iranian student, Damascus University, 4 August 2010.
68. Personal observations, Damascus University, 29 December 2009.
69. Conversation with Iranian students in Syria, Damascus first half of 2008 and 2009.
70. Conversation with Iranian student, Damascus, 2 August 2010.
71. Conversation with Iranian student, Damascus University, 1 October 2009.
72. Conversation with Iranian dentistry student, Damascus University, 4 August 2010.
73. Interview with Bassel Neyazi; Email exchange with former Syrian student in Iran, 29 January 2006.
74. Conversations with former and current Syrian students in Iran, Damascus and Tehran, 2008–2009.
75. Conversation with Iranian student, Damascus, 30 July 2010.
76. Conversations with former and current Syrian students in Iran, Damascus, Tehran and Latakia, May and June 2009, August 2010.

77. Interview with Muhammad Hassan Javid; 'Syria and Iran to Activate Technical and Scientific Cooperation', *SANA*, 15 November 2007.
78. Interview with Mehdi Khaledzadeh, Cultural attaché, Iranian Cultural Centre, Damascus, 27 September 2009.
79. 'Iran universities to open branches abroad', *Press TV*, 14 February 2009.
80. Interview with Seyyed Ali Hosseini.
81. Interview with Mehdi Khaledzadeh.
82. 'Iran universities to open branches abroad', *Press TV*, 14 February 2009. This information has not yet been verified.
83. Muhammadi was a professor of Arabic at Tehran University who became the chair of the centre at the Lebanese University when it was created in 1956. Shaery-Eisenlohr, Roschanak, *Shi'ite Lebanon, Transnational Religion and The Making of National Identities* (New York, 2008), pp. 165–7.
84. IFM year 1341–1345, K:13, D:215, file nr. 17000/57/813, date: 4 January 1964.
85. IFM year 1341–1345, K:13, D:215, file nr. 2523, date: 20/8/1342 (1963).
86. See several files of IFM year 1341–1345, K;13, D:215, correspondence between the Iranian embassy Damascus, the Syrian foreign ministry, Damascus University and Tehran University.
87. Interview with Muhammad al-Tounji, Aleppo, 1 June 2009. Leaflet about Muhammad al-Tounji's "academic production" including his CV, obtained from al-Tounji during the interview.

Chapter 7. Religious Tourism

1. Demos, Cultural Diplomacy, pp. 33–35.
2. Ibid, p. 37.
3. Jack, G. and A.M. Phipps, *Tourism and intercultural exchange: why tourism matters* (Clevedon, 2005), Chapter 1.
4. See Chapter 3.
5. 'Responsibilities and organizational structure of the Ministry of Culture and Islamic Guidance', www.iranculture.org/en/nahad/ershad.php.
6. 'Hadj and Pilgrimage Organization', www.iranculture.org/en/nahad/haj.php.
7. Böttcher: *Syrische Religionspolitik unter Asad*, pp. 22–23.
8. Ibid, p. 105.
9. 1984 cultural agreement; Iranian Foreign Ministry: *Suriyeh*, p. 241–2.
10. See for instance 'Iran, Syria review expansion of cooperation in energy, tourism', *IRNA*, 5 February 2008; 'Iran-Syria relations growing and exemplary: VP', *Tehran Times*, 1 March 2009; 'Tehran-Damascus sign economic MOU', Tehran Times, 12 January 2010.
11. Mitchell, Chapter 9.

12. 'Top Syrian official praises Iran's stand on nuclear right', *IRNA*, 27 September 2005.
13. See for instance 'Iran cultural week kicks off in Syria', *Press TV*, 8 February 2008.
14. 'Iran participating in Syria handicrafts exhibition', *IranMania*, 12 October 2008.
15. Personal observations, Iranian Cultural Tourism Week, Meridien Hotel Damascus, 7 February 2008.
16. 'Iftitah al-m'arad al-siyahi al-suri fi Tehran', *Tishrin*, 30 July 2008.
17. Chiffoleau, Sylvia and Madeouf, Anna (eds), *Les Pèlerinages au Maghreb et au Moyen-Orient. Espaces publics, espaces du public* (Beirut, 2005), Introduction.
18. Chiffoleau and Madeouf, p. 10.
19. For a detailed discussion of the visitation of the shrines of the Imams, see Nakash, Yitzhak, 'The visitation of the Shrines of the Imams and the Shi'i Mujtahids in the Early Twentieth Century' *Studia Islamica 81* (Paris, 1995), 153–64, and Nakash, Yitzhak, *The Shi'is of Iraq* (Princeton, 2003), Chapter 6.
20. Buchta, Wilfriend, *Schiiten* (München, 2004), p. 63–4.
21. Nakash: 'The visitation of the Shrines of the Imams', p. 154.
22. Pinto, Paulo, 'Pilgrimage, Commodities, and Religious Objectification: The Making of Transnational Shiism between Iran and Syria' *Comparative Studies of South Asia, Africa and the Middle East* vol.27, no.1 (2007), p. 111.
23. Chiffoleau and Madeouf, p. 14.
24. Pinto, p. 120f.
25. Ali was killed by a Kharijite. Krämer, Gudrun, *Geschichte des Islam* (Bonn, 2005), pp. 38–41; Buchta: *Schiiten*, pp. 14–16.
26. Krämer, pp. 47–49; Buchta: *Schiiten*, pp. 14–18; and Pinto, p. 111.
27. Calzoni, Irene, 'Shiite Mausoleums in Syria with particular reference to Sayyida Zaynab's Mausoleum' *La Shi'a nell'impero ottomano* (1991), pp. 199–201; Tabbaa, Yasser, 'Invented Pieties: The Rediscovery and Rebuilding of the Shrine of Sayyida Ruqayya in Damascus, 1975–2006' *Artibus Asiae* vol.67, Part 1 (2007), p. 96.
28. Alavi, Seyyed Ahmad, *Rahnama'i musavvir-e safar ziyarati suriyeh* (Qom, 1386/2007), p. 68. I bought this book at the annual book fair next to the shrine of Sayida Zaynab in June 2008.
29. Ibid, p. 40.
30. For a detailed account, see Alavi, pp. 81–112, and Calzoni, pp. 196–198.
31. Alavi, p. 114, 135–6, Calzoni, p. 199, Tabbaa, p. 96.
32. Calzoni, p. 193; Ababsa, Myriam, *Ideologies et territoires dans un front pionnier : Raqqa et le Projet de l'Euphrate en Jazire syrienne*, PhD thesis in Geography at the Université de Tours (France), (Tours, 2004), p. 414.

NOTES 247

33. Calzoni, pp. 193–194.
34. Calzoni, p. 192, Alavi, p. 134.
35. Alavi, p. 136.
36. Ibid, p. 139.
37. Map: www.lib.utexas.edu/maps/middle_east_and_asia/syria_pol_2007.jpg (marking by author).
38. Ababsa, Myriam, 'The Shi'a Mausoleums of Raqqa: Iranian proselytism and local significations' in F. Lawson (ed), *Demystifying Syria* (London, 2009), pp. 85–87; Alavi, pp. 141–144, Calzoni, pp. 191–192.
39. Conversation with Iranian student in Syria, Damascus, 22 April 2009.
40. Nakash: 'The visitation of the Shrines of the Imams', p. 154; Buchta, pp. 20–21; Mervin: 'Sayyida Zaynab', p. 150.
41. Nakash: *The Shi'is of Iraq*, pp. 164, 167–8.
42. Nakash: 'The visitation of the Shrines of the Imams', p. 159; Nakash: *The Shi'is of Iraq*, pp. 168–73; Mervin: 'Sayyida Zaynab', p. 150. See also Corboz, Elvire, *Negotiating Loyalty Across the Shi'i World: The Transnational Authority of the al-Hakim and al-Khu'i Families.* Unpublished DPhil thesis in Oriental Studies at the University of Oxford. (Oxford, 2009), p. 50f.
43. Nasr, Vali, *The Shia Revival* (New York, 2007), p. 18.
44. Pinto, p. 112.
45. See Ababsa: 'The Shi'a Mausoleums of Raqqa', p. 89.
46. Chiffoleau and Madeouf, p. 19.
47. Nasr, p. 56.
48. See table below for numbers of Iranian tourist entries to Syria.
49. IFM file file nr. 621/27, date: 31/3/1333.
50. Syrian Ministry of Tourism: Religious Sites in Damascus Countryside, The Shrine of Sayeda Zaynab. www.syriatourism.org.
51. Calzoni, p. 200. Mervin: 'Sayyida Zaynab', p. 154
52. Mervin: 'Sayyida Zaynab', p. 153; IFM files (see below).
53. IFM file nr: 2563, date: 25/11/1333.
54. See IFM files.
55. Mervin: 'Sayyida Zaynab', p. 153.
56. IFM file nr. 630/36, date: 15/4/1336.
57. IFM file nr. 896, date: 19/7/2535; IFM file nr. 244, date: 16/12/1344.
58. IFM file nr. 1194, date: 13/6/1344, Letter from Iranian ambassador to director of the Shah's office.
59. Mervin: 'Sayyida Zaynab', p. 153. She is citing an unedited document provided by Rida Murtada.
60. IFM file nr. 1099, date: 19/8/1332 (late 1953). Al-Zaman newspaper, 15/8/1332: 'al-qafas al-jadid la-darih al-sayida zaynab'; Mervin: 'Sayyida Zaynab', p. 153.

61. IFM Syrian FM file nr. (6136/62/811) 7, date: 29 June 1957.
62. Iranian Islamic architecture is often characterised by heavy ornamentation using geometrical patterns. Domes, often covered in mosaics, are a central feature.
63. IFM file nr. 1939/25, date: 21 January 1957; no nr./date; IFM file nr. 1400, date: 30 October 1957.
64. IFM file nr. 96/25 (letter from Iranian ambassador to Syrian Prime Minister), date: 13 April 1957.
65. IFM file, Letter of Syrian Prime Minister to Iranian Ambassador, May 1957; IFM file, Syrian Prime Minister's Office, file nr. 1/5149, date: 13 November 1957.
66. Tabbaa, p. 110.
67. Amiri, p. 132.
68. This assumption is based on the lack of evidence suggesting that any renovation on the shrine of Sayida Zaynab took place between the years 1973 and 1979.
69. Syrian Ministry of Tourism: Religious Sites in Damascus Countryside, The Shrine of Sayeda Zaynab. www.syriatourism.org.
70. Pinto, p. 113.
71. Ibid, p. 114; Mervin: 'Sayyida Zaynab', p. 154.
72. Ibid.
73. Tabbaa, pp. 98-9.
74. Ababsa explains the difficulties in obtaining detailed information on Iranian financial involvement; the director of awqaf in Raqqa confirmed Iranian financial participation in the construction of the shrines, but refused to give more information. Ababsa: *Ideologies et territoires*, pp. 391-2.
75. Ibid; Ababsa: 'The Shi'a Mausoleums of Raqqa', p. 86.
76. Ibid, p. 92.
77. Ababsa: *Ideologies et territoires*, p. 427.
78. Ibid, p. 398.
79. Tourist statistics for the year 2008, Syrian Ministry of Tourism, pdf nr. 20090127-054408. www.syriatourism.org.
80. al-qadimun (arab wa ajanib) hasab al-jinsiya wa marakiz al-hudud al-bariya wa al-bahariya wa al-jawiya fi aam 2007, www.syriatourism.org.
81. See table below.
82. *Syria Today*, a monthly Syrian magazine, places the annual number of Iranian pilgrims to Syria at between 400,000 and 500,000 in 2007, Basel Oudat in the al-Ahram Weekly suggests close to 600,000 tourists a year. 'Besides the tourists who visit Syria for its historical sites, beautiful cities and seaside resorts, thousands of Shia pilgrims also come to worship at shrines around

the country', *Syria Today*, November 2007; 'How strong is their alliance?', *al-Ahram Weekly*, 2008, available: http://weekly.ahram.org.eg/2008/900/re5. htm. The counsellor at the Iranian embassy in Damascus suggested that as many as one million Iranians were visiting Syria every year. Interview with Mousa Tabataba'i.

83. Tatawwur 'adad al-siyah hasab al-jinsiya wa al-sanawat min 'aam 2000–2008, al-siyah al-'arab wa al-ajanib wa al-suri al-mughtarab hasab al-jinsiya wa al-sanawat min 'aam 2002–2010, www.syriatourism.org.

84. Ababsa: *Ideologies et territoires*, p. 413–4.

85. Pinto, p. 114; 'Iranians in Syria: Sign of Close Ties', *New York Times*, 3 January 1984.

86. Mervin: 'Sayyida Zaynab', p. 149.

87. Samii, Abbas W., 'Syria and Iran: An Enduring Axis', *Mideast Monitor 2* (2) (2006).

88. Tabbaa, p. 111.

89. See Adelkhah, p. 77f.

90. Conversation with travel agents in Damascus, 22 March 2010.

91. 'Rail travel between Syria, Iran resumes after 19 years', *Associated Press*, 10 March 2001.

92. Ababsa: *Ideologies et territoires*, p. 394.

93. Bahout, Joseph, *Les Entrepreneurs Syriens. Economie, affaires et politique* (Beirut, 1994), pp. 52–54; Ababsa: *Ideologies et territoires*, p. 391.

94. 'Maqam al-sayida Zaynab muhasir min jawanibihi bi-ishghalat wa ikshaf 'ashwa'iya', *Tishrin*, 13 July 2005.

95. Ibid.

96. 'Arbakat lil-siyaha al-diniya fi dimashq.. ba'iayun wa dalalun yakhd'aun qasidi "al-sayida zaynab"...', *Tishrin*, 12 May 2009.

97. 'al-siyaha al-diniya la t'arif al-kasad...', *Tishrin*, 6 February 2009.

98. Adelkhah, p. 46; 'Besides the tourists who visit Syria for its historical sites, beautiful cities and seaside resorts, thousands of Shia pilgrims also come to worship at shrines around the country', *Syria Today*, November 2007.

99. Adelkhah, pp. 44–5.

100. 'Iran and Syria Look to Closer Ties', *IWPR*, 11 March 2010.

101. Ibid; Personal observations, Damascus March 2010; Khalili, Laleh, 'No dolls in Damascus. Globalization of another sort', *The Iranian*, 8 May 2002.

102. Pinto, p. 117.

103. Conversation with Syrian importer, Damascus, 20 February 2010.

104. For a discussion of the production and consumption of religious commodities, see Pinto, pp. 117–23.

105. Hirschfeld, p.114; 'Iran's Tourists Clash With Police in Syria', *The New York Times*, 22 March 1983.
106. Hunter: 'Iran and Syria', p. 210.
107. Hirschfeld, p. 114; 'Iranian Tourists Clash With Police in Syria'; 'Iranian tourists in Syria: a sign of political coziness', *Christian Science Monitor*, 24 February 1984.
108. Interview with Ali Montazeri, former cultural attaché, ICRO Damascus, Damascus, 19 June 2008.
109. Adelkhah, p. 52. Personal observations.
110. 'Iran and Syria Look to Closer Ties', *IWPR*, 11 March 2010.
111. Khalili.
112. Personal observation, Damascus, 25 March 2010.
113. Adelkah, p. 51.
114. Ababsa: *Ideologies et territoires*, p. 413–4.
115. Conversation with Damascene shopkeepers, Qaymariya, Damascus, February 2008.
116. Interview with Pegah Zohouri, student at St. Antony's College, Oxford, June 2010.
117. Conversation with Iranian girl visiting Damascus, February 2004.
118. See Chapter 2.

Conclusion

1. Conversation with Iranian student in Damascus, 28 July 2010.
2. Total votes: 10,378; Ahmadinejad: 7,184; Moussavi: 2,866; Rezaei: 153; Karrubi: 60. 'Detailed list of votes cast abroad in Iran election', *Press TV*, 15 June 2009.
3. Conversation with Iranian student in Damascus, 30 July 2010.
4. 'Iranians, Syrians share common cause', *CNN*, 13 April 2012.
5. 'Battle of Homs' on YouTube, last accessed 27 May 2012.
6. Personal observation, Damascus, 24 April 2012.
7. Moubayed, Sami, 'The Turkish-Iranian Struggle for Syria', *Middle East Online*, 10 March 2012.

BIBLIOGRAPHY

PRIMARY SOURCES

OFFICIAL RECORDS

Archives of the Iranian Foreign Ministry, Tehran, Iran
Folder: Iranian Embassy Damascus, Dameshgh 52, number 63 (referred to as IFM). Survey of files from the following Iranian calendar years (Gregorian calendar years in brackets): 1331–1335 (1952–1956), 1336–1340 (1957–1961), 1341–1345 (1962–1966), 1346–1350 (1967–1971), 1351–1355 (1972–1976). Files cited (dates in brackets given in Gregorian calendar years, otherwise in Iranian calendar years):
IFM year: 1331–1335, K: 4, D: 72, file nr: 203/1, date: (22 January1952).
IFM year: 1331–1335, K:4, D: 72, file nr. 158, date: (6 May 1952).
IFM year: 1331–1335, K:4, D: 72, file nr. 384/81, date: (4 June 1952).
IFM year: 1331–1335, K: 4, D: 72, file w/out nr, date: (24 May 1953).
IFM year: 1331–1335, K: 4, D: 72, file w/out nr, date: (26 June 1955).
IFM year: 1331–1335, file nr. 621/27, date: 31/3/1333 (1954).
IFM year: 1331–1335, file nr: 2563, date: 25/11/1333 (1955).
IFM year: 1331–1335, file nr. 1734, date: 29/7/1333 (1954).
IFM year: 1331–1335, file nr. 1099, date: 19/8/1332 (late 1953).
IFM year: 1336–1340, K:8, D:140–1.
IFM year: 1336–1340, K: 8, D: 144, file nr: 261/22, date: 31/02/1336 (1957).
IFM year: 1336–1340, file nr. 1187/24, date: (6 October 1957).
IFM year: 1336–1340, file nr. 630/36, date: 15/4/1336 (1957).
IFM year: 1336–1340, Syrian FM file nr. (6136/62/811) 7, date: (29 June 1957).
IFM year: 1336–1340, file nr. 1939/25, date: (21 January 1957).
IFM year: 1336–1340, file nr.1400, date: (30 October 1957).
IFM year: 1336–1340, file nr. 96/25, date: (13 April 1957).
IFM year: 1336–1340, letter from the Syrian Prime Minister to the Iranian Ambassador, (May 1957).

IFM year: 1336–1340, Syrian Prime Minister's Office, file nr. 1/5149, date: (13 November 1957).

IFM year: 1341–1345, K:19, D: 302, date: (30 January 1963).

IFM year: 1341–1345, file nr. 244, date: 16/12/1344 (1966).

IFM year: 1341–1345, file nr. 1194, date: 13/6/1344 (1965), letter from the Iranian ambassador to the director of the Shah's office.

IFM year: 1341–1345, K;13, D:215, correspondence between the Iranian embassy Damascus, the Syrian Foreign Ministry, Damascus University and Tehran University.

IFM year: 1341–1345, K:13, D:215, file nr. 17000/57/813, date: (4 January 1964).

IFM year :1341–1345, K:13, D:215, file nr. 2523, date: 20/8/1342 (1963).

IFM year: 1351–1355, K: 156, D: 2255.

IFM year: 1351–1355, file nr. 10476/17, date: 18/08/1354 (9 November 1975) [1975 cultural agreement between Syria and Iran]

IFM year: 1351–1355, K: 157, D: 2260, file nr. 2297, date: (21 January 1974).

IFM year: 1351–1355, K: 157, D: 2260, file nr. 10476/18, date: 18/08/1354 (1975).

IFM year: 1351–1355, file nr. 175, date: 07/12/1353, file nr. 2050, date: (16 March 1975).

IFM year: 1351–1355, K: 156, D: 2255.

IFM year: 1351–1355, file nr. 185, date: 14/12/1353 (1975).

IFM file nr. 896, date: 19/7/2535 (1976).

IFM file nr. 179, date: 02/07/2536 (1977).

IFM file nr. 212, date: 20/07/2536 (1977).

IFM file nr. 405, date: 27/12/2536 (1978).

Archives of the Syrian Ministry of Culture, Damascus, Syria:

1984 cultural agreement between Syria and Iran.

Cultural implementation programmes between Syria and Iran for the years 2003–04–05 and 2006–07–08.

Unpublished internal reports of the Islamic Culture and Relations Organisation (ICRO), obtained at the Organisation's central library, Tehran 3 November 2008:

Constitution of ICRO.

ICRO file nr. 98. 'Ittihadiyeh nevisandegane arab dar suriyeh' (The Arab Writers' Union in Syria), 23/01/1372 (1993).

ICRO file nr. 136. 'Fa'aliyethaye honari markaz farhangi amrika dar dameshq' (Artistic activities of the American cultural centre in Damascus), 30/08/1374 (1995).

ICRO file nr. 433/2/25. Subject not specified in title.

ICRO file nr. 444. 'Fa'aliyat raizan farhangi jomhuri eslami iran dar suriyeh dar zamineh gostaresh zaban va adabiyat farsi dar iin keshvar' (Activities of the

Iranian cultural centre in Syria in the field of Persian language and literature in this country).

ICRO file nr. 1877. 'Gozareshi az vazaiyat fa'eli tadris va adabiyat farsi dar daneshkadeh adabiyat dameshq' (Report about the situation of Persian teaching and literature at the faculty of literature in Damascus), 30/10/1372 (January 1994).

ICRO file nr. 3192. 'Ashna'i ba barnameha va fa'aliyethaye farhangi, honari, daneshgahi va pajuheshi raizan farhangi jomhuri eslami iran dar suriyeh' (Introducing cultural, artistic, university and research programmes and activities of the Iranian cultural centre in Syria).

ICRO file nr. 3269. 'Iftitah markaz amuzesh zaban-e farsi dar daneshgah halab va didar hay'at irani ba rusaye daneshgahhaye halab, tishreen va demashq' (Opening of the Persian teaching centre at Aleppo University and meeting of Iranian delegation with presidents of Aleppo, Tishreen and Damascus Universities), 30/12/1378 (February 2000).

ICRO file nr. 3699. 'Bargozari hafte farhangi jomhuri eslami iran dar lazaqiyeh' (Organising the cultural week of the Islamic Republic of Iran in Latakia).

ICRO file nr. 4932. 'Molaqatha ba shakhsiyathaye rasmi suriyeh' (Meetings with Syrian officials), 30/10/1382.

ICRO file nr. 5513. 'Gozaresh marakez farhangi khareji dar suriyeh' (Report on foreign cultural centres in Syria), 30/11/1369 (1991).

ICRO file nr. 5996. 'Hemayesh enqelab eslami va takrim nokhobegan' (Conference: the Islamic revolution and cultural elites), 27/11/1382 (2004).

ICRO file nr. 6914. 'Gozaresh safar hay'at bolandpayeh asatid-e daneshgah al-zahra beh jomhori arabi suriyeh' (Report on the trip of teachers of al-Zahra University to the Syrian Arab Republic), 28/12/1382 (March 2004).

ICRO file nr. 8043. 'Gozareshi az vazaiyat kitabkhaneh iranshenasi markaz motale'at raizani farhangi jomhuri eslami iran dar suriyeh' (Report on the situation of the Iranian studies library of the Studies Centre of the Iranian cultural centre in Syria), 31/02/1380 (2001).

ICRO file nr. 9286. 'Iraniyan muqim suriyeh v apish nevis asasnameh tashkil komiteh umur iraniyan' (Iranians resident in Syria and draft of constitution for setting up a committee for the affair of Iranians).

ICRO file nr. 10545. 'Cheshm andazi no beh vazaiyat alaviyan b'ad az riyasat aghaye bashar al-asad' (Insight into the situation of Alawis after the [start of the] presidency of Bashar al-Asad), 30/10/1381 (January 2003).

Publications of the Iranian Cultural Centre Damascus:

'Adawa' 'ala rabitat al-thaqafa wa al-'alaqat al-islamiya fi iran' (Lights on the Islamic Culture and Relations Organisation) *al-thaqafa al-islamiya* no.89 (Damascus 2002), 152–164.

'Adawa' 'ala al-usbu'a al-thaqafi al-irani al-kabir fi al-jumhuriya al-'arabiya al-suriya' (Lights on the great Iranian cultural week in the Syrian Arab Republic) *al-thaqafa al-islamiya* nr.96 (Damascus 2004), 235–261.

Amrani, Yaser, 'Fahras mawdua'i 'aam li-'adad al-thaqafa al-islamiya min al-'adad 1–100' (General index of subjects of al-thaqafa al-islamiya issues from number 1–100) *al-thaqafa al-islamiya* no.100 (Damascus 2006), 345–412.

Azarshab, Muhammad Ali, *al-alaqat al-thaqafiya al-iraniya al-'arabiya* (Damascus, 2001).

Barnamij al-nashatat al-thaqafiya (The Cultural Programme) brochures (Arabic and Persian).

Brochure (Arabic and Persian) on the Centre for Iranian-Arab Cultural Studies, Iranian Cultural Centre Damascus (Damascus 2005).

Faslnameh Farhangi (Persian). *ICRO Syria Website.* [http://damascus.icro.ir/?c=ne wsShow&NewsId=554537&t=4].

Iranian Cultural Centre Damascus official website (Arabic and Persian), http://damascus.icro.ir/.

Iranian Cultural Chancellor (ed), *Gahnameh Farhangi* 1–11 (Damascus 2003–2006).

'Liqa' hiwari m'a al-sayed wazir al-thaqafa al-suri al-doktor mahmud al-sayed' (Dialogue with the Syrian Minister of Culture, Dr Mahmud al-Sayed) *al-thaqafa al-islamiya* no.100 (Damascus 2006), 42–48.

'Liqa'at hiwariya thaqafiya hawal: "dawr al-'alaqat al-thaqafiya al-iraniya al-suriya fi t'aziz al-'alaqat al-iraniya al-'arabiya", hiwar m'a al-ustadh ahmad al-hassan wazir al-'alam al-suri al-sabiq' (Cultural dialogues about: "The role of Syrian-Iranian cultural relations in strengthening Arab-Iranian relations", dialogue with Mr. Ahmad al-Hassan, former Syrian Minister of Information) *al-thaqafa al-islamiya* no.100 (Damascus 2006), 54–65.

'Liqa'at hiwariya thaqafiya hawal: "dawr al-'alaqat al-thaqafiya al-iraniya al-suriya fi t'aziz al-'alaqat al-iraniya al-'arabiya", hiwar m'a al-doktor Ali 'Aqlah 'Arsan al-amin al-'aam li-ittihad al-kuttab al-'arab' (Cultural dialogues about: "The role of Syrian-Iranian cultural relations in strengthening Arab-Iranian relations", dialogue with Dr. Ali 'Aqlah 'Arsan, secretary general of the Arab Writers' Union) *al-thaqafa al-islamiya* no.100 (Damascus 2006), 66–88.

Maskarnejad, Jalil, 'Ahmiyat t'alim al-lugha' (The importance of language teaching) *al-thaqafa al-islamiya* no.67 (Damascus 1996), 193–197.

'Mas'ul farhangi suri: iraniyan va arab do bal-e umat islami hastand' (Syrian cultural official: Iranians and Arabs are two wings of the Islamic *umma*), ICRO Report on cultural week in Safita; [Available: http://damascus.icro.ir/?c=ne wsShow&NewsId=548355&t=4].

'Mubadi al-siyasa al-thaqafiya lil-jumhuriya al-islamiya al-iraniya' (Principles of the Iranian Islamic Republic's cultural policy) *al-thaqafa al-islamiya* nr.89 (Damascus 2002), 138–151.

Murad, Riyad Abdulhamid, *al-tabadul al-thaqafi* (Damascus, 1989).

Salmani, Abdulkarim, 'Adawa' 'ala al-lugha al-farisiya' (Lights on the Persian Language) *al-thaqafa al-islamiya* nr.100 (Damascus 2006), 109–114.

Shafi'ai, Husayn, 'Al-mustashariya al-thaqafiya al-iraniya bi-dimashq khilala rub'a qarn' (The Iranian cultural chancellery in Damascus during a quarter century) *al-thaqafa al-islamiya* nr.100 (Damascus 2006), 95–108.

Taheri, Abdallah Naseri, 'Limadha?! Kaifa?! Ila ayna?!' *al-thaqafa al-islamiya* nr. 4 (Damascus 1986), 5–10.

'al-Thawra al-islamiya wa takrim al-nukhub al-thaqafiya' (The Islamic revolution and honouring the cultural elite), pamphlet (February 2008).

'al-Usbu'a al-thaqafi al-suri fi Tehran, 28/02–08/03/2002' (The Syrian cultural week in Tehran) *al-thaqafa al-islamiya* nr.89 (Damascus 2002), 188–191.

'Waqa'ia hafl iftitah qism al-lugha al-farsiya wa adabiha fi jam'at dimashq' (The opening ceremony of the department of Persian language and literature at Damascus University) *al-thaqafa al-islamiya* nr.98 (Damascus 2005), 225–231.

'Waza'iyat zaban-e farsi dar suriyeh' (The situation of the Persian language in Syria), *pajuheshha-ye mutal'ati* nr.4 (July 2004).

'Zaban va adabiyat farsi dar suriyeh' (Persian language and literature in Syria), *Cheshm Andaz, Irtibatat Farhangi* nr. 14 (February 2006).

Publications of the Arab-Syrian Cultural Centre Tehran and of Syrian Ministries

Brochure of the Arab-Syrian cultural centre in Tehran, Arab-Syrian cultural centre (Tehran, 2007).

Pamphlet on Muhammad al-Furati by the Ministry of Culture printed on the occasion of a special remembrance seminar for al-Furati, Dayr al-Zur, 16 and 17 May 2007.

Majlis al-ta'lim al-'aali, al-qarar raqam 220, al-mada 12 (Council of Higher Education, Law nr. 220, Article 12), obtained in Damascus, 13 June 2009.

THESES, LECTURES, MANUSCRIPTS

Ababsa, Myriam, *Ideologies et territoires dans un front pionnier: Raqqa et le Projet de l'Euphrate en Jazire syrienne*, unpublished PhD thesis in Geography at the Université de Tours/France (Tours, 2004).

Corboz, Elvire, *Negotiating Loyalty Across the Shi'i World: The Transnational Authority of the al-Hakim and al-Khu'i Families*, unpublished DPhil thesis in Oriental Studies at the University of Oxford (Oxford, 2009).

al-Gharir, Musa. 'B'ad al-malamih al-asasiya lil-'alaqat al-suriya al-iraniya' (Some basic remarks about Syrian-Iranian relations), unpublished lecture given at several universities in Iran in the academic year 2005–2006. Obtained from al-Gharir, Tehran, 23 April 2006.

Al Khatib, Reem and Yazaji, Rana, *Compendium: Country Profile Syria* (unpublished manuscript).

Marschall, Christin, *Syria, Iran and the Changing Middle East Order*, unpublished MPhil thesis at the University of Oxford (Oxford, 1991).

Sadjadpour, Karim, 'Iran's Regional Position' (Panel title). University of Maryland symposium on 'Iran after the 2009 Elections: Domestic, Regional and International Dimensions', 6 November 2009. Available online: http://ms-websvr.ad.eng.umd.edu/DETSMediasite5/Viewer/?peid=35639796c7a9 4e3fbe98a418d04b5662.

Sha'ban, Buthaina. Questioned during a talk she gave at the Middle East Centre, St. Antony's College, Oxford, 17 November 2008.

SECONDARY SOURCES

Ababsa, Myriam,
'Significations territoriales et appropriations conflictuelles des mausolées chiites de Raqqa (Syrie)', in S. Chiffoleau and A. Madeouf (eds), *Les Pèlerinages au Maghreb et au Moyen-Orient. Espaces publics, espaces du public* (Beirut, 2005).
'The Shi'a Mausoleums of Raqqa: Iranian proselytism and local significations', in F. Lawson (ed), *Demystifying Syria* (London, 2009).

Abassi, Muhammad, *al-Doktor Ali Shariati* (Syria, date unknown).

Abrahamian, Ervand, *The Iranian Mojahedin* (London, 1989).

Adelkhah, Fariba. 'Économie morale du pèlerinage et société civile en Iran: les voyages religieux, commerciaux et touristiques à Damas' *Politix* vol.20, no.77 (2007), 39–54.

Adib-Moghaddam, Arshin, *The International Politics of the Persian Gulf: A Cultural Genealogy* (London, 2006).

Afrasiabi, Kaveh, *After Khomeini: new directions in Iran's foreign policy* (Boulder Co., 1994).

Agha, Hussein and Khalidi, Ahmad, *Syria and Iran: Rivalry and Cooperation* (London, 1995).

Ajami, Fouad, *The Vanished Imam: Musa al Sadr and the Shia of Lebanon* (London, 1986).

Al-e Ahmad, Jalal, *Lost in the Crowd* (Washington D.C., 1985).

Alam, Asadollah, *The Shah and I* (London, 1991).

Alavi, Seyyed Ahmad, *Rahnama'i musavvir-e safar ziyarati suriyeh* (Qom, 2007).

Alpher, Joseph, 'The Khomeini International' *The Washington Quarterly* vol. 3, no.4 (1980), 54–74.

Amirahmadi, Hooshang and Entessar, Nader,
(eds), *Iran and the Arab World* (New York, 1993).
'Iranian-Arab Relations in Transition', in H. Amirahmadi and N. Entessar (eds), *Iran and the Arab World* (New York, 1993).

Amiri, Kiumarth, *Zaban va adab farsi dar jehan; suriyeh* (Persian language and literature in the world; Syria). (Tehran, 2002).

Ansari, Ali, 'Civilizational Identity and Foreign Policy: The Case of Iran', in B. Shaffer (ed), *The Limits of Culture: Islam and Foreign Policy* (Cambridge MA, 2006), 242–262.

al-Azhari, Nada, 'Hewar m'a ra'is qism al-lugha al-'arabiya fi jami'at Tehran... Azartash Azarnoush: ta'thir al-'arabiya fi al-farisiya gharib wa mustamir' (Dialogue with the head of the Arabic language department in Tehran University... Azartash Azarnoush: the impact of Arabic on Persian is strange and continuous), *al-Hayat*, 24 June 2008.

Bahout, Joseph, *Les Entrepreneurs Syriens. Economie, affaires et politique* (Beirut, 1994).

Bakhash, Shaul, 'Iran's Foreign Policy under the Islamic Republic, 1979–2000', in C. Brown (ed), *Diplomacy in the Middle East: The International Relations of Regional and Outside Powers* (London, 2004).

Baktiari, Bahman and Bayat, Asef, 'Revolutionary Iran and Egypt: Exporting Inspirations and Anxieties' in N. Keddie and R. Matthee (eds), *Iran and the Surrounding World: Interactions in Culture and Cultural Politics* (Seattle and London, 2002).

Bates, Gill and Huang, Yanzhong, 'Sources and Limits of Chinese 'Soft Power'' *Survival* vol.48, no.2 (Summer 2006), 17–36.

Beidun, Labib, *Hayat wa dhikriyat fi hay al-amin* (Damascus, 2003).

Böttcher, Annabelle,
Syrische Religionspolitik unter Asad (Freiburg, 1998).
'Official Sunni and Shi'i Islam in Syria' *San Domenico, European University Institute working paper* (2002/3), pp.3–25.

Bound, Kirsten, Briggs, Rachel, Holden, John and Jones, Samuel, *Cultural Diplomacy* (London, 2007).

Brown, Carl (ed), *Diplomacy in the Middle East: The International Relations of Regional and Outside Powers* (London, 2004).

Buchta, Wilfried,
Die iranische Schia und die islamische Einheit 1979–1996 (Hamburg, 1997).
Who Rules Iran? The Structure of Power in the Islamic Republic (Washington D.C., 2000).
'The Failed Pan-Islamic Program of the Islamic Republic: Views of the Liberal Reformers of the Religious "Semi-Opposition"', in N. Keddie and R. Matthee (eds), *Iran and the Surrounding World: Interactions in Culture and Cultural Politics* (Seattle and London, 2002).
Schiiten (München, 2004).

Bustamante, Michael J. and Sweig, Julia E, 'Buena Vista Solidarity and the Axis of Aid: Cuban and Venezuelan Public Diplomacy' *The ANNALS of the American Academy of Political and Social Science* no.616 (March 2008), 223–256.

Calabrese, John, 'Iran II: The Damascus Connection' *The World Today* vol. 46 (October 1990).

Calzoni, Irene, 'Shiite Mausoleums in Syria with particular reference to Sayyida Zaynab's Mausoleum', in B. S. Amoretti (ed), *La Shi'a nell'impero ottomano* (Rome, 1993), 191–201.

Chehabi, H.E. (ed), *Distant Relations: Iran and Lebanon in the last 500 years* (London, 2006).

Chiffoleau, Sylvia and Madeouf, Anna (eds), *Les Pèlerinages au Maghreb et au Moyen-Orient. Espaces publics, espaces du public* (Beirut, 2005).

Chubin, Shahram and Zabih, Sepehr, *The Foreign Relations of Iran: A Developing State in a Zone of Great-Power Conflict* (Berkeley, 1974).

Dawisha, Adeed (ed), *Islam in Foreign Policy* (Cambridge, 1983).

Dawn, Ernest C, 'The Foreign Policy of Syria', in C. Brown (ed), *Diplomacy in the Middle East: The International Relations of Regional and Outside Powers* (London, 2004).

Das Palästinaproblem aus der Sicht Imam Khomeinis (Tehran, 1996).

Dehshiri, Muhammad-Rida, 'Principles and Fundamentals of Islamic Diplomacy From Imam Khomeini's Viewpoint', in M. H. Hafezian (ed), *Imam Khomeini and the International System* (Tehran, 2006).

Die Revolution Publizieren... aus der Sicht Imam Khomeinis (Tehran, 1999).

Djalili, Mohammad Reza, *Diplomatie Islamique* (Paris, 1989).

Drysdale, Alasdair and Hinnebusch, Raymond, *Syria and the Middle East Peace Process* (New York, 1991).

Ehteshami, Anoushiravan, 'The Foreign Policy of Iran', in A. Ehteshami and R. Hinnebusch (eds), *The Foreign Policies of Middle East States* (Boulder Co., 2002).

Ehteshami, Anoushiravan and Hinnebusch, Raymond,
    Syria and Iran: Middle Powers in a penetrated regional system (New York, 1997).
    (eds) *The Foreign Policies of Middle East States* (Boulder Co., 2002).

Ehteshami, Anoushiravan and Zweiri, Mahjoob (eds), *Iran's foreign policy: from Khatami to Ahmadinejad* (Reading, 2008).

Eickleman, Dale and Piscatori, James, *Muslim Politics* (Princeton, 1996).

Emami, Muhammad Ali, *Siyaset va Hukumet dar Suriyeh* [transl.: Politics and Government in Syria] (Tehran, 1997).

Encyclopedia of Islam entries:
    'Hamdanids' *Encyclopedia of Islam* vol.III (Leiden, 1971).
    'Ibn 'Asakir' *Encyclopedia of Islam* vol.III (Leiden, 1971).
    'al-Sam'ani, Abu Sa'd' *Encyclopedia of Islam* vol.VIII (Leiden, 1995).
    'Sayf al-Dawla' *Encyclopedia of Islam* vol.IX (Leiden, 1995).

Esposito, John (ed), *The Iranian Revolution: Its Global Impact* (Miami, 1990).

European Cultural Foundation, *Cultural Policies in Algeria, Egypt, Jordan, Lebanon, Morocco, Palestine, Syria and Tunisia: An Introduction.* (Amsterdam, 2011).

Foreign Broadcast Information Service (FBIS). 'Tehran Seeks To Preserve Hizballah, Weaken Peace Chances', *FBIS Trends,* 11 August 1993.

Fuller, Graham, *The center of the universe: the geopolitics of Iran* (Boulder Co., 1991).

Goethe-Institut yearbook 2008.

Goodarzi, Jubin, *Syria and Iran: Diplomatic Alliance and Power Politics in the Middle East* (London, 2006 and 2009 paperback edition with new preface).

Gregory, Bruce, 'Public Diplomacy: Sunrise of an Academic Field' *The ANNALS of the American Academy of Political and Social Science* vol. 616 (2008), 274–290.

Hafezian, Mohammad Hossein (ed), *Imam Khomeini and the International System* (Tehran, 2006).

Haigh, Anthony, *Cultural Diplomacy in Europe* (Strasbourg, 1974).

Hartig, Falk, 'Mit Konfuzius ins 21. Jahrhundert – Chinas Auswärtige Kulturpolitik', in K.-J. Maaß (ed), *Kultur- und Außenpolitik* (Baden-Baden, 2009), 401–410.

Haseeb, Khair el-Din (ed), *Arab-Iranian relations* (Beirut, 1998).

Hinnebusch, Raymond,

'The Foreign Policy of Syria', in A. Ehteshami and R. Hinnebusch (eds), *The Foreign Policies of Middle East States* (Boulder Co., 2002).

Syria: Revolution from above (London, 2002).

(ed) *Syrian Foreign Policy and the United States: From Bush to Obama* (St Andrews, 2010).

Hirschfeld, Yair, 'The odd couple: Ba'athist Syria and Khomeini's Iran', in M. Ma'oz and A. Yaniv (eds), *Syria under Assad: domestic constraints and regional risks* (London, 1986).

d'Hooghe, Ingrid, 'Public Diplomacy in the People's Republic of China', in J. Melissen (ed), *The New Public Diplomacy* (London, 2005), 88–105.

Hopwood, Derek, *Syria 1945–1986. Politics and Society* (London, 1988).

Hunter, Shireen,

Iran and the World: Continuity in a Revolutionary Decade (Indiana, 1990).

'Iran and Syria: From Hostility to Limited Alliance', in H. Amirahmadi and N. Entessar (eds), *Iran and the Arab World* (New York, 1993).

'Iran and the Arab World', in M. Rezun (ed), *Iran at the Crossroads: Global Relations in a Turbulent Decade* (Boulder Co., 1990).

International Crisis Group. 'Reshuffling the Cards? (I): Syria's Evolving Strategy'. *Crisis Group Middle East Report* nr. 92 (14 December 2009).

Iranian Diplomatic Corps Handbook of 1984.

Iranian Foreign Ministry, *Suriyeh {be sefaresh} daftar mutala'at siyasi va bein el-melli* (Tehran, 2008).

Jaber, Hala, *Hezbollah: Born With a Vengeance* (London, 1997).

Jack, G. and Phipps, A. M., *Tourism and intercultural exchange: why tourism matters* (Clevedon, 2005).

Jan Zadeh, Ali, *Doktor Ali Shariati* (Tehran, 1969).

Keddie, Nikki,

Iran and the Muslim world: resistance and revolution (Basingstoke, 1995).

Modern Iran: Roots and Results of Revolution (New Haven, 2003).

Keddie, Nikki and Gasiorowski, Mark (eds), *Neither East nor West: Iran, the Soviet Union, and the United States* (New Haven and London, 1990).

Keddie, Nikki and Matthee, Rudi (eds), *Iran and the Surrounding World: Interactions in Culture and Cultural Politics* (Seattle and London, 2002).

Al Khatib, Reem and Yazaji, Rana, 'Syria', in *Cultural Policies in Algeria, Egypt, Jordan, Lebanon, Morocco, Palestine, Syria and Tunisia* (Amsterdam, 2010).

Kienle, Eberhard, *Ba'th v Ba'th: The Conflict between Syria and Iraq 1968–1989* (London, 1990).

Korany, Bahgat, 'Defending the Faith amid Change: The Foreign Policy of Saudi Arabia', in B. Korany and A. Dessouki (eds), *The Foreign Policies of Arab States: The Challenge of Change* (Boulder Co., 1991).

Korany, Bahgat and Dessouki, Ali (eds), *The Foreign Policies of Arab States: The Challenge of Change* (Boulder Co., 1991).

Krämer, Gudrun, *Geschichte des Islam* (Bonn, 2005).

Kramer, Martin,
(ed) *Shi'ism, Resistance, and Revolution* (Boulder Co., 1987).
'Syria's Alawis and Shi'ism', in M. Kramer (ed), *Shi'ism, Resistance, and Revolution* (Boulder Co., 1987), 237–254.
'The Global Village of Islam' *Middle East Contemporary Survey* vol.16 (1992), 193–226.

Lawson, Fred,
'Syria's Relations with Iran: Managing the Dilemmas of Alliance' *The Middle East Journal* vol.61, nr.1 (Winter 2007), p.32.
Demystifying Syria (London, 2009).

Leonard, Mark, *Public Diplomacy* (London, 2002).

Lesch, David,
The new lion of Damascus: Bashar al-Asad and modern Syria (New Haven and London, 2005).
'The Role of Bashar al-Asad in Syrian Foreign Policy', in R. Hinnebusch (ed), *Syrian Foreign Policy and the United States: From Bush to Obama* (St Andrews, 2010).

Leverett, Flynt, *Inheriting Syria: Bashar's Trial by Fire* (Washington D.C., 2005).

Lipset, Seymour Martin, *Political Man: The Social Bases of Politics* (Baltimore, 1981 [expanded edition]).

Louër, Laurence,
Transnational Shia Politics: Religious and Political Networks in the Gulf (London, 2008).
Chiisme et politique au Moyen-Orient: Iran, Irak, Liban, monarchies du Golfe (Paris, 2008).

Lutzmann, Eva and Schneider, Gerd, 'Global Players – Die Auswärtige Kulturpolitik Frankreiches, Großbritanniens, Italiens, Portugals und Spaniens', in K.-J. Maaß (ed), *Kultur und Außenpolitik* (Baden-Baden, 2009), 369–378.

Maaß, Kurt-Jürgen, *Kultur und Außenpolitik* (Baden-Baden, 2009).

Ma'oz, Moshe, *Syria and Israel: From War to Peace-making* (Oxford, 1995).

Ma'oz, Moshe and Yaniv, Avner (eds), *Syria Under Assad: Domestic Constraints and Regional Risks* (London, 1986).

Marschall, Christin, *Iran's Persian Gulf Policy: From Khomeini to Khatami* (London, 2003).

McMurry, Ruth Emily and Lee, Muna, *The cultural approach: Another Way in International Relations* (Chapel Hill, 1947).

Melissen, Jan,
(ed) *The New Public Diplomacy* (London, 2005).
'Between Theory and Practice', in J. Melissen (ed), *The New Public Diplomacy* (London, 2005), 3–27.

Menashri, David,
(ed) *The Iranian Revolution and the Muslim World* (Boulder Co., 1990).

Post-revolutionary politics in Iran: religion, society and power (London, 2001).

Mervin, Sabrina,
'Sayyida Zaynab: banlieue de Damas ou nouvelle ville sainte chiite?' *CEMOTI* 22 (1996), pp.149–162.
(ed) *Les mondes chiites et l'Iran* (Paris, 2007).

Meshkin Fam, Batul, 'al-lugha al-arabiya fi iran: al-waqi'a wa al-murtaja' (The Arabic language in Iran: reality and expectations) *al-dirasat al-adabiya* nr. 48–52, (Winter 2005–06), 71–86.

Milani, Mohsen, 'Iran's active neutrality during the Kuwaiti crisis: Reasons and ramifications' *New Political Science* vol.11, nr.1 (1992), 41–60.

Mitchell, John, *International cultural relations* (London, 1986).

Mohtashemipur, Ali Akbar, *Khatirat hojjatoleslam va al-muslimin Sayyid Ali Akbar Mohtashemipur* (Tehran, 1997–9).

'Musahibe ba ustad Ahmad Aram' *Khabarname farhangistan zaban va adab farsi* nr.15–16 (Spring 1997).

Nakash, Yitzhak,
'The visitation of the Shrines of the Imams and the Shi'i Mujtahids in the Early Twentieth Century' *Studia Islamica* 81 (Paris 1995), 153–64.
The Shi'is of Iraq (Princeton, 2003).

Nasr, Vali, *The Shia Revival. How Conflicts within Islam Will Shape the Future* (New York, 2007).

Norton, Augustus R.,
Amal and the Shia: struggle for the soul of Lebanon (Austin, 1987).
Hezbollah: A Short History (Princeton, 2007).

Nye, Joseph,
The paradox of American power: why the world's only superpower can't go it alone (Oxford, 2002).
Soft Power: The means to success in world politics (New York, 2004).
'Public Diplomacy and Soft Power' *The ANNALS of the American Academy of Political and Social Science* vol.616 (2008), 94–109.

Olmert, Yosef, 'Iranian-Syrian Relations: Between Islam and Realpolitik', in D. Menashri (ed), *The Iranian Revolution and the Muslim World* (Boulder Co., 1990).

Olson, Robert, 'The Kurdish Question four years on: The policies of Turkey, Syria, Iran and Iraq' *Middle East Policy* vol.3, no.3 (October 1994), 136–144.

Palmer Harik, Judith, *Hezbollah: The Changing Face of Terrorism* (London, 2004).

Parsi, Trita, *Treacherous Alliance: The Secret Dealings of Israel, Iran, and the U.S.* (New Haven and London, 2007).

Parvini, Khalil, 'al-lugha al-'arabiya fi iran, bayn al-manahij al-jami'aiya wa al-turath al-makhtut' (The Arabic language in Iran, between university programmes and the manuscript legacy) *al-dirasat al-adabiya* nr. 48–52, (Winter 2005–06), 87–105.

Pierret, Thomas,
'Les cadres de l'élite religieuse sunnite' *Maghreb-Machrek* nr. 198 (Winter 2008–2009).

'Sunni Clergy Politics in the Cities of Ba'thi Syria', in F. Lawson (ed), *Demystifying Syria* (London, 2009).

Pinto, Paulo, 'Pilgrimage, Commodities, and Religious Objectification: The Making of Transnational Shiism between Iran and Syria' *Comparative Studies of South Asia, Africa and the Middle East* vol.27, no.1 (2007).

Rabinovich, Itamar, *The View from Damascus: State, Political Community and Foreign Relations in Twentieth-Century Syria* (London, 2008).

Rahnema, Ali, *An Islamic Utopian: A Political Biography of Ali Shari'ati* (London, 1998).

Rajaee, Farhang, 'Iranian Ideology and Worldview: The Cultural Export of the Revolution', in J. Esposito (ed), *The Iranian Revolution: Its Global Impact* (Miami, 1990).

Ramazani, Rouhollah,
Iran's Foreign Policy 1941–73 (Charlottesville, 1975).
'Khumayni's Islam in Iran's Foreign Policy', in A. Dawisha (ed.), *Islam in Foreign Policy* (Cambridge, 1983).
Revolutionary Iran: Challenge and response in the Middle East (Baltimore, 1986).
'Iran's Export of the Revolution: Politics, Ends and Means', in J. Esposito (ed), *The Iranian Revolution: Its Global Impact* (Miami, 1990).

Ranstorp, Magnus, *Hizb'allah in Lebanon: The Politics of the Western Hostage Crisis* (London, 1997).

Roche, François, *Histoires de diplomatie culturelle des origins a 1995* (Paris, 1995).

Sabbagh, Said, *Al-alaqat al-masriya al-iraniya bayna al-wasal wa al-qati'a, 1970–1981* (Cairo, 2007).

Saikal, Amin, 'Iranian Foreign Policy, 1921–1979', in P. Avery, Hambly and C. Melville (eds), *The Cambridge History of Iran, Vol.7: From Nadir Shah to the Islamic Republic* (Cambridge, 1991).

Sariolghalam, Mahmood (ed), 'Roundtable: Iran's Foreign Policy during Khatami's Presidency' *Discourse* vol.2, no.1 (Tehran 2000).

Schirazi, Asghar, *The Constitution of Iran: Politics and the State in the Islamic Republic* (London, 1998).

Seale, Patrick,
The Struggle for Syria: A Study of Post-War Arab Politics, 1945–1958 (New Haven, 1965 and new edition 1985).
Asad: The Struggle for the Middle East (Berkeley and Los Angeles, 1989).

Shaery-Eisenlohr, Roschanack, *Shi'ite Lebanon: Transnational religion and the Making of National Identities* (New York, 2008).

Shaffer, Brenda. 'The Islamic Republic of Iran: Is It Really?', in B. Shaffer (ed), *The Limits of Culture: Islam and Foreign Policy* (Cambridge MA, 2006), 219–239.

Sick, Gary, 'Iran's Foreign Policy: A Revolution in Transition', in N. Keddie and R. Matthee (eds), *Iran and the Surrounding World* (Seattle and London, 2002).

Stanley, Bruce, 'Drawing from the well: Syria in the Persian Gulf' *Journal of South Asian and Middle Eastern Studies* vol.XIV, no.2 (Winter 1990).

Suwaidi, Jamal (ed), *Iran and the Gulf: a search for stability* (Abu Dhabi, 1996).

Tabbaa, Yasser, 'Invented Pieties: The Rediscovery and Rebuilding of the Shrine of Sayyida Ruqayya in Damascus, 1975–2006' *Artibus Asiae* vol. 67, no. 1 (2007), 95–112.

Talhamy, Yvette, 'The Syrian Muslim Brothers and the Syrian-Iranian Relationship' *Middle East Journal* vol.63, nr. 4 (Autumn 2009), 561–580.

van Dam, Nikolaos, *The Struggle for Power in Syria: Politics and Society under Asad and the Bath Party* (London, 1996 and 2011).

Wang, Jian, 'Localising public diplomacy: the role of sub-national actors in nation branding' *Place Branding* 2, no.1 (2006), 32–42.

Wedeen, Lisa, *Ambiguities of domination: politics, rhetoric, and symbols in contemporary Syria* (Chicago, 1999).

Zisser, Eyal,
  Asad's Legacy: Syria in Transition (London, 2001).
  Commanding Syria: Bashar al-Asad and the first years in power (London, 2007).

WEBSITES OF INSTITUTIONS AND INDIVIDUALS, AND WEB PAGES CONSULTED

ahl al-bayt World Assembly website: www.ahl-ul-bait.org.

Short biography of Dr. Aynevand,
www.adabefarsi.ir/Default.aspx?page=5357&section=pfitem&id=37035.

British Council website: www.britishcouncil.org.

Confucius Institutes website: http://college.chinese.cn/en/node_1979.htm.

Damascus University website: www.damasuniv.shern.net.

Farhangserai melal website: www.fsm.ir.

French Cultural Centre Damascus website: www.ccf-damas.org.

French Embassy Tehran website: www.ambafrance-ir.org.

Goethe-Institut website: www.goethe.de.

Hadj and Pilgrimage Organization website: www.iranculture.org/en/nahad/haj.php.

Hanban website: http://english.hanban.edu.cn.

Iranian Association of Arabic Language and Literature website: www.iaal.ir/history.htm.

Institut français du Proche Orient website: www.ifporient.org.

Iranian cultural centre Damascus website: www.damascus.icro.ir.

Iranian parliament website (Syrian-Iranian friendship group): http://mellat.majlis.ir/PARLIAMENTARY%2OFERIENDSHIP%20GROUPS/SOORIEH.HTM.

Islamic Culture and Relations Organisation (ICRO) website: www.icro.ir.

Italian Cultural Centre Damascus website: www.iicdamasco.esteri.it.

Iranian Red Crescent Society website: www.rcs.ir.

Iran Language Institute website: www.kanoonzaban.net.

Österreichisches Kulturforum Teheran website: www.austria-iran.com.
Secretariat of Supreme Council of Cultural Revolution website: www.iranculture.
    org.
Society for the Defence of the Palestinian Nation website, www.pngo.ir.
Spanish Cultural Centre Damascus website: http://damasco.cervantes.es.
Syrian Ministry of Tourism website: www.syriatourism.org.

NEWS ARTICLES

Survey of news articles from the following publications:
AFP
Ba'th Newspaper
Charlie Rose Interview
Christian Science Monitor
The Daily Star
The Economist
Etemaad
Fars News Agency
IRNA
Jerusalem Post
MidEast Mirror (via BBC Summary of World Broadcast)
Press TV
Radio Monte Carlo (via BBC Summary of World Broadcast)
Reuters
SANA
Syria Today
Syrian Arab Republic Radio (via BBC Summary of World Broadcast)
Syrian Arab TV (via BBC Summary of World Broadcast)
Tehran Times
al-Thawra Newspaper
Tishrin Newspaper
al-Vefagh
Xinhua News Agency

MAPS

Map 1: Map of Central Damascus: Syrian Ministry of Tourism,
www.syriatourism.org.
Map 2: Map of Syria:
www.lib.utexas.edu/maps/middle_east_and_asia/syria_pol_2007.jpg.

INDEX

www.ingramcontent.com/pod-product-compliance
Lightning Source LLC
Chambersburg PA
CBHW070610270326
41926CB00013B/2488